ABSOLUTE BEGINNER'S GUIDE

TO

Adobe® Photoshop® Elements 2

Lisa Lee

201 West 103rd Street,
Indianapolis, Indiana 46290

Absolute Beginner's Guide to Adobe® Photoshop® Elements 2

International Standard Book Number: 0-7897-2831-1

Library of Congress Catalog Card Number: 2002110926

Printed in the United States of America

First Printing: October 2002

05   04   03   4   3

Trademarks

Warning and Disclaimer

Associate Publisher
Greg Wiegand

Executive Editor
Candy Hall

Acquisitions Editor
Candy Hall

Development Editor
Laura Norman

Managing Editor
Thomas F. Hayes

Project Editor
Tonya Simpson

Copy Editor
Cheri Clark

Indexer
Rebecca Salerno

Proofreader
Kellie Cotner

Technical Editor
Rima Regas

Team Coordinator
Cindy Teeters

Interior Designer
Anne Jones

Cover Designer
Anne Jones

Page Layout
Julie Parks

Contents at a Glance

Table of Contents

About the Author

Lisa Lee is the author of several best-selling computer books on topics ranging from Macintosh computers to Adobe Photoshop and Photoshop Elements. She also has written more than 1,000 tutorials about all kinds of consumer hardware products, operating systems, and applications.

When she's not writing, she is an amateur photographer and artist. Visit her Web site at `www.flatfishfactory.com` to check out her latest projects.

Dedication

This book is dedicated to Mike Neil.

Acknowledgments

This book would not be possible without the fabulous Photoshop Elements team at Adobe. Thanks to all who worked on Photoshop Elements 2 to make it even better than version 1.0.

Thanks to all of my fellow photographers who contributed to this book. Sairam Suresh, Bobby Joe, Neal Tucker, Kieca Mahoney, and especially Julie Ann Lee: You are all great photographers. Thanks for giving me permission to use your photos in my book!

Thank you, Mom, for trusting me with so many of your sacred photos. And, special thanks to Marta Justak for being such a supportive, invaluable agent and friend.

A big thank you to the wonderful team at Que Publishing for being so helpful, and for helping me put together such a great book. Thanks to Candy Hall for asking me to write this book. Special thanks to Laura Norman for being such an expert editor and manager of this book's layout and design, and Tyler and Rima Regas for their much-appreciated technical expertise. Finally, thanks to all the teams at Que who helped put this book together and make it out into the world.

We Want to Hear from You!

As the reader of this book, *you* are our most important critic and commentator. We value your opinion and want to know what we're doing right, what we could do better, what areas you'd like to see us publish in, and any other words of wisdom you're willing to pass our way.

As an associate publisher for Que, I welcome your comments. You can email or write me directly to let me know what you did or didn't like about this book—as well as what we can do to make our books better.

Please note that I cannot help you with technical problems related to the *topic* of this book. We do have a User Services group, however, where I will forward specific technical questions related to the book.

When you write, please be sure to include this book's title and author as well as your name, email address, and phone number. I will carefully review your comments and share them with the author and editors who worked on the book.

Email: feedback@quepublishing.com

Mail: Greg Wiegand
Que Publishing
201 West 103rd Street
Indianapolis, IN 46290 USA

For more information about this book or another Que title, visit our Web site at www.quepublishing.com. Type the ISBN (excluding hyphens) or the title of a book in the Search field to find the page you're looking for.

INTRODUCTION

Photoshop Elements is Adobe's replacement for Photoshop LE, which was commonly bundled with scanners, cameras, and computers. Adobe introduced Photoshop Elements 1 in the spring of 2001, and it has been a huge success. Version 2, which is the latest release, has full support for Mac OS X and Windows XP, plus revisions to many of the cool features in Photoshop Elements 1. Although Photoshop Elements 2 doesn't have all the features you'll find in Photoshop, it does contain a few things you won't find in Photoshop, such as a shortcuts toolbar, Red Eye Brush Tool, the Quick Fix window, Selection Brush, Send to Email shortcut, Save As PDF shortcut, and the Photomerge Wizard. There are also tools such as Adjust Backlighting and Fill Flash that enable you to darken or lighten midtones in an image, and the automatic color-correction command. What's most important, Photoshop Elements enables you to apply many of the same top-notch photo-editing techniques that make Photoshop so popular.

About *Absolute Beginner's Guide to Adobe Photoshop Elements 2*

Digital imaging has evolved from simple bitmap graphics, such as the first icons used with Macintosh computers, to full-blown, full-color, high-resolution, still-frame and digital video editing. Since those early days of black-and-white bit flipping, high-cost scanners and digital cameras have plummeted in price while exponentially improving in image quality, performance, and features. Today, people can use digital cameras to instantly share exciting, fresh images on printed paper or on the Web, or convert old, damaged photos into digital data using a flatbed or film scanner. Photoshop Elements enables you to correct colors, repair and enhance images, and share the results. For example, you can put together an old yearbook online or digitize your family tree without having to worry about dirt, dust, and aging affecting your digital images.

I can't believe how many years I've been learning about digital images and trying to improve my digital-imaging editing skills. First, I spent years experimenting with black-and-white and color photography. Years ago, I remember how disappointed I was when I took my first 640×480 digital pictures with Apple's QuickTime camera. Today, I have a three-megapixel camera, and I take only digital pictures.

The point I want to make is that working with digital images is much easier and affordable today than it ever was. Programs such as Photoshop Elements make it easy to learn to work with digital images and produce satisfying results. However, easy doesn't necessarily mean fast. Photoshop Elements provides the tools that enable you to spend a lot of quality time perfecting an image and experimenting with images, new and old.

Photoshop Elements is both an easy-to-use and a sophisticated application. You can try a quick fix on an image, as well as perform some heavy-duty image editing, beginning with hours of experimentation, which extends into days of fine-tuning. Keeping this range of tasks in mind, I've designed this book for those who have opened their first scanner or digital camera and have little experience working with digital images. Or, if you already have a scanner or digital camera, and have upgraded to Photoshop Elements from another application, you'll learn how to use combinations of tools to improve or create new digital images.

Whom This Book Is For

My hope is that you, the reader, can sit down and start doing something with Photoshop Elements by first understanding some of the basic concepts of digital imaging, and then following a set of steps, or a variation on a set of steps, in this book. I'd also like to think the examples in this book will inspire you to extend your creativity. I try to write books that teach some useful skills, produce tangible results, and show you that computers can do great things if you take the time to explore what's possible.

Like Photoshop Elements, this book isn't for the complete novice—someone just sitting down with his or her very first computer. If you're familiar with a Windows or Macintosh computer and new to Photoshop Elements or digital photography, this book is for you. If you're new to Photoshop Elements or version 2.0, this book can show you how to perform many of those swanky Photoshop techniques with Photoshop Elements 2.

What's New in Version 2?

Photoshop Elements 2 improves upon many of the cool features that were in the first version. The Web Photo Gallery has several new Web page layouts and options, Photomerge enables you to create more dynamic panoramas, and the File Browser is even easier to use. Following is a brief list of features that changed in Photoshop Elements 2:

- The Quick Start window has been redesigned and is called the *Welcome window.*
- The shortcuts bar has been redesigned with new buttons, such as the Attach to Email, Browse, and Quick Fix buttons, and the Search text box.

- The Selection Brush Tool is new, and some of the tools in the Toolbox have been relocated. Color buttons are new to each of the shortcut and options buttons, and the Toolbox tools too! Move the cursor over each button to see each icon in color.

- There are more shapes, layer styles, and recipes, and improved tutorials.

- The Variations dialog box has been dubbed the Color Variations dialog box, and has a whole new look.

- The Recipes palette has been renamed the *How To* palette, and the History palette is called the *Undo History* palette.

- The Auto Color Correction, Quick Fix, and Selection Brush tools are a few of the new features that appear in 2.0.

- JPEG 2000 is a new file format you can use to create customized JPEG files. You can open and edit JPEG 2000 files only with Photoshop Elements 2.

How to Use This Book

I had two goals in mind when I put this book together. Because this book is about Photoshop Elements, my first goal was to introduce you to the digital-imaging features in the program. The examples and steps in this book are just some of the many ways you can work with digital images. My second goal was to introduce you to working with digital images. This involves using a small combination of tools, observation skills, and a little creativity. With a little luck, my examples will help you design and create your own pictures that you can share with others.

This book is divided into four parts. The first two parts show you how to get images into and out of Photoshop Elements 2. These are basic skills that you might already be familiar with if you've used other graphics applications. The latter two parts make up the larger portion of the book. They show you how to do some basic, simple tasks, and grow on those skills to perform more complicated, advanced tasks. You can read this book from cover to cover, use it as a reference, or go to any particular chapter you like.

Except for the system requirements and installation sections, all the screenshots created for this book were created with Windows XP Pro and Photoshop Elements 2. The Macintosh and Windows versions of Photoshop Elements 2 are similar, so Mac users should be able to follow along. Tool shortcuts and menu command shortcuts are included for both Windows and Mac. Macintosh keyboard keys and shortcuts appear as (Command-C), and Windows keyboard keys and shortcuts appear as [Ctrl+C].

You'll find tips, notes, cautions, and sidebars throughout this book. Each contains a different kind of helpful hints. Some chapters also contain variations on a set of steps, which take a particular skill, such as color correcting, and show you how to adjust the exposure and hot spots in an image in addition to how to fine-tune brightness and contrast settings for an image.

tip

Tips highlight something new, something cool, something helpful, and something true.

Cautions warn you about potential pitfalls or tell you ways to troubleshoot a potential problem.

note

Notes point out a related tidbit of information about a chapter topic.

YOUR MILEAGE CAN VARY

In a perfect world, this book would be all things to all Photoshop Elements owners. I realize, however, that I'll fall short explaining a technical doodad, or skimp on coverage about filter effects. Hey, if you want to see what all the filters look like in Photoshop Elements, open the Filters palette and choose All from the drop-down menu. You won't find out how to use every single one in this book! Because I'm cutting to the chase, I might as well tell you that there's no coverage of how to create Jackson Pollack–style brushes, or how to create the perfect collage or montage.

Also, sidebars point out some interesting factoids that are related to the local chapter topic.

The Contents of This Book

Absolute Beginner's Guide to Adobe Photoshop Elements 2 takes you from simple tasks to complex ones. The book begins by taking you through some of the more elementary features, such as understanding the work area, and some simple tasks such as resizing or auto-correcting the tonal range of an image. It then gradually introduces you to using combinations of tools to correct, repair, and combine digital images into animation or panoramic photos.

Most of the book focuses on building on fundamental techniques for improving, correcting, combining, or creating great-looking digital pictures. Each part of this book introduces you to a different digital-imaging element of the program, from scanning and printing images to color correction and animation.

Part I—Photoshop Elements Setup

It doesn't take a rocket scientist to set up Photoshop Elements. In fact, you can skip to Part II if you aren't interested in how the work area is laid out, or how different tools and windows are related to one another in the work area. If you do want to customize a preference or turn off a setting, you can always come back and revisit these chapters.

Chapter 1—Familiarize yourself with all the tools, menus, and windows in the work area.

Chapter 2—Find out how to customize the color, tool, and program settings.

Chapter 3—Learn how to connect, view, and download images from a digital camera or scanner.

Part II—Opening, Saving, and Printing Images

For those of you who take photos that look great as is, you can learn how to view, save, and print them in Photoshop Elements. I've also thrown in some simple tweaking tasks, so you can quickly straighten or automatically correct an image.

Chapter 4—Open sesame, or Open As sesame. Find out how to open and convert image files. Image modes and resolution for printers, monitors, scanners, and cameras are also explained.

Chapter 5—Explore the exciting world of file formats and learn how to optimize and save the right file for printing or for the Web. Also, find out how to upload images to a Web server.

Chapter 6—Get the scoop on how to print images with grayscale or color printers. Print a folder of files to a contact sheet using the built-in Automate command. Also, learn how to create picture packages showing one picture multiple times in different sizes, all on the same page.

Part III—Correcting and Combining Images

Start taking a walk on the wild side of digital imaging. Take a scanned or camera-captured image and learn how to work with color. You also learn how to fix numerous kinds of color-related problems using the arsenal of tools in the Toolbox and menus.

Chapter 7—Take a short course and learn how to interpret all the colors in front of your eyes. Work with the palettes that enable you to control color for any open image.

Chapter 8—Jump into a slew of color-correction techniques, and consider a few variations that can help bring an old photo alive.

Chapter 9—Experiment with filters and effects to enhance digital pictures. Learn how to hide things you don't want to see, and bring out objects or areas in a picture.

Chapter 10—Combine, remove, and perform advanced correction techniques by taking full advantage of layers, copy and paste commands, and the Clipboard.

Chapter 11—Add a title, or enhance text by putting an image inside each character. Use the shape and drawing tools to make your mark on an image.

Chapter 12—Repair old photos scanned in from negatives or damaged photo paper.

Chapter 13—Create complex pictures and recipes that can help you experiment with any previous set of tasks to pump up an image.

Part IV—Designing Complex Images

After you've primed and polished your images, you can go the distance and learn more advanced tasks, such as animating your images or creating a Web photo gallery.

Chapter 14—Put together two or more images to create complex images.

Chapter 15—Learn to create animation, or more precisely, an animated GIF.

Chapter 16—Stitch together two or more pictures and create a panorama. Photoshop Elements has a built-in tool, the Photo Merge Wizard, that magically combines similar photos to create a panorama.

Chapter 17—Create a slideshow and Web photo gallery out of any folder full of images. Photoshop Elements can generate HTML and JavaScript code, as well as resize your image files.

Glossary—You'll find definitions for most of the acronyms and Photoshop Elements terms used in this book in the glossary.

PART i

PHOTOSHOP ELEMENTS SETUP

1

NAVIGATING THE WORK AREA

The Welcome window, menu bar, tools, palettes, image window, short-cuts bar, and options bar compose the work area. Each brings a unique set of features to Photoshop Elements. As you work with different image files, you will find that there are several workflow processes you can follow. Before taking a look at how you want to use Photoshop Elements to explore these workflow processes, you'll take a tour of the work area. Workflow processes are covered in more detail in Parts III and IV of this book.

You'll also learn how to open and save an image file—two tasks you'll find yourself doing almost every time you use Photoshop Elements. You can open an image to determine its dimensions, to combine it with other images, or to simply view or print it. Of course, you also can modify any image using the Toolbox or palette tools. Finally, you might want to save the image in one or more image file formats so that you can preserve a work in progress or publish the image on a Web site or print it.

Comparing the Macintosh and Windows Work Areas

The Mac and Windows versions of Photoshop Elements have more in common than you'd think. Virtually all the Toolbox tools, shortcuts, options, and palettes are identical, except for one or two check boxes and options that are specific to Mac and Windows. To help you distinguish the differences as you read through this book, I've noted which menu commands, dialog boxes, and controls are available for either Mac or Windows.

The differences between the Mac and Windows versions are largely due to the differences between these two operating systems. Windows programs open with a large window connected to the menu bar. You can resize the work area by resizing this background window. If you close this window, Photoshop Elements exits to the desktop. The status bar and image information are located at the bottom of the work area. On a Mac, the work area is shared with the desktop. Document information and status bar information are located at the bottom of the active image window.

In addition to the three-dimensional buttons and beautifully designed windows, window controls, shortcut menus, menu bars, and other user interface elements, you'll find that the menus on Mac OS X are organized differently than those on Mac OS 9 and Windows. For example, there's a **Photoshop Elements** menu in Mac OS X. The **About Photoshop Elements**, **Color Settings**, **Preferences**, **Hide/Show Photoshop Elements**, and **Quit** commands are stored in the Photoshop Elements menu. Some of the menu commands, such as the **Window, Images, Bring All to Front** command, are available only on Mac OS X. Others, such as the **Window, Status Bar** command, are available only on Windows.

Like Mac OS 9, Mac OS X has an Apple menu, although the menu commands differ between Mac OS 9 and Mac OS X. The **Start** menu in Windows is similar to the Apple menu in Mac OS. Aside from the differences between operating systems, not many things are different between the Mac and Windows versions of Photoshop Elements. If you're familiar with Mac OS or Windows, you should have no problems using either one to get stuff done with Photoshop Elements.

Getting Familiar with the Welcome Window

When you start Photoshop Elements, the Welcome window will appear in the middle of the work area. You can open it by choosing Welcome from the Window menu. There are six buttons you can choose from; each enables you to jump to a palette window, perform a menu command, or exit the Welcome window. The following list explains each button in the Welcome window (see Figure 1.1):

■ **New File**—Create and open a new document window and choose the dimensions, resolution, and color mode of the document. The **Preset Sizes** drop-down menu enables you to configure the document to specific paper, screen, or print dimensions.

■ **Browse for File**—Open the **File Browser** palette and navigate your hard drive to preview any image you want to open.

FIGURE 1.1

Bring an image into the work area with a single click, or access tutorials or help from the Welcome window.

■ **Connect to Camera or Scanner**—Control a scanner or camera and download an image into a new image window.

■ **Common Issues**—Open the **How To** palette and view common Photoshop Elements issues.

■ **Tutorial**—Learn how to use some of the advanced features in Photoshop Elements.

■ **Exit Welcome Screen**—Click this button to close the Welcome window.

Creating a New File

Click the **New File** button in the Welcome window to create an empty document window. Before you type in the width and height of the document, select the unit of measurement you want to use to determine the size of the document. Choose from pixels, inches, centimeters, points, or picas. The example in Figure 1.2 shows the dimensions in pixels, which is the typical unit of measurement for an image. Fill in the rest of the settings you want for your new window, and then click **OK**. A blank image window will appear in the work area.

tip

You can replace the sunflower with your own custom image. Create a 300×310 pixel image at a resolution of 72 ppi and name it `PS_Elemements Quickstart_06.jpg`. Rename the existing file in the `HTMLPalettes\Welcome\Images` folder located in the `Photoshop Elements 2` folder. Exit Photoshop Elements, and then relaunch the program to view your custom image in the Welcome window.

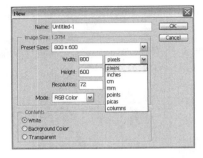

The Welcome window provides three ways to open an image window in the work area. You can click the **New File** button, **Browse for File** button, or **Connect to Camera or Scanner** button. The **New File** button enables you to create a new image window. The **Browse for File** button enables you to open the **File Browser** palette or window.

As its name implies, the **Connect to Camera or Scanner** button enables you to import images from cameras and scanners. The **Connect to Camera or Scanner** button opens a dialog box that contains a list of installed TWAIN plug-ins. View and select a TWAIN plug-in from the Import Source window list, and then use the digital camera's software to download an image from the external device into a new window in the work area.

note

If you do not want the Welcome window to appear when you start Photoshop Elements 2, uncheck the Show This Screen at Startup check box.

Browsing Files

Click on the **Browse for Files** button to open the **File Browser** palette (see Figure 1.3). The **File Browser** palette enables you to select one or more photos by navigating folders and previewing files stored on your local hard drive, network server, or removable media such as a CD, DVD, or Zip cartridge. You can view thumbnails of all the image files stored in a particular folder. The first time you preview images in the File Browser, it may take a few seconds for each thumbnail to draw. Faster computers and hard disks enable Photoshop Elements to draw thumbnails more speedily in the File Browser.

To open an image file double-click a thumbnail. Alternatively, you can (**Ctrl-click**) [**right-click**] on a thumbnail and choose the Open command to open an image file in the work area. To select more than one image, hold down the (**Option**) [**Alt**] key and click on each image you want to select. Double-click any of the selected thumbnails to open the group of selected images.

Click once on an image to select it. The selected image will appear on the middle-left side of the File Browser window. The EXIF (Exchangeable Image File format), or camera-specific information for the photo, will appear in the lower-left corner of the File Browser window, enabling you to see the height, width, image file format, name, and camera settings for each photo. EXIF is the standard format used by most digital cameras to store interchangeable information, such as the date, time, shutter speed, exposure setting, metering system, and other camera-specific data used for a particular photo. EXIF information is commonly referred to as an EXIF annotation.

note

For Windows users, to open a file in a different file format, you have to use the **Open As** command from the **File** menu.

FIGURE 1.3

The File Browser enables you to navigate and preview photos stored on local hard drives, removable media, CDs, and network server.

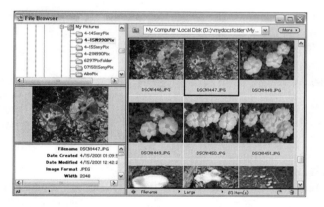

Connecting to a Camera or Scanner

Before you can use the **Acquire** command to control a camera or scanner, you must install the TWAIN plug-in for that device. You also will need to connect a USB or serial cable to the digital device and computer, and power on the device.

Some vendors provide a separate installer program for the TWAIN plug-in, and others install it as part of a software application that comes bundled with the camera or scanner. Most camera and scanner vendors advertise whether a TWAIN plug-in is bundled with a camera or scanner product. If you're shopping for a camera or scanner and don't plan to use a card reader to copy your files to your computer, purchase a camera or scanner that comes with a TWAIN plug-in. This will enable you to control the device using Photoshop Elements.

Click the **Connect to Camera or Scanner** button in the Welcome window to access any connected devices, as shown in Figure 1.4. The Select Import Source window will open. A list of TWAIN plug-in files installed on your hard drive will appear in the window list. Choose a device from the Select Import Source window, and bring an image directly into the work area.

FIGURE 1.4

A list of TWAIN plug-ins appears in the Select Import Source window if you click the Acquire button in the Welcome window.

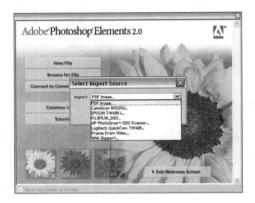

The software that opens from the Select Import Source dialog box is the software created specifically for a particular model of a digital camera or scanner. Select the images you want to view or save from the device's software window. Then download them to your hard drive.

The rate at which an image is acquired depends on what kind of cable is used to connect the camera or scanner to the computer. Most of the newer cameras and scanners have a USB connector, which supports a faster data transfer rate than its predecessor, the serial port. Some of the higher-end scanners, in the $1,000 price range, also have a FireWire (officially called IEEE 1394) port available for connecting to a computer. FireWire ports can support the faster data transfer rates between a digital device and a computer. If the computer does not have a USB port, you will need to download images over the serial port. Most digital cameras will include a USB-to-serial adapter cable. However, newer cameras tend to support only USB connections. If you own a computer that doesn't have a USB port, you can easily and

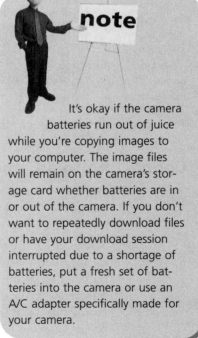

note

It's okay if the camera batteries run out of juice while you're copying images to your computer. The image files will remain on the camera's storage card whether batteries are in or out of the camera. If you don't want to repeatedly download files or have your download session interrupted due to a shortage of batteries, put a fresh set of batteries into the camera or use an A/C adapter specifically made for your camera.

inexpensively add USB to your system by purchasing a serial-to-USB or PC card adapter peripheral.

Accessing Common Issues

The **Common Issues** button opens the common issues information in the **How To** palette. Each issue appears as a link. Click on a link to view more information about each issue (see Figure 1.5). Click on the drop-down menu in the How To palette and choose **Download New Adobe Recipes** to connect to Adobe's Web site and update the list of common issues in the **How To** palette.

FIGURE 1.5

Access the How To information on common issues by clicking the **Common Issues** button in the Welcome window.

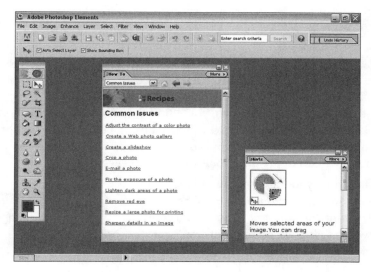

Viewing Tutorials

Click the **Tutorial** button to learn how to use some of the more advanced features (see Figure 1.6). You can, for example, walk through some basic step-by-step examples in a browser application that show you how to use layers, create a multi-picture panorama, or produce an animation. You also can jump to Adobe's Web site and view more online tutorials there. Of course, this book contains all that and more, so read on!

Introducing the Work Area

Some of the first things you'll notice are the menu bar, shortcuts, and options bars located at the top of the work area. The menu bar itself contains a healthy total of 10 menus. Located directly below the menu bar is the shortcuts bar, which holds (you guessed it) shortcuts to tasks such as printing, browsing, saving, and going to Adobe Online. Just below the shortcuts bar, you'll find the options bar. The options bar's contents change depending on which tool is selected in the Toolbox.

FIGURE 1.6

A few advanced tutorials are installed with Photoshop Elements. Click the **Tutorial** button to view the tutorials in a browser application.

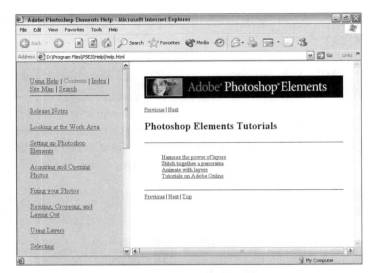

Over to the left of the work area, you'll find the indispensable Toolbox. If you've seen Photoshop or other graphics applications, the tool buttons might look familiar to you. You'll find selection, drawing, editing, and color-selection tools in the Toolbox. You can apply these tools to any image window.

Another thing you might notice are the floating window palettes. A *palette* is a type of window that you can drag around and combine with other palettes, but that won't get lost in a crowd of windows. A palette is always in front of all the other image windows in the work area. The palette well (on the right end of the shortcuts bar) houses all the palettes when they aren't in use. To use a palette, you can choose the palette name from the **Window** menu, or click its tab and drag it from the palette well onto the work area (see Figure 1.7).

tip

Move the **Hints** palette to the lower-right corner of the work area. By default it opens in the upper-right corner, which makes it disappear when you select a tab in the palette well.

The status bar is located at the bottom of the work area if you're running Windows. On a Mac, the status bar information appears at the bottom of each image window. The status bar displays information about the image window, such as how much disk space it's occupying or its dimensions. You can customize the status bar to show one of the following data items: document dimensions, document sizes, document profile, scratch size, efficiency, timing, and current tool. If you're running Windows, you can view help text for the selected tool in the right portion of the status bar. The next section explores the tools in the shortcuts and options bars.

FIGURE 1.7

The palette well resides in the shortcuts bar alongside the shortcut icons.

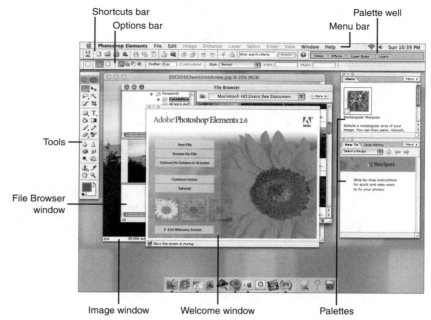

Shortcuts bar
Options bar
Palette well
Menu bar
Tools
File Browser window
Image window
Welcome window
Palettes

Using the Shortcuts and Options Bars

The shortcuts bar brings some of the most frequently selected menu commands to the work area. You can quickly open, save, or print a document with a single mouse click instead of having to click and select a menu command or learn a keyboard shortcut. You can also open the Quick Fix, Color Variations dialog box or send a photo in email.

Shortcuts not only help you save time, but also are smart! Each shortcut button becomes selectable only when certain conditions are met. For example, most shortcuts require an open image window.

Each shortcut button has two states, active and inactive. For example, if you haven't made any changes to an image in the image window, the Save shortcut button will appear grayed out in the shortcuts bar and will not be selectable. Similarly, if you haven't modified an image file, the Step Forward shortcut will be unselectable.

note

You can close a palette by clicking in its Close box. The **x** button in each palette and image window represents the Close box if you're running Windows or Mac OS X. Mac OS 9 users can click the left square in the title bar of the palette or image window.

HOW TO SHOW AND HIDE PALETTES

You can hide or show the shortcuts and options bars, as well as the tools and palettes by choosing the **Shortcuts** or **Options** command from the **Window** menu. Choose **Window, Tools** if you want to show or hide the Toolbox. A check will appear beside each Window menu item that is visible onscreen.

If you press the **Tab** button once, you can hide all palettes, plus the Toolbox, shortcuts bar, and options bar. Press the **Tab** button once more, and presto—they're back!

The following list (starting from the left side of the shortcuts bar) gives you a brief description of each button and its function:

- **Adobe.com**—Click this button to visit Adobe's Web site. You will need to click the links to locate and view the latest information available about Photoshop Elements, including information about software updates and third-party plug-in information.

- **New Document**—Open a new document window by clicking this shortcut button.

- **Open Document**—Navigate your hard drive and select an existing image file to open in the work area.

- **Browse**—Open the File Browser window to navigate images on your hard drive or network and select the file you want to open.

- **Import**—Open the Select Import Source dialog box and select a scanner, camera, or video clip to import an image into the work area.

- **Save Document**—If you've made any changes to an image file, click this shortcut button to save your changes.

- **Save for Web**—The Save for Web window enables you to customize a file you want to save for the Web. Select a Web file format for an image, and preview settings in the Save for Web window by clicking this button.

- **Save As PDF**—Enables you to save an image as an encoded ZIP or JPEG file. You can use the Adobe Acrobat browser plug-in or another graphics program to view PDF files on a Windows or Macintosh computer.

- **Attach to Email**—Opens the Attach to Email dialog box. Auto-convert an image to a 1,200×900-pixel (6×8-inch) image or send it as is. After you choose an email option, Photoshop Elements creates a new email message and attaches the photo. All you need to do is add a list of recipients, type a message, and send it off to the Internet.

- **Online Services**—Opens the Online Services Assistant dialog box. You can download new recipes and other Photoshop Elements files from Adobe's Web site using the Online Services Assistant.

■ **Print Document**—When you're ready to print your image, click this shortcut button to send the image file to a color or black-and-white printer.

■ **Print Preview Document**—Preview a document before sending it to the printer by clicking the Print Preview shortcut button.

■ **Step Backward/Step Forward**—Clicking one of these buttons moves you backward or forward through tasks performed on the document, logged in the History palette.

■ **Quick Fix**—Opens the Quick Fix dialog box. Correct colors, adjust brightness/contrast, and modify focus and rotation of the image using the options in the Quick Fix dialog box.

■ **Color Variations**—The Color Variations window enables you to preview and modify red, green, blue, and saturation color changes to the active image window.

■ **Search**—Type one or more words into the Search text box to let Photoshop Elements find How To, Help, and Tutorial information on a particular topic. Any matching results will appear in the Search Results palette.

■ **Help Contents**—Clicking the Help button opens a browser window and brings up the HTML-based Help contents for Photoshop Elements.

SEPARATED AT BIRTH?

The options bar works right alongside each tool located in the Toolbox. That is, the buttons, text boxes, drop-down menus, and check boxes in the options bar change depending on which tool is selected. After a tool is selected, you can adjust any available settings from the options bar. Click in a text box, click and drag a slider control, or select an item from a drop-down menu list to customize the selected tool.

Introducing the Toolbox

The Toolbox contains two vertical columns of tools. Although this window opens by default on the left side of the work area, you can drag and drop it anywhere on your desktop. If you have two monitors connected to your computer, you can place the Toolbox on one monitor and the image window on the other screen. You can choose **Tools** from the **Window** menu if you want to hide or show tools in the work area.

Before you start clicking away on those tools, remember that only one tool at a time can be applied to an image window. Also, some tools, such as the Dodge, Burn, and Clone Stamp tools, require an image to be in RGB mode before you can use them. Other tools, such as the Clone Stamp and Selection Brush tools, work with special keys, such as the Alt (Option) or Caps Lock keys, to enable a feature in the tool. The foreground and background colors, shown at the bottom of the Toolbox, can also affect the way the tool can be applied to an image. Most tools, except for the Eraser Tool, apply the foreground color to the image window.

A total of 40 tools are available in the Toolbox, but you can see only 24 of them. Why? Well, some tools are hidden in the Toolbox. Simply click and hold down the mouse over the desired tool to view its hidden alternatives. A small arrow appears in the lower-right corner of the tool if any hidden tools share that space.

For example, the Rectangle Marquee Tool, located in the upper-left corner of the Toolbox, shares its space in the Toolbox with the Elliptical Marquee Tool. When you're using the Rectangle Marquee Tool, the Elliptical Marquee Tool remains hidden in the Toolbox.

Fortunately, each tool in the Toolbox has a shortcut key. Quickly select a tool by pressing a key on the keyboard. You don't have to hunt for an icon and then click the tool's icon every time you want to pick a new tool. If more than one tool shares a shortcut, you can hold down the Shift key and then press the shortcut key to cycle through each tool that shares the same keyboard shortcut. For example, if you want to select the Rectangular Marquee Tool, press the letter M on the keyboard. If you want to choose the Elliptical Marquee Tool, hold down the Shift key and press M again. The icon in the Toolbox will change as you cycle through each tool that shares a particular keyboard shortcut.

The tools in the Toolbox, shown in Figure 1.8, can be grouped into five categories: selection, drawing, effects, miscellaneous, and Color-Picker tools. The following list summarizes the five groups of tools:

- **Selection Tools**—Select an area by shape, define a shape with a lasso tool, or select pixels by color using these handy tools. These tools are located at the top of the Toolbox.

- **Drawing Tools**—Choose the Brush or Pencil Tool and customize the brush settings and other options before you draw or paint on an image. Shape tools enable you to add simple geometric shapes to any image window or photo.

- **Effects Tools**—Remove red-eye, or apply a blur or sharpen tool to an image with a custom-size brush or darken or lighten (burn or dodge) pixels in the image window. There are several effects tools from which you can choose.

- **Miscellaneous Tools**—Magnify or zoom out from the contents in the image window; move an image around in the image window.

- **Color-Picker Tools**—Select a foreground or background color, or clone a pattern of pixels to another part of a photo. This group of additional tools consists of the tools located at the bottom of the Toolbox.

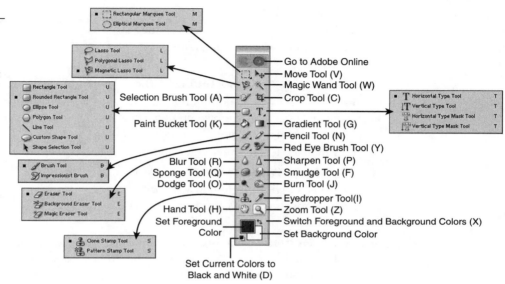

FIGURE 1.8
Forty tools are
stored in the
Toolbox. Click
an icon to select
a tool.

Choosing Pixels with Selection Tools

Selection tools enable you to choose all the pixels in an image, or one or two pixels. Six kinds of selection tools are available. Each one can help you quickly select all or part of the pixels in a layer of the image window. After pixels are selected, you can edit them by applying a menu command, tonal range, color correction, or filter tool to the selected pixels.

NO TOOL IS AN ISLAND

After you select a tool, take a peek at the options bar, located just below the shortcuts bar below the menu bar. Some tools have more options than others. But these options, which also can be viewed from the **Preset Manager** window, enable you to customize the way a tool works.

But wait, there's more! You can find out more about a tool from the Hints palette. The **Hints** palette automatically opens in the upper-right corner of the work area when you first start Photoshop Elements. If you want to manually open or close it, choose **Show Hints** from the **Window** menu, or select the **Hints** tab from the palette well located in the short-cuts bar.

The following list explains what each selection tool can do (see Figure 1.8):

■ **Marquee Tool (M)**—Select an area in a rectangle or circular shape with this tool. The Elliptical Marquee Tool shares this space in the Toolbox.

- **Move Tool (V)**—Click and drag one or more image objects in the image window with this frequently used tool.

- **Lasso Tool (L)**—The Polygonal and Magnetic Lasso tools enable you to click around the shape or color of an object you want to select in the image window.

- **Magic Wand Tool (W)**—Click on a color with this tool to select all touching pixels of that color in an image window.

- **Selection Brush Tool (A)**—Use this brush to select pixels or add or remove pixels from a selection. You can use either a rubylith (red mask) or marching ants (selection) mode to view the selected area created by this brush.

- **Crop Tool (C)**—Select part of an image by applying the Crop Tool to an image file. The Crop Tool enables you to select a rectangular area of an image and removes any image area outside the cropped area.

> **tip**
>
> Beside each tool name is the command-key shortcut you can use to quickly select that tool from the Toolbox. To view a tool's name and short-cut, place the cursor over a tool button. Let it hover over the tool for a few seconds. The tool tip will appear, and the shortcut letter will appear to the right of the tool's name. Press the shortcut key to select a tool.

Working with an Image in the Image Window

Before you can use the selection tools, you'll need to create a new image window or open an image file. When an image window is open, you can pick a tool from the Toolbox and experiment with selecting, drawing, or editing images. The drawing and shape tools enable you to work with vector and bitmap graphics and combine them with an image.

What are vector and bitmap images? Vector images are mathematically calculated graphics such as shapes, or line art–type images created by programs such as Adobe Illustrator. Vector images can be resized without losing image clarity. The mathematical algorithm works with a rasterizer to draw the vector graphics onscreen or on paper. On the other hand, bitmap images, including digital photos, consist of groups, or matrices, of pixels. Bitmap images are not easily scaled up in size. For example, if you try to enlarge a bitmap image, you'll start to see squarish chunks of colors appear. This is called *pixelation*. In contrast, vector graphics are more adept at rising to this occasion.

Of all the tools in the Toolbox, drawing tools offer you the most freedom to be creative (see Figure 1.9). In addition to using the Brush, Shape, and Pencil tools, you can add text, apply a gradient (a range of two or more colors that blend together), use a layer style, or blend layers of images together with the Photoshop Elements tools.

FIGURE 1.9

A tool tip for each tool appears in the Hints palette, or if you hover the cursor over a tool button.

Clone Stamp tool

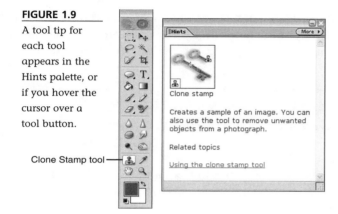

The following list provides a brief description of each of the drawing tools:

- **Shape Tool (U)**—Add a vector graphic to an image using one of six shape tools: Rectangle, Rounded Rectangle, Ellipse, Polygon, Line, or Custom Shape. Or modify a shape with the Shape Selection Tool.

- **Type Tool (T)**—Text objects are a special kind of vector graphic. You can continue to modify text after you add it to a document by selecting the Horizontal or Vertical Text tools, and then selecting the text you want to modify from the image window. After you convert the text into a bitmap, though, you won't be able to use the Type Tool to modify the bitmap text. The Type Mask tools enable you to add text directly to an image layer. Horizontal and Vertical Type generates bitmap text, which is not editable. After you add it to an image, you can't change it, but you can always Undo.

- **Paint Bucket Tool (K)**—Fill an area with a solid color using the foreground color from the color well combined with the Paint Bucket Tool.

- **Gradient Tool (G)**—A gradient consists of two colors in which one fades gently into the other from one end of the selected area to the opposite end. You can use the Gradient Tool to create a virtual sunset, focused lighting, or other

tip

To find out more about how to add text and graphics to an image, see Chapter 11, "Adding Text and Shapes to Images."

effects by placing a gradient over the Fill area of a shape or graphic in the image window.

- **Brush Tool (B)**—Experiment with different brush sizes, tips, and colors with either the paint brush or the Impressionist brush. You can choose a custom brush tip for this tool from the options bar. The Impressionist brush enables you to paint with stylized brush strokes. You can customize the brush, blending mode, opacity, style, fidelity, area, and spacing of the tool in the options bar.

- **Pencil Tool (P)**—If you don't need a straight line, or want to replace one colored pixel with a new color, try using this tool.

- **Eraser Tool (E)**—This shares its space with the Background Eraser and the Magic Eraser. The Eraser Tool can be applied to a single layer or across all layers in the image window. The Background Eraser can remove the contents in the background layer of the image. The Magic Eraser replaces the color you click with the foreground color in the image window.

- **Red-Eye Brush Tool (Y)**—Click and drag this tool over a photo of someone with red-eye, and wipe the red away!

Except for the Shape and Type tools most tools in the Toolbox are bitmap tools. The Shape and Type tools create vector graphics, meaning you can dramatically shrink or grow the image without losing the clarity and crispness of the graphic. Bitmaps can be reduced in size. The number of pixels in a bitmap is fixed. As you increase the size of the bitmap, the pixels grow in size, but the clarity of the image doesn't scale, resulting in a pixelated or blocky-looking graphic. Figure 1.10 shows a Shape Tool placed over the bitmap image in the image window. As you draw or add graphics to an image, a new layer is created for each graphic object in the Layers palette. You can combine vector and bitmap graphics into the same image file.

Shape tool   Vector graphic

FIGURE 1.10

Add a vector graphic object to an image file by applying a shape tool to the image window.

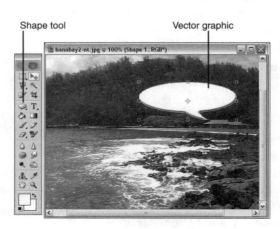

VECTOR AND BITMAP GRAPHICS

Vector and bitmap graphics are equally easy to work with. However, vector graphics are mathematically calculated whereas bitmaps are made up of static pixels. You can apply sophisticated tonal range and color tools, as well as filters and effects to bitmap graphics in Photoshop Elements. Vector graphics enable you to format various font options. For example, you can customize the font family, font size, and font style as often as you like. Text and shape objects are vector objects in Photoshop Elements. Although there are no limits to the size of a bitmap or vector graphic, vector graphics tend to create smaller-size image files. Why do vector graphics generate smaller files? Vector graphics are created with a mathematical algorithm, enabling a program to store less information to generate the final graphic, whereas bitmap fonts are stored pixel by pixel.

Several effect-related tools are also located in the Toolbox. Some of these tools, such as the Blur and Sharpen tools, can also be found in the **Filter** menu. The Red-Eye Brush Tool is one of the new, cool features in Photoshop Elements. The effect-related tools are as listed here:

- **Blur Tool (R)**—Add a localized blur effect to a particular set of pixels by applying this tool to an area of pixels.

- **Sharpen Tool (P)**—Like its big brother the Sharpen filter, this tool compares like-minded pixels and changes their color to try to create the illusion of a sharper, crisper image.

- **Sponge Tool (Q)**—With the right color and blending setting, this tool can act like a wet sponge. Click a color, and then drag this tool over a different color to sponge the first color onto the next one.

- **Smudge Tool (F)**—Click and drag this tool to smudge colors in an image layer. Some of the pixels below the original position of the tool will remain, whereas others move along with the brush to create a smear, or smudge effect.

- **Dodge Tool (O)**—Lighten the shadows, midtones, or highlights of an image using these handy tools.

- **Burn Tool (J)**—Darken the shadows, midtones, or highlights of an image using these handy tools.

tip

As you work on an image, it's possible to lose sight of your original goal for the image. If you want to undo or go back to a previous state of the image (as long as you don't close the image file), you can open the **History** palette and select a previous state of the document and jump back in time. Scroll and zoom changes are not saved in the **History** palette.

In addition to the invaluable effect tools, don't forget to try the Clone Stamp and Pattern Stamp tools. These tools enable you to quickly duplicate a pattern or matrix of pixels in an image, and then apply that pattern elsewhere in the same image. Other tools that can help you select and control key elements are briefly explained in the following list:

- **Clone Stamp/Pattern Stamp Tool (S)**—Hold down the **(Option)** [**Alt**] key and click the cursor over an area of an open image file you want to clone. This becomes the sample point for the tool. You can apply the tool to another location in the open image, and the sampled pixels will be applied wherever you click and drag the tool in the selected layer of the image window (see Figure 1.11). The Pattern Stamp Tool enables you to apply a pattern as a brush in the image window.

- **Eyedropper Tool (I)**—Use this tool to pick a foreground or background color in the image window.

- **Hand Tool (H)**—If you're working on a large or magnified document, select this tool to move the image around within the viewable area of the image window.

- **Zoom Tool (Z)**—Magnify a specific area of an image by selecting this tool, and then clicking in the image window. Hold down the **(Option)** [**Alt**] key to demagnify the image. Double-click this tool to restore the view to 100%.

- **Foreground Color**—The left color square displays the color of a shape, pen, or pencil. It can be added to the selected layer in the image window using the Brush or Paint Bucket tools.

- **Background Color**—This is the color square located immediately to the right of the foreground color. This color appears when you select and delete an area in the image window.

FIGURE 1.11

The Clone Stamp Tool enables you to perform some amazing bitmap cloning. In this example, I've created a clone of the sheep on the right.

Original bitmap

Cloned bitmap

Different Ways to Apply the Clone Stamp Tool

Some of the tools in the Toolbox can sample pixels across all layers. Although most of the examples in this book apply the Clone Stamp Tool across layers, you can do the same with the Magic Wand, Smudge, Blur, and Sharpen tools. The following list describes the Clone Stamp Tool settings available in the options bar:

- **Brush Settings**—Click the brush stroke to open a drop-down menu. Choose a new brush size or stroke, or customize and save your own brushes.

- **Blending Mode**—Choose the blending mode to be applied when the Clone Stamp Tool applies the sampled pixels. See Chapter 10 to find out more about blending modes.

- **Opacity**—Set the transparency level of the applied pixels for the Clone Stamp Tool. Lower values add more transparency.

- **Alignment**—Apply the entire sampled area once to the target area. When the mouse is released, any other areas you choose to apply the tool to are relative to the first area where you applied the tool. Uncheck this option if you want to apply a particular sampled area multiple times to different images.

- **Use All Layers**—Check this option if you want to sample pixels from across layers in the image window. But apply the Clone Stamp Tool only to a correction layer.

THE PATTERN STAMP TOOL

The Pattern Stamp Tool is located with the Clone Stamp Tool in the Toolbox. You can apply a pattern, selectable from the options bar, to the image window with the Pattern Stamp Tool. As with the Clone Stamp Tool, you can choose a custom brush size, and adjust the blending mode and opacity settings for the Pattern Stamp Tool.

Working with Palettes

Tucked away in the palette well are 11 palettes. Each palette has a unique tab, and each tab can be pulled away from the palette well and opened into a standalone palette window in the work area. To activate a palette, click its tab. When a palette window is closed, its tab will reappear in the palette well. If a palette window is open in the work area, you can view or use it as you like. You can also drag and drop palettes one on top of another to create shared palette windows.

Palette windows are designed to make it easier for you to access features in Photoshop Elements. For example, the **File Browser** window enables you to view a thumbnail image of a previously viewed file. Simply double-click an image to open it in the work area (see Figure 1.12).

FIGURE 1.12

The File Browser enables you to preview photos and double-click a thumbnail image to open a file.

GROUPING AND UNGROUPING PALETTES

If you like a particular combination of palettes, you can click and drag each one onto a single palette window to group them together. Each palette window can host additional palettes if you drag and drop one palette window over another. Similarly, you can separate grouped palettes by dragging a palette tab away from its shared window.

The following sections explore the palette windows you'll find in the work area. You'll find out more about how to use a palette as you read through the rest of this book and work through the sample exercises.

Introducing Palettes

You can access each palette from the **Window** menu or from the palette well. Each palette performs a specific function. For example, the **File Browser** palette enables you to preview, select, and open an image file. The **Hints** and **How To** palettes contain helpful information about the tools in the Toolbox and how to use them to correct color and apply effects to an image.

Palettes also share some common features. For example, the **More** menu button is located in the upper-right corner of each palette. A right-arrow icon appears in the tab of a palette located in the palette well, or as the **More** button icon in the floating palette window. Click the **More** button to view unique menu commands for each palette. Some palette windows, such as the **Layers**, **Filters**, and **Swatches** palettes, also have a small set of icon buttons located at the bottom. You can click each button to change the view of the contents in the palette or to perform a special command.

TAKE A PEEK AT THE PALETTE MENU

If you see a right-arrow icon in a palette's tab, this means that the palette contains a drop-down More menu. Click the arrow icon to view the More menu list. Items in the menu list can vary from palette to palette.

The following list introduces you to each of the palette windows in Photoshop Elements:

- **File Browser**—View and open an image file stored on any local or networked drive on your computer. You can use this palette to navigate the image files stored on a hard drive or CD-ROM.

- **Navigator**—You can adjust the view of the image as it appears in the image window. Click and drag the red rectangle in this palette window to pan to different areas of an image.

- **Info**—View X and Y coordinates for your cursor as it hovers over any area in the image, or view the color information below the cursor.

- **Hints**—Read all about any tool you select from the Toolbox or any palette in the palette well. This palette is a floating dictionary!

- **How To**—Learn how to apply one or more tools in Photoshop Elements by following the steps in this palette window. Choose a set of recipes from the drop-down menu, and then click a link to view the set of steps for a particular task.

- **Undo History**—As you apply tools, menu commands, or changes from a palette to an image, each task is logged as an entry in the **History** palette. Click an entry to revert the document to a previous state.

- **Swatches**—Store groups of colors in custom palettes in this handy palette window (see Figure 1.13). You can pick a color from an existing color palette or add your own custom colors to a color palette.

FIGURE 1.13

Create and experiment with custom colors using the Swatches palette.

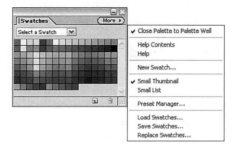

- **Layers**—The **Layers** palette enables you to view each image object, hidden or showing in the image window. Layers enable you to modify images in separate layers, preserving the original image until you're ready to flatten and optimize the final image. You can add, view, or remove layers using the buttons at the bottom of the palette.

■ **Layer Styles**—Customize the way a selected object looks by choosing a layer style. You can apply layer styles to bitmap or vector graphics.

■ **Filters**—Preview or apply filters to the selected area of an image by clicking a button in this palette window.

■ **Effects**—Preview or apply an effect from this palette.

Using the Info, Undo History, and Navigator Palettes

Although each palette window can be used as a standalone tool, two or three can work together to help you get more done faster by streamlining your workflow (see Figure 1.14). For example, if you want to view color information and navigate around an image file, you can open the Navigator and Info palettes in their own separate windows. Simply glance at the open palette window to find out a particular color in an image, or zoom into or out of a picture. You also can keep track of the changes you make to an image by opening the History palette.

FIGURE 1.14

View document information in the **Info**, **Navigator**, and **Undo History** palettes.

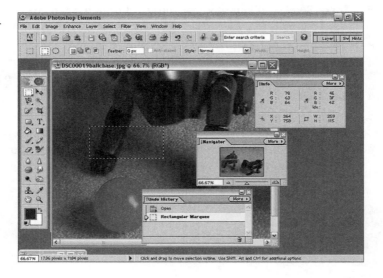

The Info palette enables you to view location and color information in the image window. If you want to pinpoint the location of a particular pixel or create an exact match for a color, you can use the Eyedropper Tool, combined with the Info palette, to get the job done! Click the tab for the Info palette, and then select the Eyedropper Tool from the Toolbox. Move the Eyedropper Tool over the active image window. The cursor location and RGB and hexadecimal color information update as you move the cursor around the image window.

Most tasks you perform in Photoshop Elements are stored as states in the Undo History palette. The **Undo History** palette records the tasks you perform only while it's open in the work area. If you choose a different image window, or save or close the file, and then reopen it, Photoshop Elements will clear all history states. You can click an item in the **Undo History** palette's window list to revert the image window to a previous state. You also can drag and drop a history state over the image window to revert the image to a previous state.

The **Navigator** palette enables you to change the view of the open image. A thumbnail image of the open document appears in the **Navigation** palette. You can drag the slider control to zoom into or away from the contents of the image window, or you can type a number into the **View text** box to change the view in the image window. A red rectangle marks the current view in the palette. You can click and drag the rectangle to pan to a new location of the image in the image window.

tip

You can combine two or more palettes into a single palette window. Click the tab of a palette and drag and drop it over the tab area of a second palette window if you want both palettes to share the same window.

Drag and drop the second palette toward the bottom of a palette window if you want to stack two palette windows one above the other in the work area.

EVERY STEP YOU TAKE

The **Undo History**, **Info**, and **Navigator** palettes enable you to find out precisely what you're looking at (in terms of color, document history, and magnification level) in the image window.

Customizing Images with the How To, Filters, and Effects Palettes

Filters and effects enable you to customize an image. You can preview each filter or effect from the palette window (see Figure 1.15). A filter or an effect can be applied once, or multiple times, to the same image. You also can apply more than one filter or effect to any image. The image window must be in RGB mode before you apply a filter or an effect.

A filter is less complex than an effect. Fifteen groups of filters are installed with Photoshop Elements. Each filter has a unique way of changing an image. Effects, on the other hand, are made up of several filters and a few other items. Four groups of effects are available in the **Effects** palette. Drag and drop a filter or an effect onto the image window to watch it go.

If you want to follow step-by-step instructions to use a particular tool or command, open the **How To** palette. The **How To** palette contains groups of recipes that can show you, for example, how to apply the Red-Eye Brush Tool, correct color, retouch photos, and create Web graphics.

Viewing Objects in the Layers Palette

Any image opened in Photoshop Elements is opened in a single layer, called the *Background layer*. If you copy or create a new layer or paste another image into the image window, a new layer is created for each image object. Each new layer is placed above the background layer.

FIGURE 1.15

Preview effects and filters before applying them to an image. Recipes also enable you to apply a task to all or part of an image.

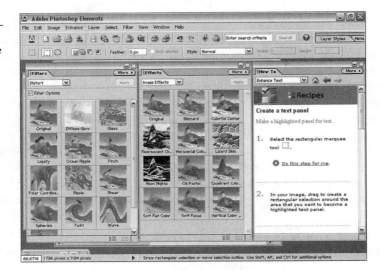

You can view all layers in a document in the Layers palette (see Figure 1.16). The Layers palette enables you to select a specific layer, as well as adjust transparency settings and blending modes for one or all layers. You also can drag and drop layers within the Layers palette to change the order of layers in the document.

FIGURE 1.16

Each object or adjustment layer in a document appears in the Layers palette.

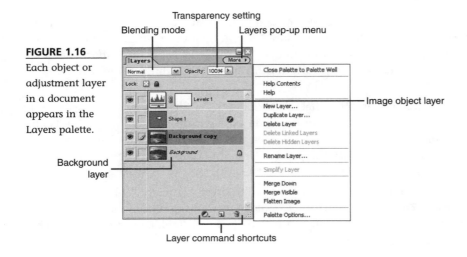

A Closer Look at the Image Window

You might have noticed that the image window is the center of attention in the work area. But it's pretty obvious that you can't do much with Photoshop Elements if you don't have an image file open. In addition to presenting the bitmap, text, or vector graphics, the image window can also display some general information about the image file (see Figure 1.17). Each image window can also sport standard scroll and size controls enabling you to resize or view any part of the image.

FIGURE 1.17

You can view some general information about each image file open in the work area. The filename and color mode of the image window appear in the title bar. The document size of the active window appears on the left side of the status bar.

Viewing Color Mode and Image Size Information

The image window displays the size of the open image, as well as its image mode. Photoshop Elements supports four image modes: RGB, grayscale, indexed color, and bitmap. Each image mode has its own way of managing the color information for the open image. In most cases, a scanned image, or an image from a digital camera, is created as an RGB image and opened in RGB image mode in Photoshop Elements.

When you open an image file, Photoshop Elements changes the document view (also known as the *magnification level*) so that you can view the entire image in the work area. The actual width and height of the image, in pixels and inches, can be viewed by holding down the

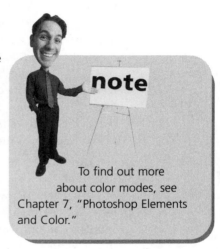

note

To find out more about color modes, see Chapter 7, "Photoshop Elements and Color."

mouse button while the cursor is over the middle section of the status bar (see Figure 1.18).

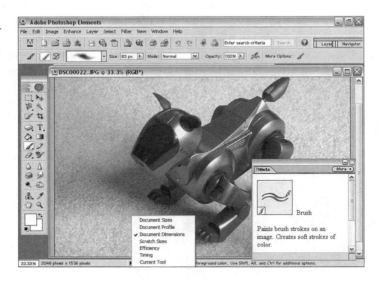

Working with the Image Window

Each document window, which I also call an *image window*, can be moved, resized, hidden, opened, or closed. When a new document is created or an existing image file is opened, Photoshop Elements places the image into a background layer and opens the contents of the file into memory. As you change an image, your changes are stored on a scratch disk on the hard drive.

The name of the image file appears in the title bar of the window. You can move a window by clicking in the window's title bar and dragging it to a new location in the work area. The status bar located at the bottom of the window can be configured to show information about the open file, such as its file size or dimensions. The Macintosh version of Photoshop Elements shows the document status at the bottom of each image window. The Windows version shows the status of the active window in the status bar located at the bottom of the work area.

You can have more than one image window open at once in the work area. The text in the title bar of the active window will be black (or will appear as the color chosen for an active window in Windows or Mac OS), and not gray. The active image window usually is the front window in the

note

To find out more about how to save files, go to Chapter 5, "Saving and Sharing Files."

work area. You can apply tools and commands only to the active image window. Any windows open behind or beside the active window are—you guessed it—inactive. If you don't plan to work with an inactive window, you might want to close it to free up memory.

If you modify the image, Photoshop Elements will ask whether you want to save the changes to the file on your hard drive when you close the image window or exit Photoshop Elements. If you want to preserve any layer information or custom Photoshop settings and pick up where you left off when you next work with this image file, you can save the file as a Photoshop file. You also can save the image file in one of many commonly used graphics file formats for Web or print.

Navigating Menu Commands

The menu bar consists of 10 menus in the work area. Each menu in the menu bar represents a group of commands that can enable you to apply a specific graphics tool to all or part of an image. For example, the **Filters** menu contains groups of filters and effects that, when applied to an image, can create cool-looking effects. The following sections give you an overview of each menu command in Photoshop Elements.

Introducing File Menu Commands

Some of the menu commands, such as **New**, **Open**, and (**Quit**) [**Exit**] will be familiar to you if you've used other Windows or Mac OS applications. Photoshop Elements has an extended set of commands in its **File** menu, more so than most applications. For example, you can optimize an image for the Web by choosing the Save for Web command, or preview an image by choosing the Print Preview command. The following list introduces you to each command that resides in the File menu:

Mac OS X folks will have two additional menus (aren't you lucky!): Apple and Photoshop Elements. However, with a few exceptions, the Mac and the Windows versions have almost identical menu commands.

- ■ **New**—Opens the New document window, enabling you to define the exact dimensions, image mode, and resolution.
- ■ **New from Clipboard**—Pastes the contents of the Clipboard into a new image window. Use the **Edit**, **Copy** command in Photoshop Elements or another program to place text or graphics in the Clipboard. Choose **File**, **New** from Clipboard to paste the Clipboard contents into a new, custom-tailored image window.

■ **Open/Open As**—Opens an image file. The **Open As** command enables you to convert an image file into a supported Photoshop Elements file format. For a complete list of supported file formats, see Chapter 4, "Creating, Opening, and Converting Images."

OPEN SESAME

There are a few more ways you can open an image file in the work area. You can use the **Copy** command in Photoshop Elements or another application to move a file to the Clipboard and then paste it into a new image window.

You also can choose the **Open Recent** command from the **File** menu. A list of previously opened files will appear in the menu list. Click on a file to open it.

If you want to create a panorama, choose the **Photomerge** command from the **File** menu. To find out how to create a panorama, go to Chapter 16, "Stitching Together a Panorama."

■ **Browse**—Opens the **File Browser** palette or File Browser window (if the palette is detached from the palette well).

■ **Open Recent**—Brings up a submenu containing the 10 most recently opened image files.

■ **Create Photomerge**—Opens the Photomerge window that enables you to create horizontal or vertical panoramas.

■ **Close**—Closes the active, open window.

■ **Close All**—Closes all open windows.

■ **Save**—Saves the active image window. If this command is used on a new image window, the Save dialog box will appear, enabling you to name the image, navigate to the folder where you want to save the file, and choose a file format.

> **note**
>
> If you're eager to play with digital images and don't want to get familiar with all the menu commands in Photoshop Elements, skip ahead to the next chapter, or to Part III of this book.

■ **Save/Save As**—Use this command, and use it often, to save a native Photoshop file or any other supported file format. For a complete list of supported file formats, see Chapter 5, "Saving and Sharing Files." The Save As command enables you to choose a new name and file format for the file you want to save.

■ **Save for Web**—Optimize an image for the Web by opening the Save for Web window. You can save a GIF, JPEG, PNG-8, PNG-24, or animated GIF from this window.

- **Revert**—Removes any changes made to the document, returning it to its original contents when it was first opened. This tool can revert the document to only its last-saved state.

- **Attach to Email**—Opens a dialog box enabling you to resize or send the image as is to your default email program.

- **Create Web Photo Gallery**—Opens the Web Photo Gallery dialog box. Select the layout and photos you want to use to create a photo gallery you can view on CD-ROM or on your Web site.

- **Online Services**—Enables you to update Photoshop Elements and get the latest bug fixes and software changes.

- **Place**—Enables you to place an imported PDF, Illustrator, or EPS file, or an image stored in the Clipboard, into a specific place in the image window.

- **Import**—Select this command to control a scanner or camera device that works with installed TWAIN software. A list of installed TWAIN plug-ins can be found in the Import menu.

- **Export**—Save an image file using the **Export** menu command. You can install plug-in files that enable you to export an image file to a custom file format.

- **Batch Processing**—Opens the Batch window that enables you to resize, rename, or convert one or more image files automatically.

- **Automation Tools**—Choose from creating an automated contact sheet, picture package, or Web photo gallery, or run a simple automated task, such as resizing photos on a batch of image files.

- **File Info**—Add caption, copyright, URL, and EXIF information to a document. EXIF information displays camera, scanner, or other device-specific information related to the image file.

- **Print Preview/Print**—Print commands enable you to preview the page layout, configure the way the document will print, and then send the image to the printer as a print job. For best results, check the **Scale to Fit Media** check box to retain high-resolution image quality and print the image to any height and width. Preview the image in the left window pane.

- **Page Setup**—Enables you to choose portrait or landscape orientation for the open image file and select the paper size and scale of the active image window.

- **Print Layouts**—Choose a picture package if you want to print a photo at different sizes on a single sheet of paper. Select **Contact Sheet** to print thumbnail images of images stored on your hard drive.

- **(Quit) [Exit]**—Terminates the Photoshop Elements application. This command is located in the Photoshop Elements menu in Mac OS X.

Exploring Edit Menu Commands

Commands in the Edit menu might seem even more familiar to you if you're a big cut, copy, and paste user. If these commands don't ring a bell, don't worry; you'll learn how to use them soon enough! The following list summarizes what each of these handy commands can do:

- **Undo/Redo/Can't Undo**—Select this command once to reverse the previous task or command performed on the image window. You can perform multiple undo commands. Set the number of undo tasks from the General Preferences window.

- **Step Forward/Backward**—Redo the previously undone task by choosing **Step Forward**. Undo the previous task by choosing **Step Backward**.

- **Cut**—Removes the selected area from the image window and puts it into the Clipboard. The Clipboard is a part of the Windows and Mac operating system used to store temporary data.

- **Copy/Copy Merged**—Creates a copy of the selected area in the image window and places it in the Clipboard. Copy Merged enables you to copy all the layers in the selected area.

- **Paste/Paste Into**—Places the image stored in the Clipboard into a new layer in the image window. The Paste Into command places the image from the Clipboard into a selected area in the image window.

- **Clear**—Deletes the selected image and its layer from the image window. However, you can revert the document by opening the **History** palette or by choosing the **Undo** command from the **Edit** menu.

- **Fill/Stroke**—The **Fill** command enables you to adjust content and blending settings for the fill or color after you've applied a tool to an image. The **Stroke** command enables you to customize a stroke after it has been applied to an image.

- **Define Brush/Pattern**—These commands enable you to select a customized brush stroke or pattern and save it as a custom brush or pattern.

- **Purge**—Clear the **Undo**, **Clipboard**, **Histories**, or all three types of settings from the Purge command's submenu.

- **Color Settings/Preset Manager/Preferences**—Customize the color management, tools, and your work preferences by choosing these menu commands. To find out more about how to use these valuable features, go to Chapter 2, "Customizing Adobe Photoshop Elements." These commands are located in the Photoshop Elements menu in Mac OS X.

Image Menu Commands

Perform the equivalent of a facelift or liposuction with one or more of the commands you'll find in the Image menu. Go to Chapter 8, "Tonal Range and Color Correction," to find out how to use the Image menu commands with your images. Each selection in the Image menu list contains a short list of mission-critical tools that can make your images look marvelous!

The following list provides a brief explanation of what each menu item can do:

- **Duplicate Image**—Creates an exact copy of the selected image object.
- **Rotate**—Flip or turn an image on its side by choosing one of the commands from this menu.
- **Transform**—Skew or distort an image, or change a selected image's perspective. Choose the **Free Transform** command to apply the Skew, Distort, or Perspective effects in tandem.
- **Crop**—Use this tool to define new boundaries for the open image and reduce its dimensions.
- **Resize**—Adjust the image or canvas size of an image by choosing the **Image Size** or **Canvas Size** commands from this menu. Choose **Scale** to adjust the size of the selected area in the image window. Or choose **Reveal All** to show any hidden images stored in the **Layers** palette.
- **Adjustments**—Choose one of the commands in this menu to reduce the number of pixels in an image by defining a reduced set of colors to apply to the open image.
- **Histogram**—Enables you to view the distribution of darker and lighter pixels (shadows and highlights) for each or all color channels in the open image. An RGB image contains red, green, and blue channels. You can view each channel separately or view all three at once in the Histogram dialog box.
- **Mode**—Change the number of colors available to an image. Choose from RGB, Grayscale, Bitmap, or Indexed Color modes.

Adjusting Images with the Enhance Menu Commands

Image is everything in Photoshop Elements. Even if your image looks great, you can use the tools in the Enhance menu to make it look even better. It's sort of the equivalent of adding makeup to a facelift. After all, the devil is in the details, right?

The following list contains a brief description of each menu item in the Enhance menu:

- **Quick Fix**—Opens the Quick Fix dialog box. Access the brightness/contrast, color correction, focus, and rotate tools.

- **Auto Levels**—Photoshop Elements will automatically correct the tonal range of colors in an image when this option is selected. Sometimes, this feature can save you time by quickly correcting colors rather than your having to do it manually.

- **Auto Contrast**—Automatically correct the contrast levels in an image with this command.

- **Auto Color Correction**—Automatically correct color in an image set to RGB image mode.

- **Adjust Lighting**—The **Fill Flash** and **Adjust Backlighting** commands are located in the Adjust Lighting submenu.

- **Fill Flash**—Brighten shadowed areas of an image with this command. It is located in the Adjust Lighting submenu.

- **Adjust Backlighting**—Manually adjust washed-out colors in the background of an image using this feature. It is located in the Adjust Lighting submenu.

- **Adjust Color**—Open the Color Cast, Hue/Saturation, Remove Color, or Color Variations tools from this menu. Use the Hue, Saturation, and Lightness dialog box to adjust RGB or CYK colors in an image. Replace or remove colors using the Color menu commands.

- **Color Variations**—The Variations window enables you to experiment with color adjustment. You can make changes to Shadows, Midtones, Highlights, and Saturation, and view the results as you manually adjust colors. This menu command is located in the Adjust Color submenu.

- **Adjust Brightness/Contrast**—Manually adjust the brightness and contrast levels of an image with this command. The submenu options in this menu command open the Brightness/Contrast dialog box or Levels dialog box for making the adjustments.

Layer Menu Commands

Layers enable you to organize, combine, and edit images in a document. Although you can use the Layers palette to adjust many of the layers settings, there are many more commands in the Layers menu and Layers palette. The following list summarizes the Layer menu commands:

- **New**—Create one of four possible kinds of new layers.

- **Duplicate Layer**—Create a copy of a layer by selecting a layer, and then choosing this menu command.

- **Delete Layer**—Remove a layer from a document.

- **Rename Layer**—Give each layer a unique name so you can easily find each graphic element in an image window. You also can double-click a layer to open the Layer Properties window. Then, type in a new name for the selected layer.

- **Layer Style**—Apply or modify a layer style by choosing one of the commands in this submenu.

- **New Fill Layer**—Add a solid-color, gradient, or pattern layer to a document.

- **New Adjustment Layer**—Experiment with Levels, Brightness/Contrast, Hue/Saturation, Gradient Map, Invert, Threshold, and Posterize settings to adjust the tonal ranges of an image.

- **Layer Content Options**—The Change Layer Content and Layer Content commands enable you to modify adjustment or fill layers that exist in the Layers palette.

- **Type**—Format a text layer in a document by choosing one of the commands in this menu. The **Warp Text** command enables you to create some cool-looking text effects.

- **Simplify Layer**—Some layers can contain more than one element. Choose this command to merge complex layers into a simple, single-object layer.

- **Group with Previous/Ungroup**—Keep layers together or apart by choosing one of these two commands.

- **Arrange**—Change the order of the selected layer in the Layers palette. The Background layer cannot be moved, although any other layer can be moved freely.

- **Merge Layers**—Merge all layers below the selected layer in the Layers palette.

- **Merge Visible**—Combine all layers marked with the eye icon into a single layer. Invisible layers will remain unchanged.

- **Flatten Image**—Merge all layers in a document into a single layer.

Using the Select Menu Commands

Before you can view or edit part of an image, you'll need to select it. The selection commands enable you to easily shrink, grow, reverse, or smooth the edge pixels of a selection in the active image window. The following list provides a brief summary of the Selection menu commands:

- **All**—Select everything in the active image window.

- **Deselect**—Deselect everything in the active image window.

- **Reselect**—Well, you get the picture by now. This command reselects the previously selected image.

- **Inverse**—Select all parts of the image except for the currently selected area.

- **Feather**—Blend the edges of the selected image object into the pixels surrounding the selected area.

- **Modify**—Adjust the border, or expand, smooth, or contract a selected area of an image.

- **Grow**—Extend the edges of the selected area.

- **Similar**—Change the pixels of the edges of the selected area to be more like the color of the surrounding pixels.

- **Load/Save/Delete Selection**—Choose the **Save Selection** command to store a selection. Deselect the selection and apply any other tools or commands to the image window. Select the **Load Selection** command to reselect the saved selection. You can choose from a list of saved selections. Use the **Delete Selection** command to remove a selection from the Selection dropdown menu.

Adding Effects from the Filter Menu

Wow! Have you ever seen so many menu options in a menu list? The Filter menu stores all the plug-in files installed with Photoshop Elements. Plug-in files can be used to extend the capabilities of Photoshop Elements. Select an image layer in the Layers palette, and then choose one of the many commands in the Filter menu to stylize an image. The following list provides a brief overview of each group of filters and effects installed with Photoshop Elements:

- **Repeat Last Effect**—The previously selected filter or effect will appear at the top of the Filter menu. Press (**Command-F**) [**Ctrl+F**] to reapply the filter or effect to the selected area of the document.

- **Artistic**—Apply neon glow, colored pencil, smudge stick, rough pastels, and other artistic stroke effects to an image.

- **Blur**—These filters smooth out pixels by averaging the color of pixels located beside hard edges, lines, or shaded areas.

- **Brush Strokes**—Apply another variation of brush strokes to an image, similar to the artistic effects.

- **Distort**—Each distort effect takes a shape, such as a sphere, and applies a specific effect, such as pinch, ripple, or shear, combined with the shape to distort an image. One of the more powerful tools in Photoshop Elements, the Liquify Tool, is located in the **Distort** menu.

- **Noise**—Add pixels to an image to reduce the clarity of an image. This filter can be used to minimize sharp color or tonal contrasts in an image.

- **Pixelate**—Group pixels to a specific shape or size to create a unique effect.

- **Render**—Add a lens flare, lighting effect, or 3D effect to an image by applying a render effect.

- **Sharpen**—Sharpen filters work in contrast to Blur filters, increasing the contrast of nearby pixels to bring out an image.

- **Sketch**—Apply a texture or stroke to an image to enhance it. Works similarly to the Artistic and Brush Stroke filters.

- **Stylize**—Apply a painted effect to an image with options such as Emboss, Diffuse, Solarize, Glowing Edges, Trace Contour, or Wind filter.

- **Texture**—Intensify the depth or substance of an image by applying selections such as Grain, Patchwork, Stained Glass, or Texturizer filters to an image.

- **Video**—De-interlace or change an image to NTSC colors with video filters.

- **Other**—Create your own filter effects by choosing the Custom filter, or choose DitherBox, High Pass, Maximum, Minimum, or Offset filter to apply a color adjustment filter to an image.

- **Digimarc**—Image files can be saved with a unique identification, or watermark. This filter enables you to search for a digimarc watermark in an image.

Customizing Output with the View Menu Commands

View commands enable you to change the way an image appears in the image window. As you work with an image, you might need to magnify part of it, zoom out, or measure a certain area. The commands in the View menu enable you to do just that. The following list describes each menu option and its use:

- **New View**—Opens a second, duplicate window of the image in the active window.

- **Zoom In**—Magnifies the image in the image window.

- **Zoom Out**—Reduces the size of the image in the image window.

- **Fit on Screen**—Adjusts the size so that the full image fits in the image window.

- **Actual Pixels**—Changes the view to 100%, or the unaltered view of the image in the image window.

- **Print Size**—Defines the printed dimensions of the image file. Changes the image in the image window to the way it will appear if printed.

- **Selection**—Enables you to view or not view a dash-line marquee when a selection tool is applied to the image window.
- **Rulers**—Shows or hides a horizontal and vertical ruler on the image window.
- **Grid**—Adds or removes a grid in the image window.
- **Annotations**—If an image contains annotation data, you can view or hide this information by selecting this command.
- **Snap To Grid**—Helps align an object being placed in the image to the nearest grid cell.

Opening and Closing Palettes with the Window Command

Photoshop Elements enables you to work with more than one image file at a time. Windows folks can use the commands in the **Window** menu to help organize all the open documents in the work area. Each palette window also can be selected from the **Window** menu. The following list contains a brief description of the commands in the **Window** menu. The palette commands are not included in this list; you'll find these commands in the previous section.

- **Images**—A list of any open image windows appears in this menu, along with the following menu commands.
- **Cascade**—Overlaps each window from the left corner of the work area toward the right. This menu item is available only in the Windows version of Photoshop Elements.
- **Arrange Icons**—A Windows-only menu option. This command aligns any minimized windows along the lower-left corner of the work area.
- **Close All**—Another Windows-only menu command. This one closes all open image windows.
- **Tile**—Resizes each open window so that you can view each open image in the work area. This menu item is available only in the Windows version of Photoshop Elements.
- **Minimize**—Reduces the size of the active window to a small title bar and relocates it to the bottom-left corner of the work area. (**Command-M**) [**Ctrl+M**] is the shortcut key for this menu command.
- **Bring All to Front**—Sorry Windows folks, this menu command is only in the Mac version of Photoshop Elements. It brings the selected window to the foreground.
- **Show/Hide Tools**—Shows or hides the Toolbox.
- **Show/Hide Options**—Shows or hides the options bar.
- **Show/Hide Shortcuts**—Shows or hides the shortcuts bar.

- **Show/Hide Welcome**—Opens or closes the Quick Start window.
- **Show/Hide Search Results**—Shows or hides the **Search Results** palette.
- **Reset Palette Locations**—Returns the palette windows to their original locations in the work area.

2

Customizing Adobe Photoshop Elements

Using just the default settings in Photoshop Elements will enable you to perform all kinds of digital magic on your photos. As you become more familiar with the way the tools and features work, you might want to customize some of the settings. For starters, you can customize the way an image file is opened or saved, or choose whether the cursor matches the brush size or remains constant regardless of how many pixels a tool applies to an image.

Photoshop Elements has three general groups of customizable settings. The first group, color settings, enables you to choose the type of color management used with every image. The second group, the Preset Manager, enables you to create and choose custom brush, gradient, and pattern-related settings. And last but not least, the Preferences dialog box enables you to customize eight windows of user preference settings.

Adjusting Color-Management Settings

Somehow, a term involving color combined with management just doesn't sit well with me. When I think of color, I think of red, blue, and yellow. When I think of management, I think of a business, desks, payroll, a water cooler, phones, and a photocopier.

If you think about how a computer manages color, and compare that to the way a monitor, printer, camera, or scanner manages color, it might seem as though each device is running its own color-management business. For example, if you pick a certain green color on your computer monitor, it might look light blue when you print it to your color printer. Similarly, if you take a picture of a red apple with a camera, it might appear red on your computer screen, but greener when you print to a color printer. The accuracy of color between your computer monitor and printer all depends on how you calibrate the color software for your computer's monitor and printer. On the other hand, if you don't use color management, you risk losing some of the color information in an image. With digital images, each color is stored as a number. Color profiles enable a computer and peripheral devices to translate a color value from one color space, such as RGB (red, green, and blue), into another color space, such as HSB (hue, saturation, and brightness) or CMYK (cyan, magenta, yellow, and black).

The following sections explain how color-management settings work in Photoshop Elements. If you're not sure which setting to choose, choose the default setting: **No Color Management**. Even though you choose the **No Color Management** option, Photoshop Elements will assign a color profile to each image file you open. As you edit and save the image file, Photoshop Elements will use the color profile to manage color. The color profile Photoshop Elements assigns to the image will no doubt be different from the color profile used by the scanner or camera to generate the original colors.

BACK UP ORIGINAL IMAGES

Before you get all excited about working with color images and start modifying an image with Photoshop Elements, make a copy of that file onto your hard drive. If you plan to make several modifications to an image file, it's helpful to keep a backup of the original nearby on your local hard drive.

However, the best method for backing up a file is to copy it to an external drive, such as a Zip disk or CD-R media, or to a tape backup drive connected to your computer over a network. If the hard drive stops working, you can always install Photoshop Elements on a new computer, restore your backup files, and continue working on your image files. After you've created a copy of the original image file, you can make all the changes you like without worrying about making an irreversible mistake. If you make a mistake, you can always start over with the original.

Operating System Color Settings

Some operating systems, such as Mac OS 9 or Mac OS X, support color management for input and output devices, such as a scanner or printer. This is important in that it helps to ensure that the colors you are seeing onscreen when you create your images are the same colors that appear when the image is seen in print or on the Web. To customize the color settings for Mac OS, open the Color Sync control panel.

Windows does not have an equivalent technology to Color Sync. However, Photoshop Elements enables you to save an image file with an ICC color profile, which, in essence, does the same thing.

CHOOSING A COLOR PROFILE FOR WINDOWS

Right-click the desktop, and choose Properties to open the Display control panel window. Click the Settings tab, and then click the Advanced button. The Multiple Monitors window opens. Click the Color Management tab, and then click the Add button to choose a color profile for your computer monitor. The color profile files end with an .icm extension. These files are installed in the Windows operating system folder on your hard drive. You can choose the sRGB Color Space Profile or the AdobeRGB1998 color profile for your monitor; both profiles are common to Windows, Mac, and Photoshop Elements.

If you haven't chosen a color profile for your Windows or Macintosh operating system, you can set the color profile in Photoshop Elements. Open the Color Settings dialog box located in the **Edit** menu (**Command-Shift-K**) [**Ctrl+Shift+K**], shown in Figure 2.1. Choose Limited color to save an sRGB IEC61966-2.1–compatible color profile with images intended for the Web. Although No Color Management is the default for the color settings, your color images might still print colors fairly close to the way they appear onscreen.

FIGURE 2.1

Make a color setting selection.

The Limited Color Management setting will give you the option, on the Save or Save As dialog box, to save an sRGB IEC61966-2.1 color profile for a Web image. The sRGB color profile is the standard default color space for Web pages. It was created by the ICC, an international consortium of businesses and color experts.

An alternative to the sRGB color profile is the Adobe RGB color profile. The Adobe RGB Color profile is generally more suitable for working with print devices. Click the **Full Color Management** radio button to save an Adobe RGB (1998) Color profile to an image you want to print. Photoshop Elements will provide the Adobe RGB color profile as the ICC profile option when you save an image file.

In addition to choosing a color management setting for Photoshop Elements, you can customize the operating system settings on your computer monitor so that you can view as many colors as you like. The maximum number of colors you can view on your monitor is limited by the amount of video memory installed on the monitor or on your computer. To adjust the number of colors viewable on your computer, open the Display Settings control panel if you're using Windows, or open the Monitors (or Monitors & Sound) control panel if you're using a Mac. Choose a minimum of thousands (16-bit) or millions (24-bit) of colors.

tip

ICC is an acronym for the International Color Consortium, which defines standards for consistent color across output devices. Find out more about the sRGB color space by visiting `http://www.w3.org/Graphics/Color/sRGB.html`.

The size of your desktop affects how much of an image file you can view. Choose a minimum desktop size of 800×600 pixels. Depending on the average size of the image you'll be working on (the average two-megapixel camera creates a 1024-×768-pixel image file), choose a desktop size that displays the most colors. This provides the best processor performance in addition to a healthy dose of desktop real estate.

WHAT'S THE SIZE OF YOUR DESKTOP?

The desktop size represents the number of pixels that you can view on your computer monitor. However, the larger the desktop size, the smaller each pixel will become. The result? Eyestrain.

In a nutshell, it's tough to work with large image files on a small computer monitor's desktop (for example, 13- or 15-inch monitors). Although you might be able to view the full color spectrum on any size monitor, smaller monitors limit how much of the image you can view and access.

If working with small pixels or squinting your eyes appeals to you, choose a larger desktop size for your computer screen. I use a 1,600×1,200-pixel desktop on a 17-inch monitor with one of my Windows computers.

Choosing a Color Profile

Photoshop Elements can work with a wide range of color profiles. Some digital camera software may install custom color management software onto your computer. A Kodak digital camera may install Kodak's CMS (color management system). Windows computers can work with more than one color management system. To select the color profile for your computer, open the Properties window for the My Computer icon. Click the **Settings** tab, and click the **Advanced** button to access the color profile configurations settings for the graphics card installed on your computer. You can also use a color calibration program installed on your computer to select a color profile and calibrate the color settings for your computer monitor. To find out how to calibrate your monitor with Adobe's Gamma control panel, go to Chapter 7, "Photoshop Elements and Color."

Choosing Settings in the Preset Manager

Customize settings for brushes, swatches, gradients, and patterns from the Preset Manager window. Choose **Preset Manager** from the **Edit** menu to open the Preset Manager window. The Preset Type drop-down menu contains Brushes, Swatches, Gradients, and Patterns. Each of these menu options changes the available settings that appear in the Preset Manager window.

The **More** button is located in the upper-right corner of the Preset Manager dialog box. Click this button to view a drop-down menu for each Preset. You can change the window list view, load another group of settings into the window list, or choose a custom command specific to each preset. The **Load** and **Save Set** buttons enable you to save and open custom settings so you can reuse your presets with other documents or share them with other Photoshop Elements users.

Each set of brushes, gradients, swatches, or patterns is stored in a folder located in the Presets folder of the Adobe Photoshop Elements folder on your hard drive. For example, each set of brushes is stored in a separate file in the Presets\Brushes folder. To create a new set of brushes, patterns, gradients, or swatches, select one of the items in the window list, and then click the Save Set button. Type a name for the file, and save the file to your hard drive. Brushes are saved as .abr files, patterns as .pat files, gradients as .grd files, and swatches as .aco files. When the file is placed in the corresponding Brushes,

note

If Limited Color Management is selected in the Color Settings window, Photoshop Elements will attach an sRGB IEC61966-2.1 color profile to the image being saved. sRGB IEC61966-2.1 will appear beside the ICC Profile check box name in the Save As dialog box. If you open this image file in another graphics application, it will be capable of producing a more accurate set of colors than if the color profile had not been saved with the file.

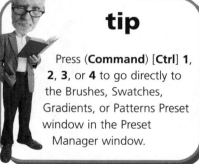

tip

Press (**Command**) [**Ctrl**] **1**, **2**, **3**, or **4** to go directly to the Brushes, Swatches, Gradients, or Patterns Preset window in the Preset Manager window.

Gradients, Color Swatches, or Patterns folder in the Presets folder, its name will appear in the drop-down menu list in the Preset Manager window.

Selecting Brushes in the Preset Manager

You can choose the default brush settings for the Brush tool (B) from the **Brushes Preset Manager** window. Upon first glance, you'll notice that each type of brush setting has a number below it. The number represents the number of pixels that brush will apply to the canvas. Click a brush in the window to pick the style or stroke settings you want to use.

Double-click a setting to open its **Brush Name** window. View the name of the brush, or type a new name into the **Name** text box.

The menu for the Brushes Preset Manager enables you to reset or replace brushes, choose a custom view for the window list, or load several brushes (Assorted Brushes, Calligraphic Brushes, Drop Shadow Brushes, Faux Finish Brushes, Natural Brushes 2, Natural Brushes, or Square Brushes) into the window list. You can view only one group of presets at a time in the **Preset Manager** window (see Figure 2.2).

note

Each group of brushes that appears in the drop-down list in the Preset Manager window is stored on your hard drive in the Presets, Brushes folder in the Photoshop Elements folder. Photoshop Elements stores brush files as ABR files.

FIGURE 2.2

Choose from a huge list of brush sizes and strokes in the Preset Manager window.

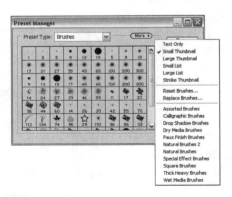

Choosing Swatches in the Preset Manager

The **Swatches Preset Manager** window determines which set of swatches appears in the Swatches palette (see Figure 2.3). Photoshop Elements includes seven sets of swatches you can load into the Swatches palette: Mac OS, VisiBone, VisiBone2, Web Hues, Web Safe Colors, Web Spectrum, and Windows.

FIGURE 2.3

Choose a group of colors to work with from the Swatches Preset Manager window.

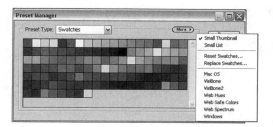

Click the arrow button to view each swatch set, and select an item from the menu list to change the swatch set in the **Preset Manager** window. Each swatch set represents a group of colors stored in a file in the Color Swatches folder, located in the Presets folder. Click the **Save Set** button to create your own swatch set and save it as a file on your hard drive. Click the **Load** button to select a swatch set file stored on your hard drive.

To view the hexadecimal value of a color, click a color square in the **Swatches** window. The tool tip for the color contains the hexadecimal value of the color. You also can double-click a color to view its hexadecimal value.

The drop-down menu for the Swatches contains two view options, **Small Thumbnail** and **Small List**. You also can reset or replace swatches from the drop-down menu.

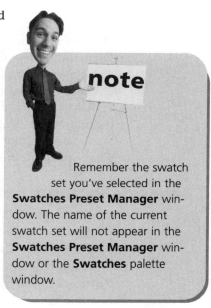

note

Remember the swatch set you've selected in the **Swatches Preset Manager** window. The name of the current swatch set will not appear in the **Swatches Preset Manager** window or the **Swatches** palette window.

Selecting Gradients in the Preset Manager

A *gradient* consists of two or more colors that gradually blend into each other. When Gradients is selected as the Preset Type, each square in the window contains a gradient map (see Figure 2.4). When you select the Gradient tool (G) from the Toolbox, you can assign a gradient map to the selected area in the image window. You can choose the default gradient maps that appear in the options bar settings from the Gradients Preset Manager window.

Each group of brushes that appears in the drop-down list in the Preset Manager window is stored on your hard drive in the Presets\Gradients folder in the Photoshop Elements 2 folder. Photoshop Elements stores groups of gradients in GRD files. Choose the **Save Set** button in the **Preset Manager** window to create a custom group of gradients.

FIGURE 2.4

Select a set of gradients to work with from the **Gradient Preset Manager** window.

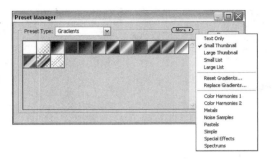

View gradient maps in one of five views: Text Only, Small Thumbnail, Large Thumbnail, Small List, or Large List. You can access these views from the arrow drop-down menu. You also can reset or replace gradients by choosing the **Reset Gradients** or **Replace Gradients** commands from the drop-down menu list. Click the **Load** button and select a gradient file, or choose one of the gradient sets from the drop-down menu to load one of eight built-in gradient map sets: Color Harmonies 1, Color Harmonies 2, Metals, Noise Samples, Pastels, Simple, Special Effects, or Spectrums.

Choosing Patterns in the Preset Manager

You can apply the Patterns in the **Preset Manager** window (see Figure 2.5) to an image by adding a pattern Fill Layer to it. You can choose from two preinstalled groups of patterns: **Patterns** and **Patterns 2**. You can reset or replace patterns from the arrow drop-down menu or change the format of the view for the **Patterns** window list.

Each group of patterns that appears in the drop-down list in the **Preset Manager** window is stored on your hard drive in the Presets\Patterns folder in the Photoshop Elements 2 folder. Photoshop Elements stores patterns in the PAT file format. PostScript patterns are stored as AI, or Adobe Illustrator, files. You can use Photoshop Elements to create your own custom patterns, too!

note

You cannot apply gradient tools to images in Bitmap, Indexed-Color, or 16-bits per channel mode.

FIGURE 2.5

You can choose from two groups of patterns in the **Patterns Preset Manager** window.

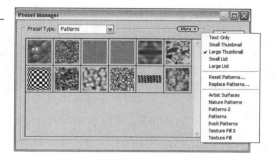

Personalizing Your Preferences

Photoshop Elements enables you to customize the way a document opens, how the cursor behaves with tools, how transparent areas are visualized in the document window, how rulers and grids behave, how the program uses memory, and which hard drives are used as scratch disks. All these settings are grouped into eight preference windows. Each setting can be accessed one at a time from the Preferences window.

The following sections introduce you to the preference settings. Each Preferences window contains a set of five buttons located to the right of the Preferences window. Click the **Prev** or **Next** button to view the next set of preferences. If you want to view the HTML help files in a browser window, click the **Help** button. Click the **OK** button to save your changes, or click **Cancel** to exit the **Preferences** window without saving any of your changes.

General Preferences

To open the **Preferences** window, choose **Preferences** from the **Edit** menu or press (**Command-K**) [**Ctrl+K**]. The **General preferences** window contains settings for the Color Picker and Undo feature, 13 check boxes you can choose from to customize various ways the work area behaves, and two buttons that enable you to reset warning messages and tools (see Figure 2.6).

tip

If you're using Mac OS X, you may want to check the Use **System Shortcut Keys** box if you want to use **Command-H** (instead of **Ctrl-Command-H**) to hide Photoshop Elements.

FIGURE 2.6

Choose from a long list of check boxes to customize the way the work area behaves. You also can choose the Color Picker or set the number of undo steps and history states.

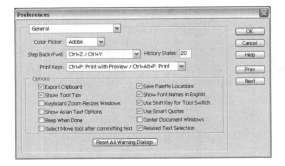

Preferences for Saving Files

Change the way image files are saved in the **Saving Files Preferences** window. For example, when you save a file, Photoshop Elements creates a thumbnail image along with the image file. On a Mac, the image file's icon becomes a tiny thumbnail image of the actual picture. On a Windows computer, you can preview each image in the Open dialog box.

In the **Saving Files Preferences** window, you can tell Photoshop Elements to ask when saving, or never save a thumbnail image with a file. You also can change the formatting of the file extension, choose file compatibility with older versions of Photoshop files, and set how many recently opened files appear in the **File**, **Open Recent** submenu (see Figure 2.7).

Customizing Display and Cursors

The cursor changes depending on which tool is selected. For example, the selection, drawing, and text tools use unique tool pointers to enable you to apply the tool to the image. Selection tools use crosshairs for tool pointers, the Text Tool uses an I-beam, and drawing tools use the Brush Size icon.

note

If you're using the Macintosh version of Photoshop Elements, you'll find a few more check boxes in the Saving Files Preferences window. You can save a Macintosh or Windows Thumbnail preview image for the file's icon. Check the corresponding Icon, Macintosh Thumbnail, or Windows Thumbnail check box to choose the settings you want.

You also have the option of always, never, or being asked whether you want to add the file extension to the name of the image file being saved.

FIGURE 2.7

Adjust your image previews, file extension-naming scheme, and Photoshop file compatibility in the Saving Files Preferences window.

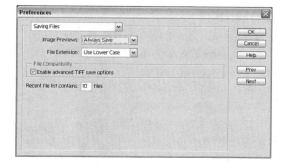

You also adjust the appearance of tool pointers in the **Display & Cursors Preferences** window. Choose **Standard** if you want the cursor to remain a constant size as you use a tool, or choose Precise if you want to use a crosshair cursor to represent the location of the brush (see Figure 2.8). Choose the **Brush Size** radio button if you want the Painting Cursors to change to match the number of pixels of the selected brush size that will be applied to the canvas.

If you hold down (**Option**) [**Alt**] when the Red Eye Brush, Brush, or Pencil Tool is selected, the cursor will change from the drawing tool to the eyedropper tool. If you choose **Precise** in the **Other Cursors** section of the **Display & Cursors Preferences** window, the eyedropper icon will change to an arrow cursor.

Navigate through the eight preferences windows by clicking in the drop-down menu window, and then pressing the up or down arrow keys on your keyboard. You also can use the (**Command**) [**Ctrl**] **1–8** keys to go directly to a preference window.

FIGURE 2.8

View the current Display & Cursors settings to change the way tool pointers appear.

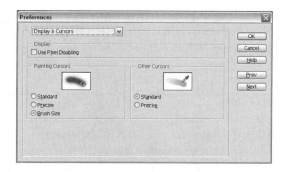

Adjusting Transparency Settings

Transparency represents the absence of color in an image—typically the background layer. You can adjust the transparency of an image layer by increasing or decreasing its opacity value from the Layers palette. A value of zero renders a transparent (or invisible) image. Photoshop Elements uses a default gray-and-white checkered pattern to represent transparency. You can customize the grid size and colors in the **Transparency Preferences** window (see Figure 2.9). Choose from a small, medium, or large grid, or change the grid colors as you like. Preview the transparency pattern in the square on the right.

tip

Press the **Caps Lock** key to switch between standard and precise cursors if you're using a selection, drawing, or text tool from the Toolbox.

FIGURE 2.9

Edit the default gray-and-white transparency pattern to suit your needs.

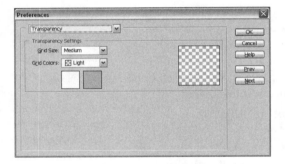

Units & Rulers Preferences

You can adjust the units of the ruler in the Units & Rulers Preferences window (see Figure 2.10). Choose the measurement and type formats for the units of a ruler, or adjust preset resolutions for Print and screen. If you've added columns to a document, you can adjust the width and gutter sizes of the columns in this preferences window, too. Choose **View**, **Rulers** to add rulers to an image window. You can open the **Units & Rulers Preferences** window and preview your changes in the active image window.

PICAS, POINTS, AND POSTSCRIPT

Type size can be measured in *picas* or *points*. A point is approximately 1/72 of an image in a 72 pixel-per-inch (ppi) image. 72-point text in a 72dpi image appears as a 1-inch-tall image. A pica is approximately 12 points in a 72ppi image.

The **Point/Pica size** option in the **Units & Rulers Preferences** window enables you to choose the point size definition for printing. If you're printing to a PostScript printer, choose **PostScript** (72 points per inch) in the **Units & Rulers Preferences** window. If you're not printing to a PostScript printer, choose **traditional** (72.27 points per inch).

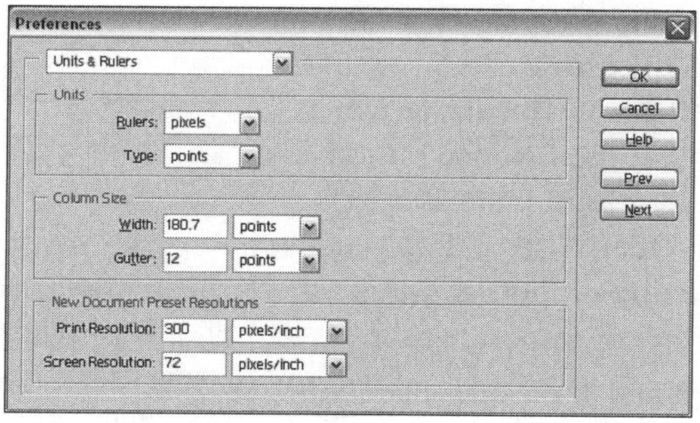

FIGURE 2.10

You can customize the rulers, column size, and point/pica size in the **Units & Rulers Preferences** window.

Personalizing Grid Settings

Each window can show or hide a grid to help you align your objects. You can view the grid by choosing **Show Grid** from the **View** menu. To have your images snap to the grid, choose **Snap** from the **View** menu. Customize the color, style, gridlines, and subdivisions of the grid in the **Grid Preferences** window (see Figure 2.11). Click each drop-down menu to view or choose new settings.

FIGURE 2.11

Create a custom grid if you need to align images to create a custom document, such as a contact sheet.

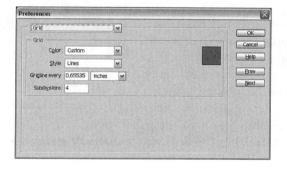

Setting Plug-Ins and Scratch Disk Preferences

Adobe designed the plug-in file format as a way to extend the capabilities of Photoshop Elements. There is a `Plug-Ins` folder located in the `Photoshop Elements 2` folder on your hard drive. Any plug-in files located in the `Plug-Ins` folder will appear in the **Filter** menu, **Filters** palette, or in the **File**, **Import** menu. If you take a closer look at the Plug-Ins folder, you'll notice that plug-in files are grouped into folders. The TWAIN plug-ins, which are explained in more detail in Chapter 3, "Acquiring Images from Scanners and Digital Cameras," are stored in the `Import/Export` folder of the `Plug-Ins` folder. If you click the **File**, **Import** menu, you'll see each TWAIN plug-in file in the Import menu list.

If you want to use an additional plug-in folder, you can check the **Additional Plug-Ins Directory** check box in the **Plug-Ins & Scratch Disks Preferences** window (see Figure 2.12). Click the **Choose** button and navigate through your hard drive to select the secondary plug-ins folder. A secondary plug-in folder enables you to access another group of plug-in files from the Filter or Import menus.

As you work with an image, Photoshop Elements uses available hard disk space as a scratch disk. The scratch disk works similarly to virtual memory, storing information about the original image, as well as any edits you make to it. Naturally, the scratch disk size will grow as you continue to modify or combine images. Each image you open, and each layer you create and modify, increases the overall size of the scratch disk.

By default, Photoshop Elements chooses the startup drive as the primary scratch disk. You might want to choose an external, or second internal drive, to use as the secondary scratch disk. You can select up to four scratch disks, enabling you to work on a single image longer, or a larger image faster, without running out of disk space on a single drive. Choose each scratch disk from the **Plug-Ins & Scratch Disks Preferences** window.

> If an error message appears saying your hard drive is full, Photoshop Elements is telling you it has run out of scratch disk space. You might not be able to save the file on which you're working. You can free up some disk space by closing other open image files or by deleting other files on your hard drive. Be sure to back up any files before deleting them!
>
> If you want to avoid running out of scratch disk space, you can attach an external drive and assign it as a second or third scratch disk before you start working with Photoshop Elements.

FIGURE 2.12

Add a second directory to extend filter effect or TWAIN plug-ins available to the work area, or assign additional scratch disks to Photoshop Elements from this Preferences window.

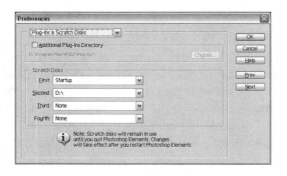

Memory and Image Cache Preferences

If the previous section about scratch disks didn't give you a hint about how large image files can be, the **Memory & Image Cache Preferences** window will give you some hard numbers to work with. If you're using Mac OS 9, you'll only be able to adjust the Cache settings from this preferences window. You can adjust the amount of memory allocated to Photoshop, as well as the cache settings with Windows and Mac OS X. Figure 2.13 shows that 114MB, or 50% of the memory on my PC, is allocated to run Photoshop Elements 2. Click the arrow button in the Maximum Used by Photoshop Elements text box and drag the slider to the right to increase the amount of available RAM dedicated to Photoshop Elements 2.

note

You must (**Quit**) [**Exit**] Photoshop Elements, and then restart the application to use the secondary plug-ins or additional scratch disks selected in the Preferences window.

FIGURE 2.13

Adjust the cache settings and the amount of memory available to Photoshop Elements 2 from the **Memory & Image Cache Preferences** window.

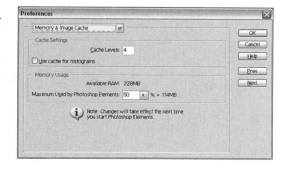

HOW MUCH MEMORY IS ENOUGH?

Assume that the average picture scanned in or captured by a digital camera is stored in a 1MB file. When Photoshop Elements opens this file, it creates red, green, and blue channels for the image. Each channel comprises about one third of the image. Most 1MB files grow into 9MB files in the work area. As you edit it or add new layers with other images, the file size can grow larger and larger.

If you plan to work on large image files, you can improve Photoshop Elements' performance by increasing the amount of memory allocated to the program when it starts. On a Windows PC, you can set how much memory on the computer can be dedicated to Photoshop Elements in the **Memory & Image Cache Preferences** window. On a Mac, select the Photoshop Elements icon, and then choose **Get Info** from the **File** menu. Select **Memory** from the **Show** pop-up menu, and then double or triple the amount of memory in the **Preferred Size** text box.

If you're still wondering how much memory is enough, remember that you can never have enough memory installed on your computer. However, a ballpark estimate is to double the amount of memory you'll think you'll need and buy as much memory as you can afford.

Photoshop Elements creates a cache to store frequently used data, such as a histogram. See Chapter 8, "Tonal Range and Color Correction," for an explanation about histograms. Each time you need to view an item stored in the cache, Photoshop Elements displays the cached information instead of recalculating the data each time you open a histogram window or access a frequently used image layer. By using the cache, Photoshop Elements can perform tasks faster, which is a good thing.

3

Acquiring Images from Scanners and Digital Cameras

Photoshop Elements enables you to import images from a scanner or digital camera. Install software, connect a cable, and power on a scanner or camera to enable Photoshop Elements to acquire photos. After you have it all set up, you're free to download as many photos as you like. Available memory, processor speed, and disk space are the only limits to how many photos you can bring into your computer! This chapter shows you how to get a scanner or digital camera up and running with Photoshop Elements.

Installing Plug-In Files

To bring your images into Photoshop Elements from a scanner or digital camera, you'll need to install a TWAIN plug-in. All plug-in files are located in the Plug-Ins folder, in the Photoshop Elements 2 folder. The (Import/Export) [Import-Export] folder is where TWAIN plug-ins are stored. TWAIN plug-ins enable you to acquire images from the **File**, **Import** menu or **Welcome** window into the work area.

The following sections show you how to install a TWAIN plug-in for an HP scanner device. However, these steps are similar for installing any TWAIN plug-in with Photoshop Elements.

Installing Plug-In Software

If you're using Windows 98 Special Edition, Windows 2000, or Windows XP, plug your scanner or camera into your computer's parallel, serial, USB, or FireWire port. Windows will notice that a new device is connected to the computer and open the Found New Hardware Wizard (see Figure 3.1). Insert the CD for the scanner or camera into the CD-ROM drive, and then click the Next button. Mac OS 9 and Mac OS X users can install the TWAIN plug-in software by running the Mac software installer program, or by placing the TWAIN plug-in file in the Plug-Ins, (Import/Export) [Import-Export] folder, in the Adobe Photoshop Elements folder.

FIGURE 3.1

When you first connect a scanner or camera to your computer, Windows will try to install software for the new hardware.

For Windows users, here are the steps for using the New Hardware Wizard to install software drivers for a scanner or camera:

1. There are two screens in the wizard that ask you how you want Windows to locate the driver software for the new device. Choose the radio button that searches for a suitable driver for the device in the **Install Device Drivers** window.

2. Click the **Next** button, and then check the CD-ROM Drive check box in the **Locate Driver Files** window. Be sure you have the CD-ROM from your hardware (scanner or camera) in the drive.

3. Click the **Next** button, and Windows searches the CD-ROM for the software driver. If a TWAIN plug-in file is on the CD, Windows installs both the driver and the TWAIN plug-in file (see Figure 3.2).

FIGURE 3.2

If Windows can locate a driver for the device, it will install the driver.

4. If Windows installs the files successfully, you'll see the Completing the Found New Hardware Wizard window. Click the **Finish** button to exit the wizard.

Accessing a New Plug-In in Photoshop Elements

Photoshop Elements scans the Plug-Ins folder only when the application starts. You must (**Quit**) [**Exit**] Photoshop Elements before you can use a newly installed TWAIN plug-in file. Click on the **File**, **Import** menu to view the list of installed plug-in files.

Before choosing a plug-in, power on the scanner or camera, and then connect the device to the computer. If you haven't already done so, start Photoshop Elements. To access any of the TWAIN plug-in files, choose **File**, **Import**. A submenu containing a list of devices appears, as shown in Figure 3.3. Select one of the TWAIN plug-in files from the **Import** menu list. The TWAIN plug-in opens a device-specific window in the Photoshop Elements work area. Use the device software to preview and download images into the work area.

TROUBLESHOOTING CONNECTIONS

Not all cameras and scanners come bundled with TWAIN plug-in files. If your device does not have a TWAIN plug-in file, you'll need to use the software that comes with the device to create an image on your computer. In either case, visit the vendor's Web site to see whether a TWAIN plug-in is available for your scanner or digital camera. Mac OS X and Windows XP include some software that may enable a camera or scanner to download images to the computer. Mac OS X users can use iPhoto to see whether the camera or scanner can be recognized by Mac OS X. Plug the USB, FireWire, or serial cable into the Windows XP computer to see whether Windows is able to recognize the device. Save the images as JPEG or TIFF files so that you can open them in Photoshop Elements.

FIGURE 3.3

Choose Import from the File menu to view a list of installed TWAIN plug-in files.

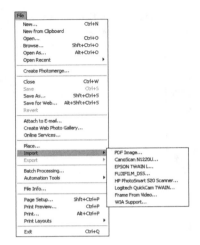

Adjusting Scanner Settings

Scanner software has many options that enable you to determine how much image information is downloaded to your computer. To access all the software options, preview and scan a photo into your computer. This section will show you how to choose a resolution for scanning photos into Photoshop Elements.

If you're using a flatbed scanner, place a photo or a piece of paper with text or graphics face down on the glass surface of the scanner. If you're using another type of scanner, insert a scannable document into the scanner device. Some scanners, such as the Epson 640U, automatically scan and choose the settings for you. The HP Photo Smart scanner starts scanning when you insert a photo, filmstrip, or slide (see Figure 3.4). Other scanners require you to click a button in the work area to start the scan.

FIGURE 3.4

Create a preview scan to get a rough idea of how the scanner software sees the scanned photo.

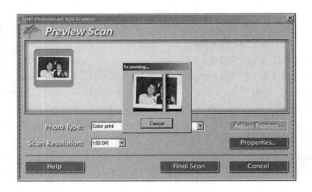

WHAT IS THE BEST RESOLUTION FOR SCANNING?

Most scanners are capable of scanning within a limited range of resolutions. Assuming you have a more recent scanner capable of scanning up to 2400 dpi, try scanning an image at 600 dpi. Then compare that scan to the same image scanned at 720, 1200, or 2400 dpi. Usually the higher dpi setting will produce the sharpest scanned image. Save the highest-quality image to your hard drive.

If you cannot see a difference between the resulting images, save each one to your hard drive. Then compare the file size of each scan. Use the Zoom tool to determine how much more image information is added to the higher-resolution images. If the 600 dpi scan looks great and creates the smallest file size of the scanned image, you might want to consider working with this setting when you scan other images.

Choosing a Resolution

If you want to scan several images into the computer with the same resolution setting, you can choose the resolution and scanner settings for one photo and scan the rest without making any changes. However, if you have a diverse set of colors, or old and new photos, you might want to set aside a big chunk of time if you want to get the best results for each scanned image.

Consider the following issues when trying to set the optimal resolution for scanned images:

- What kind of image are you trying to scan? Consider the size of the image, and decide which resolution would be able to capture the most detail without creating an unusually large file.

- How many colors does the image have? If you're scanning a color image, you might need to configure the scanner software to capture thousands of colors instead of 256. On the other hand, you can see what happens if you scan in a color image as a grayscale or black-and-white image.

- What is the highest non-interpolated resolution supported by the scanner? Some scanners work with bundled software to capture higher resolutions than the scanner hardware is capable of creating. You might want to compare the software-enhanced, high-resolution scans with the same image scanned at a lower resolution without the aid of the software interpolator.

- Does the computer have any display limitations that might limit your ability to view beyond a certain resolution? You might need to change your computer monitor's settings to display more colors if you want to see as much of the scanner output as possible. The computer's performance can slow down if you set it to display 24-bit color, compared to 256, or 16-bit color. The more colors the monitor has to display, the more processing power is required from the computer.

Choose a resolution in the scanner software window. Look for a resolution setting that enables you to set the spi or dpi of the image. Some software breaks down the resolution settings into horizontal and vertical resolution settings. The horizontal resolution affects the optics in the scan bar, and the vertical resolution affects how far the bar will move as it scans each line of the image.

Adjusting the Color Depth and Scan Area

The number of colors, or *color depth*, of the scanned image affects the quality of the resulting captured image. Most scanners automatically scan an image in color, even if the image has no color. You can adjust the software settings to scan a black-and-white image if you like. The scanner does not have any sensors built into its optical array that can distinguish a color image from a black-and-white one; it simply captures the image placed on the glass.

Although most scanners rely on the CCD and scanner hardware to determine how many colors can be scanned, each uses its own software and terminology to describe color depth. For example, the CanoScan N1220U uses the term Color Mode to describe its color depth settings: Black and White, Grayscale, Color (Photos), Color (Documents), or Text Enhanced. The Epson 640U uses the term Image Type to describe its color depth options: Color Photo, Color Document, Black & White Photo, or Black & White Document.

The important thing to remember here is that you want to pick a color depth that matches the photo placed on the scanner. For example, if you're scanning a black-and-white image, choose a grayscale or black-and-white color depth. If you're not sure which color depth to choose, choose a setting as close to 16- or 24-bit

tip

Be sure to adjust the color settings for your computer's operating system and monitor before you scan an image. Both Windows and Mac OS enable you to customize the resolution or desktop size. You also can set the color depth, or number of colors that can be displayed onscreen. If you want to learn more about how to work with color, see Chapter 7, "Photoshop Elements and Color."

color as possible. The higher the color depth value, the more color data will be captured when the image is scanned. For example, scanning an image at 24 bits will capture more color information than scanning at 16 bits.

Experiment with different color depth settings with different kinds of images. You can scan photos, line art, sketches, text, two-color images, or full-color images at different color depth settings to see how your scanner reacts to different capture modes. I capture almost all my images in color, and remove or add colors with Photoshop Elements.

The resolution setting also affects how the image will be scanned. The higher the resolution, the more color information the scanner will try to capture. If you're not sure at what resolution to start scanning an image, choose 600 dpi. Scan and save the image, and then change the resolution to 1200 or 2400 dpi and save this second image. Open each image and place them side-by-side on your desktop. If you cannot see any improvement in the 1200 or 2400 dpi image, you might want to continue to scan additional images at 600 dpi. However, if you plan to edit images, the higher resolution scan will enable you to do more precise image editing than an image scanned at a lower resolution.

COMPARING SPI TO PPI

Scanners capture images using the measurement of samples per inch (spi). However, your computer monitor displays an image in pixels, or 72 pixels per inch. You might wonder whether a sample and a pixel are the same size.

Sadly, the answer is no, they are not the same size. In fact, there isn't an easy way to compare the quality of a scanned image to an image viewed on your computer monitor. The final results depend on the output of your printer, the settings and capabilities of your computer monitor, and your ability to choose the software settings that create the best possible images.

Previewing and Setting Up for the Scan

To create a preview of an image, before you actually scan it into your computer, click the **Preview Scan** or **Preview** button in the scanner software window. Don't be surprised if your scanner does not have a preview option available. If the scanner software doesn't support a preview mode, click the Scan button and wait for the image to be scanned into the work area.

Some scanner applications, such as the Epson 640U, enable you to let the scanner do all the thinking for you with a full-service auto-scan feature. You might need to turn or flip the image on the scanner bed if you want to straighten the scanned image. If you want to avoid creating unnecessary scans, check to see whether the scanner you are planning to buy includes a preview option in its software package.

After you have created the preview scan, you can apply the selection tools to choose the specific area you want to scan into the work area (see Figure 3.5). Reducing the area being scanned reduces the amount of time you must wait for the scanner to complete its job.

FIGURE 3.5

If the scanner software provides tools, you can select the area you want to scan.

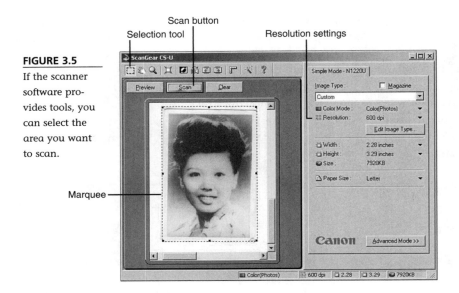

After the scanned image is captured and viewable in the work area (see Figure 3.6), you can save it to your hard drive. Choose **Save** from the **File** menu, and then type a name for the image file and save it to your hard drive. Now you can experiment with the image by applying one of the tools in the Toolbox, or add a new layer to the image file if you don't want to make any permanent changes to the original image.

FIGURE 3.6

The resulting file contains the image you selected in the scanner software window.

Photoshop Elements opens scanned images in RGB mode, enabling you to work with red, green, and blue color information. You can apply any menu command or tool to any part of an image in RGB mode. To find out more about the image modes in Photoshop Elements, go to Chapter 7.

SHOULDN'T THIS LOOK PRETTIER?

Scanners might be able to create luscious 36-bit and 48-bit color images, but most monitors are capable of displaying 24-bit color, or millions of colors. You might not be able to see the additional colors captured by the scanner, but Photoshop Elements enables you to work with all the color information captured by the scanner. You will see the difference when you edit or print the image.

Scanning Different Kinds of Images

Film, slides, color photos, or old monochrome photos all can be scanned into Photoshop Elements. After you scan a few images, you might start to notice something they all have in common: dust. You might need to gently dust the surface of the print or negative, as well as the glass surface on the scanner, before placing and scanning the image. Try to avoid using your hands, cloth, or tissue to remove dust from the surface of the scanner. For best results, hold a can of compressed air about 6 to 10 inches from the glass and use the canned air to clear the surface of the scanner.

As you scan images, try not to touch the glass on a flatbed scanner with your hand or fingers. The oil from your hand or fingertips can leave marks on the glass that will be scanned in along with your images.

Choose the scanner settings you want to apply to the scanned image. Then preview the image in Photoshop Elements. If the image is slightly crooked, you can try to straighten it in the scanner. However, you also can use Photoshop Elements to vertically or horizontally correct an image's alignment.

If you're working with a damaged, bent, or warped photo, try to flatten the image by placing it in a plastic jacket or folder. A flat image is optimal for scanning. It encourages the scanner to produce consistent, accurate colors throughout the captured image. Don't hesitate to run several preview scans, and try to scan the best possible image you can.

If you don't want to worry about adding glare to the scan by adding the plastic layer to the image, scan a test image to see how the scanner captures the damaged areas of the photo (see Figure 3.7). Then add the plastic cover to see whether you can identify any differences between the two preview images.

Experiment with scanning at different resolutions and with different color or grayscale settings. If you want to simulate creating a color image, try scanning an image in grayscale. Then hand-tint the image in Photoshop Elements by adding red, blue, and green adjustment layers to create a custom color image.

FIGURE 3.7
A test scan can help you optimize settings if you're scanning worn or damaged photos.

Scanning the Final Image

Adjust the photo and the scanner settings until you're satisfied with the scanner output. Then, click the Scan button to bring the image into Photoshop Elements. For best results, use a photo scanner to convert a color negative into a full-color, non-negative–looking image.

The scanner software will bring the image into the work area in a new document window. If you're scanning a negative, the image might be difficult to recognize at first (see Figure 3.8). When the image is in the work area, you can save it as a file or apply a tool or command. For example, you can open the Quick Fix dialog box, apply a filter, or resize the image.

FIGURE 3.8
Scan a negative into Photoshop Elements and convert it into a black-and-white or color photo.

Checking Image Quality

The size of the scanned image will vary depending on the size and quality of the original image, as well as the scanner settings selected in the scanner driver software. Use the Zoom tool to magnify the digital image to compare it to the original.

If you're disappointed by dust specs, dirt, or torn areas of the photo, you can learn how to correct these glitches in Part III of this book (see Figure 3.9).

FIGURE 3.9

You can scan damaged photos into a computer and remove dust, dirt, or damaged areas of the image using Photoshop Elements.

To change a black-and-white negative into a regular black-and-white (actually grayscale) image, first make the image window the active window. Then choose the **Invert** command from the **Image**, **Adjustments** menu. View the image in the work area, and save it if you like.

Accessing Images on the Camera

Importing images from a camera is similar to importing images from a scanner in Photoshop Elements. The basic steps involve connecting the camera to the computer, installing the camera software drivers and TWAIN plug-ins, and then choosing the TWAIN plug-in in Photoshop Elements. This section shows you how to bring images from a digital camera into Photoshop Elements.

The first thing to do is plug the serial or USB cable into your computer. Connecting a camera to a computer creates a physical hardware connection between the two devices. Next, you'll need to install software that enables your computer to communicate with the software on your camera. You can install the software from the CD-ROM that comes bundled with the camera or download the software from the camera manufacturer's Web site.

Setting Up the Software

Some cameras are bundled with TWAIN plug-in software, which will enable you to control the camera within the Photoshop Elements work area (see "Installing Plug-In Files" at the beginning of this chapter for more information). Other cameras have their own custom software you must use to download images from the camera onto your computer. If your camera falls into the latter category, follow the instructions that came with your camera, and download the image files onto your computer's hard drive. Then skip ahead to the next chapter.

Downloading Images to Your Computer

Controlling a camera in the Photoshop Elements work area is similar to the way you work with a scanner.

There are two ways you can open the Select Import Source dialog box: Click the **Import** button in the shortcuts bar or click the **Connect to Camera or Scanner** button on the **Welcome** window. After the **File**, **Import** submenu or Select Import Source dialog box is open, select a camera from the list. Then, wait for the camera's software window to open in the Photoshop Elements work area.

The user interface varies depending on the camera you're using. Usually, the software user interface is very simple. When Photoshop Elements first connects to the camera, a thumbnail image of each picture on the camera is downloaded to the computer. If you want to copy the file from the camera to the computer, click the **Acquire** button (see Figure 3.10).

note

Windows XP may enable you to download images using an Explorer window. Mac OS X users can try to use iPhoto to connect to and download images from a digital camera.

FIGURE 3.10

Download images from your camera to your computer in Photoshop Elements.

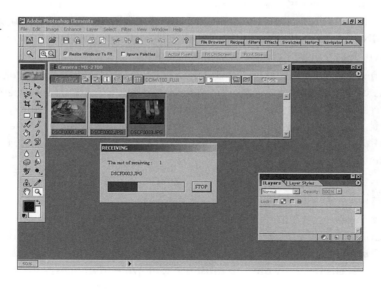

You might find that downloading images over a cable takes more time than you'd like. It will also drain your camera's batteries. If you want to copy all the files from the storage card in your camera directly onto your computer's hard drive, without viewing any of the files, you can insert the storage card into a media reader or PC Card adapter. If you're using a media card reader, you'll need to install additional software on your desktop computer so that it can recognize the USB device.

If you're using a PC Card adapter, you probably won't need to install any additional software to view or copy files from the storage card to your computer. However, some PC Card adapters require you to install software to work with a particular version of Windows or Mac OS. Windows 98, 2000, and XP, as well as Mac OS 9 and X, all have built-in support for reading files from CompactFlash, SmartMedia, and Sony Memory Stick storage cards (see Figure 3.11).

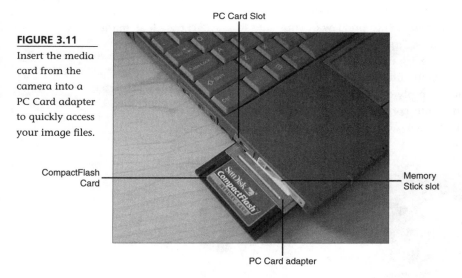

PC Card Slot

FIGURE 3.11
Insert the media card from the camera into a PC Card adapter to quickly access your image files.

CompactFlash Card

Memory Stick slot

PC Card adapter

Saving Images

After you've downloaded an image from a camera to your computer, it's a good idea to save a copy of the original image to your hard drive before you start modifying the image. After a file is saved, you can experiment with color correction or filter effects without having to worry about losing or damaging the original.

To save a file, make the file the active window in the work area. Choose **Save** from the **File** menu. Then type a name into the Save dialog box. Click on the **Format** drop-down menu and choose **JPEG**. Navigate to a folder location on your hard drive in the Save dialog box. Finally, click the **Save** button to save the image. Photoshop Elements will create a new image file on your hard drive.

Viewing the File Format

If you want to view an image on a camera without downloading it to your hard drive, you can use the File Browser in Photoshop Elements or the custom software that is bundled with the camera to preview thumbnails. Figure 3.12 shows the photo viewer application, Visual Flow, that opens when you insert a Memory Stick into a Sony computer. Each image scrolls up the photo view window as you move your cursor in the main window. Click on a picture to view it in more detail.

If you don't want to use an application to access image files, you can use Explorer (Windows) or the Finder (Mac OS) to preview or copy files to your computer. Figure 3.13 shows each image on the Memory Stick card. The camera gives each image a unique filename, along with the .jpg file extension. Simply copy the files from the Memory Stick onto your computer. Then you can use Photoshop Elements to view or modify them as you like.

note

Not sure which file format to use when saving your file? Choose the JPEG file format, with the highest level of image preservation (in Photoshop Elements, choose **Maximum**, or **12**).

To find out more about saving files, as well as Photoshop Elements–supported file formats, see Chapter 5, "Saving and Sharing Files."

FIGURE 3.12

When you insert a Memory Stick into a Sony VAIO laptop, you can navigate through thumbnail images of the files stored on the card. PC Card and USB Memory Stick readers are also available for Mac and Windows computers.

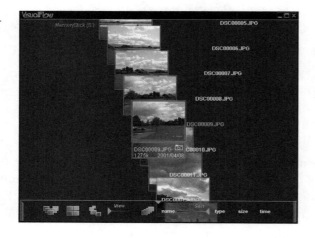

FIGURE 3.13

Files stored on a media card can be copied to your hard drive just as you copy any other document.

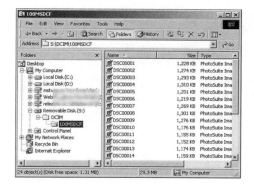

WHICH FILE FORMAT IS BEST?

Most cameras capture images and then save them as JPEG files. Although some cameras also support TIFF, and multimedia file formats, such as MPEG or AVI, the best file format to use for still image files is JPEG. You'll get the smallest, best-looking file sizes by using the JPEG file format on your camera, your computer, and, in most cases, your Web site, too.

After you've saved or copied a file to your computer, open it to see whether the file was properly saved. Choose **Open** from the **File** menu to view the Open dialog box. Select the file you just saved, and then click Open. The image opens in the Photoshop Elements work area.

If the image is larger than your desktop, Photoshop Elements resizes the full image to fit on your screen. The magnification level of the image appears in the title bar of each image window. You can use the Navigator palette to adjust the view of each image window, or select the Zoom Tool from the Toolbox. Click in the image window to increase the magnification level of the image window. Or hold down the [**Alt**] (**Option**) key to zoom away from the image. If the image opens and looks as good as the original, close it.

note

If you're using Windows, you might not see the .jpg extension if Windows is set to hide file extension names in Explorer windows.

Selecting Devices

If your digital camera or scanner has a TWAIN plug-in installed on your computer, you can work with each device one at a time or alternate between them. There are two ways you can select a device in the work area. You can choose the device from the **File**, **Import** menu list, or you can click the **Connect to Camera or**

Scanner button in the **Welcome** window. The Select Import Source dialog box opens only if you click the **Connect to Camera or Scanner** button or the **Import** button located in the shortcuts bar. You can access the TWAIN plug-in–related software of each scanner or camera from the Select Import Source dialog box (see Figure 3.14), or from the **File**, **Import** menu list. After you select a device, you can't perform any other tasks in Photoshop Elements. You must exit the camera's software window before you can access any other features in the work area.

FIGURE 3.14

Select a device.

Be sure the device is connected to your computer before selecting it in the Select Import Source dialog box. If the software cannot locate the device, it asks you to connect the device. You'll need to reselect the camera from the Import submenu to reestablish a connection with the camera.

If the software is able to locate your camera or scanner, you can preview the images in the work area. The preview image is usually much larger than the image shown in the software window. If you want to scan or download several images, it might take a while.

You can view additional information about an image, or about the camera or scanner device, if the device software provides these options. Figure 3.15 shows an information window from Fuji's MX 2700 digital camera software. This information is also accessible in Photoshop Elements. Choose **File**, **File Info** to open the File Info dialog box. Select the **EXIF** option in the **Section** drop-down menu to view image description information for the active image window in the work area.

FIGURE 3.15

Different cameras offer different software features. The Fuji camera software enables you to view camera information in Photoshop Elements.

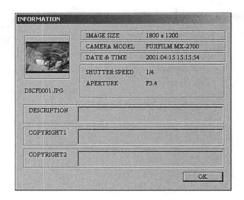

PART I

Opening, Saving, and Printing Images

4

Creating, Opening, and Converting Images

If there's anything an image absolutely has to have in Photoshop Elements, it's a window. Photoshop Elements creates a new image window whenever you open an image file or create a new one from scratch. A new or modified image window represents an unsaved document: a potential file that can be stored on your hard drive. You can open more than one image window if you want to work on more than one image at the same time or compare variations of the same image side by side. You can also duplicate an image window if you want to view the same image in different windows at different magnification levels.

Opening an image window and creating new files are the first things to learn if you want to be an image wizard. Adobe created the Welcome window to enable you to create a new file or open an existing one with a single click. You can open an image window in four ways: create a new file, paste an image from the Clipboard, browse and open existing images, or import an image by connecting to a scanner or camera. The Welcome window enables you to open the New, File Browser, or Select Import Source dialog boxes by clicking on the New File, Browse for File, or Connect to Camera or Scanner buttons. This chapter shows you several ways you can create new documents and open image files.

Creating a New Document

The image window is the heart of image editing in Photoshop Elements. Photoshop Elements enables you to set the specific width, height, and resolution of each image window. The width and height settings in the New dialog box define the size of the canvas area of the image file. You can grow or shrink the window regardless of the size of the canvas. However, more memory and scratch disk space will be required as the canvas area, resolution, and number of image layers increase.

You can use **File** menu commands and shortcut buttons as well as the buttons in the Welcome window to create a new image window. If you want to create a new image window, choose **File**, **New (Command-N) [Ctrl+N]** or click the **New** button in the shortcuts bar. The New dialog box will open. You can manually choose a preset size, such as 8×10 or 640×480, or type the width and height of the new window, as well as setting the resolution of the window, image mode, and canvas color.

If you want to create a new window that matches the dimensions of a specific image or other graphic, you can use the **File**, **New from Clipboard** command to transfer the image from the Clipboard. When you do so, Photoshop Elements will automatically set the width and height values in the New dialog box to match the contents of the Clipboard (see Figure 4.1) and place the copied image into a new window.

FIGURE 4.1

Choose a preset size or type a number to set the width and height. Choose an image mode, resolution, and contents for your new image window.

Located at the bottom of the New dialog box are three radio buttons that enable you to choose the content for the new window. You can set the color of the canvas in the background layer of the document, or choose transparent if you don't want a background added to the window. If you choose **White**, Photoshop Elements creates a background layer filled with pure white. Choose **Transparent** if you want to create a completely empty image window. You'll see a gray-and-white checkerboard pattern in the new window. This pattern represents transparent areas in the image window.

If you choose the **Background Color** radio button, the background layer of the new window will become the color displayed in the background swatch in the Toolbox. If you're working with graphics intended for Web pages, you can set the background color to match the background color of a Web page. This can help you coordinate the colors of other images you create in the image window with the colors used on a Web page.

ART DIRECTORS TOOLKIT X 2.2

Mac OS X users can use the Art Directors Toolkit to convert fractions to decimals, inches to centimeters, or points to picas. This handy utility program can also help you estimate the file size, based on print size, of an RGB, grayscale, or bitmap image. It can also compare font point sizes to inches, centimeters, points, or picas, and help you visualize columns for a page layout. Run, don't walk, to this tool to estimate page layout, file size, and resolution settings for an image file you want to create in Photoshop Elements.

By default, Photoshop Elements creates a document in RGB color mode. Almost all the examples in this book require an image to be in RGB mode, which supports millions of colors. Also, most of the tools and commands in Photoshop Elements won't work unless the image is in RGB mode. The other color modes—Grayscale, Indexed Color, and Bitmap—support 256 or fewer shades of color.

note

You can remove the background layer by first converting it to a regular layer, and then deleting the unlocked layer. To do so, double-click on the background layer, and then click **OK** in the **New Layer** window. The locked background layer will become a regular layer. Select the new layer in the Layers palette, and then click the **Trash** button located at the bottom of the **Layers** palette. The selected layer will be deleted from the image window.

Understanding the New Dialog Box

There are several settings you can customize in the New dialog box (see Figure 4.1). To create a new document, you need to review and input preset sizes or manually type the width and height, resolution, mode, and content settings in the New dialog box. The following list contains a brief description of each text box, drop-down menu, and radio button available in the New dialog box:

- **Filename**—Enter the name of the new document in the Name text box.
- **Image Size**—View the file size and set the width and height of the canvas area, not the image, in the New dialog box. Documents can be created in pixels, inches, centimeters, millimeters, points, picas, and columns.

- **Preset Sizes**—Choose a preconfigured width and height for the document you want to create, such as Letter, 5×7, 800×600, A3, or 740×540 Std. NTSC 601.

- **Resolution**—Enter the pixels per inch for the image window. You can also set this to pixels per centimeter. Note that 300 dpi is the standard resolution for a printed image, and 72 dpi is the standard resolution for a Web-ready image.

- **Mode**—Choose the image mode for the new document. Select RGB Color, Bitmap (black and white), or Grayscale (256 shades of gray).

- **Contents**—Choose a color or no color (Transparent) for the background layer of the new window.

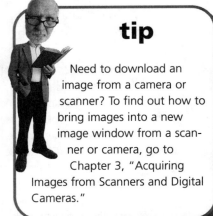

tip

Need to download an image from a camera or scanner? To find out how to bring images into a new image window from a scanner or camera, go to Chapter 3, "Acquiring Images from Scanners and Digital Cameras."

Demystifying Resolution and Image Size

Many of the settings in the New dialog box are also available in the Image, Resize, Image Size dialog box. Determining the width and height of the canvas is fairly straightforward, especially when you use the **File**, **New from Clipboard** command. The more complex settings to consider when creating a new window are the resolution and image size settings.

There's more than one definition for both of these terms. *Resolution* can be used to describe the dimensions of an image, the scale of measurement for an image, or the size of a computer desktop. *Image size* can refer to the size of the document in memory, the size of the file in pixels, or the size of the file on the hard disk. The following sections contain brief descriptions of each of these definitions of resolution and image size.

What Is Resolution?

The following list summarizes the three most commonly confused uses of the term *resolution*:

- **Dimensions of the image**—The actual number of pixels wide and tall of an image. The dimensions of the image can be larger or smaller than the canvas area of the image window.

- **Number of pixels per inch**—Some monitors display images at 96 dots per inch (dpi). Older Macintosh monitors have a resolution of 72 dpi. Photoshop

Elements uses the measurement of pixels per inch to represent the number of pixels displayed for each inch of a computer monitor. Scanned images may be set to 300, 600, or higher ppi.

- **Resolution of the display**—Set the size of your computer's desktop area from the (**Display**) [**Monitors**] **Control Panel** window. The resolution of your desktop, combined with the actual size of your display screen, determines how much of the image you can view on your computer monitor.

What Is Image Size?

The following list explains three definitions of image size:

- **Document size**—The canvas area of the image window.
- **Pixel size**—The actual number of pixels wide and tall of an image.
- **File size**—The size of the image file on the hard drive.

Customizing the Canvas Size

Each document you create in Photoshop Elements can have a canvas. When you open an existing image file, the canvas area matches the width and height of the image being opened. If a color canvas was created with the document, a separate layer will appear in the **Layers** palette. If the canvas is transparent, represented by a gray-and-white checkered pattern indicating the absence of color, no additional layers will appear in the **Layers** palette.

You can view the size of the canvas by choosing the **Canvas Size** command from the **Image**, **Resize** menu. The Canvas Size dialog box will open. The current file size appears at the top of the window, followed by its width and height. You can type a width and height into the text boxes. If you want the canvas to grow in a particular direction, click on one of the **Anchor** buttons to indicate where the existing canvas will be located in relation to the new area.

Increasing the size of the canvas will not affect the size of any images in the image window. However, if you decrease the size of the canvas, Photoshop Elements will remove any areas of the image that are not located on the smaller-sized canvas.

When you resize or create a new image window, the width and height settings define the canvas area in addition to the dimensions of the window and image. The canvas represents the printable or publishable area of the image window. The following describes each setting in the Canvas Size dialog box:

- **New Size**—The new file size is calculated based on the new width and height values you enter into the text boxes.

- **Width and Height**—Enter a new value into the text box. Choose from percent, pixels, inches, centimeters, points, picas, or columns for the canvas measurement.

- **Anchor**—Determines the location and direction of the new canvas area. Click on a square to choose where the current document will reside when the canvas area is extended.

Document Settings for Print

Although the width and height settings determine the dimensions of an image file, the resolution setting in the New dialog box ultimately has the biggest impact on how the image will appear onscreen and in print. Printers use the measurement of *dots per inch* (dpi). "Dots" refers to the way the printer places ink or toner powder onto a page to re-create the image being sent from your computer. To print a document, first you must view it on a computer screen. However, computer monitors use the pixel as their most basic form of measurement. Dots and pixels have no common ancestor, although Photoshop Elements makes it relatively easy to convert an image intended for print into an image targeted for the Web.

Computer monitors use the measurement of *pixels per inch* (ppi). The size of a pixel is different from the size of the dots referenced by printers. Digital cameras use *megapixels*, a combination of the total number of horizontal and vertical pixels captured, to determine resolution. However, when you open an image created by a digital camera, the resolution will be set to 72 pixels per inch—the same settings as a computer screen. In the next section, I'll say more about why digital cameras and publishing to the Web are much more straightforward than printing digital images.

Scanners, on the other hand, use samples per inch to measure the data captured by the 600 to 1200 sensors located on the scanner's scan bar (below the glass on a flatbed scanner). The data captured by the sensors is combined with the vertical distance between each line of captured data. For example, you can create an image that's scanned into your computer with a resolution of 1200 dpi.

After you've scanned an image into the work area, you can click on the status bar in the work area to view the image's information (see Figure 4.2). Click the middle-left area of the status bar, located at the bottom of the work area (or bottom of the window for Mac users). A pop-up window will appear displaying the dimensions of the image, as well as its image mode and resolution. Clicking on the status bar is a nice, quick way to determine the size and resolution of the image you're modifying.

FIGURE 4.2

Click on the status bar to view the current image's information.

IMAGE AND PRINT SIZES

If you plan to share a scanned image on the Web, you can modify the scanned image at a high resolution, such as 600 dpi, and then resize it to 72 or 96 dpi (see Figure 4.3). The print dimensions of the document will not change, although the size of the image window might shrink quite a bit. Double-click on the Zoom Tool (Z) in the Toolbox to resize the image to a 100% view.

FIGURE 4.3

Resize an image by changing the resolution in the Image Size dialog box. The image on the right is 72 dpi, whereas the image on the left was scanned in at 2400 dpi.

Document Settings for Web Images

If you're creating a new document for use on the Web, consider the width and height of the Web page for which you are designing the image or graphics. Most images for Web pages are created at 72 or 96 dpi, because the Web visitors can view Web pages at these resolutions on their monitors—regardless of whether the image is actually a higher dpi in its electronic format.

The dimensions of the image file will affect the overall size of the Web page. You are also limited by the connection speed of the Web visitor; the larger the image, the longer the download time for the Web page. Web pages should contain smaller, rather than larger, image files, enabling your Web visitors to experience your Web graphics without waiting too long for them to download. Find out more about how to optimize Web graphics in Chapter 5, "Saving and Sharing Files."

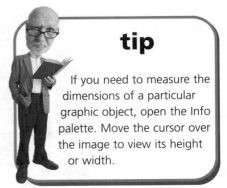

tip

If you need to measure the dimensions of a particular graphic object, open the Info palette. Move the cursor over the image to view its height or width.

Consider the following issues when creating a new document for use on the Web:

- Create an image file that fits within the desktop area of the Web page. I usually save my images as 640×480 files (see Figure 4.4), expecting visitors to my Web site to have at minimum an 800×600 pixel desktop. If a visitor arrives at your Web site and has only a 640×480 desktop, they will be able to see only part of your Web page onscreen at once. They will have to scroll around the browser window to view the full 640×480 image. If you want each visitor to view the full size of each photograph, consider creating a smaller thumbnail image for each larger image.

- A resolution setting of 72 dpi will work fine for Web graphics. In most cases, you don't have to adjust the resolution of your images captured with your digital camera to put them on a Web page.

- Set the background color of the document window to be colored or transparent. For most images, you're better off choosing a transparent background for a new image window. Alternatively, you could choose a background color for the canvas if you want to create graphics that blend in with the Web page.

note

You can use Photoshop Elements to create great-looking images for the Web. However, you'll need a text editor to create the Web page. Web pages use HTML (Hypertext Markup Language) to format text and embed images in the HTML file. To share your images on a Web site, you will upload the image file and the HTML file onto your Web server.

FIGURE 4.4

The width and height of a Web document should fall within the size of the desktop and work well with a 72 ppi resolution setting.

Width: 640 pixels (8.889 inches)
Height: 480 pixels (6.667 inches)
Channels: 3 (RGB Color)
Resolution: 72 pixels/inch

Photoshop Elements enables you to create images and graphics you can share with others. Click on the Attach to Email button in the shortcuts bar to send a photo in an email message. You can create a single-file slideshow from a folder of image files by choosing the **PDF Slideshow** menu command from **File**, **Automation Tools**. If you want to share your images on the Web, choose **Create File**, **Web Photo Gallery** to create a photo album that you can share on the Web. You can view your digital images on your computer, or upload them to a Web site and share them with friends and family over the Internet. To find out more about Web pages, image files, and how to create a Web photo album, go to Chapter 17, "Creating a Slideshow and Web Photo Gallery."

note

Many Web sites offer to convert your 35mm film to digital images for use on the Web. You can create a digital photo album if you use this type of service, and simply download the images from the Web if you want to make any color adjustments, or combine images to create new pictures.

Opening and Browsing Image Files

To open an image file, go to the **File** menu and choose one of four menu commands: **Open**, **Open As**, **Open Recent**, or **Browse**. Choose **File**, **Open** (**Command-O**) [**Ctrl+O**] when you want to open an image file in its current file format. If you want to convert a file to a different image file format, use the **File**, **Open As** command (**Command-O**) [**Alt+Ctrl+O**]. One of the reasons to use the **Open As** command is to save time. For example, if you know you want to combine two JPEG files, you can use the **Open As** command to open the first image as a PSD file, and then copy the second JPEG image into the PSD file. Each image will reside in its own editable layer.

A PSD file is the native file format used by Photoshop Elements. Why edit images as PSD files? Because this file format will preserve all layer information you generate as you apply tools, use menu commands, and click away on an image.

You also can open an image file by dragging and dropping its icon onto the Photoshop Elements application icon on your desktop. To open a recently used file, select the **File, Open Recent submenu**, which contains a list of the last 10 files that were open in the work area.

If you want to preview all the images in a folder, click the Browse button in the shortcuts bar, or select **File**, **Browse (Command-Shift-N)** [**Ctrl+Shift+N**]. The **File Browser** palette will open. Double-click on a thumbnail image to open a photo. If you click and drag the File Browser away from the palette well, it will change into a floating window. Choose **Dock to Palette Well** from the **More** drop-down menu to move the File Browser back to the palette well.

> **tip**
>
> You can use a separate program to organize and catalog your digital photos. Mac OS X users can use iPhoto to view and organize images. Click and drag any image from the iPhoto window to the desktop or another folder on your hard drive to create a copy of the image file. Open the original or copy of the image file in Photoshop Elements and edit, modify, or print the photo.

ATTENTION MACINTOSH USERS

The Macintosh version of Photoshop Elements does not have an Open As command in the File menu. Instead, you can perform this task in the **Open** window. Choose **File**, **Open**, and the Open dialog box will appear. Click on the image file you want to open. Then, choose a file format from the **Format** pop-up menu. The selected file will open in the format you choose in the Format menu list. For example, if you want to open a JPEG file as a PSD file, highlight a JPEG file in the window list. Choose **Photoshop PDF** from the **Format** pop-up menu. Click on the **Open** button, and the JPEG file will open as a native Photoshop document.

When you first open an image file, you should decide whether the quality of the image is good enough. For example, if you're scanning an image, it's better to rescan an iffy-looking image before spending hours trying to correct what could have been prevented by creating a better quality scanned image.

Working with Scanned Images

You can open an image file created by a scanner the same way you open any image file. However, depending on the resolution, dimensions, and file size of an image, it might not quite fit into the work area. If you're planning to repair or correct a scanned image, you'll want to keep the image at a higher resolution (see Figure 4.5). If you plan to print the scanned image, you probably don't need to change the resolution of the image file. If you plan to use the image for a Web page, you can change its resolution to 72 dpi after correcting or modifying it.

FIGURE 4.5

One of the benefits of working with a scanned image is that you can scan the image into Photoshop Elements at a high resolution, making it easier to work with.

WHEN BIGGER IS BETTER

Scanning an image into Photoshop Elements enables you to make detailed edits before scaling it down to a smaller size for printing or publishing to the Web. Be forewarned that the larger the document, the larger the size of the image file. This means the image takes up more space on your hard drive and will download very slowly on the Web.

For example, I scanned in a color negative at 2400 dpi and ended up saving a 3GB file. The same image scanned in at 1200 dpi is less than 1GB.

I also scanned in a 4×6 photo at 1200 dpi, which resulted in a 4GB file. This file opens as a 60MB image in Photoshop Elements!

Opening Images Created by a Digital Camera

Most files created by digital cameras are JPEG files, although some cameras also can create TIFF, MPEG, WMP, or AVI files. The latter three file formats are multimedia file formats. The multimedia files usually are smaller 320×240 pixel images compared to the larger 2000×1600 pixel still images. You cannot open multimedia files in Photoshop Elements, only import a single-frame image from multimedia files.

Choose **Open** from the shortcuts bar or from the **File** menu to view the Open dialog box. The Open dialog box looks slightly different on Windows than on a Macintosh computer. However, both dialog boxes perform the same core task of opening image files. You can open any of the file formats that appear in the **Files of Type** drop-down menu. To find out more about the supported file formats in Photoshop Elements, go to Chapter 5.

The Windows Open dialog box enables you to preview some JPEG files if a thumbnail is stored along with the full-size image (see Figure 4.6). The file size appears below the thumbnail image. Sorry, Mac users, you can preview images as a thumbnail icon on your desktop, but not in the Open dialog box.

If your camera can capture one-, two-, or three-megapixel images, you can open them with Photoshop Elements. When you open a megapixel image, it might seem as though your desktop is a little too small to display the full-size image. This is a good thing, because it's better to have a larger image than a smaller one, especially when you want to edit the image. Photoshop Elements will adjust the magnification level of the image so that you can view the entire image in the work area. You can view the file size, resolution, width, or height of an image by clicking on the status bar of the open image in the Photoshop Elements work area.

> **tip**
>
> If you want to open more than one image at a time, hold down the **Shift** or **Ctrl** keys and click on more than one file in the Open dialog box or the File Browser palette window.

FIGURE 4.6

The Open dialog box enables you to view one or all image file formats supported by Photoshop Elements.

If you want to reduce the dimensions of the digital image, choose **Image Size** from the **Image**, **Resize** menu. Enter a smaller number into the width and height text boxes. By default, the link icon that appears to the right of these text boxes will maintain the original proportions of the image file. You can type in a new number for the width of the document, and Photoshop Elements will automatically calculate the new height of the image.

IMPORTING VERSUS OPENING

Importing enables you to select specific settings for an image file being opened in the work area. For example, TWAIN plug-ins enable you to run device-specific (such as scanners or digital cameras) software in the Photoshop Elements work area, allowing you to customize an image with the device before opening it in the work area. Similarly, you can use the PDF Image command to import each image from a PDF (Portable Document Format) file. If you opened the PDF file with the Open command, the entire document will open in the image window. To find out more about the PDF file format, see Chapter 5. To find out how to import images from a scanner or camera, go to Chapter 3.

Resizing an Image

Photoshop Elements opens a photo in its original dimensions, although it may automatically change the view so you can see the entire image in the work area. You can change the view of the image displayed in the image window to zoom in or away from the image. If you want to permanently resize the image (see Figure 4.7), change the width and height values in the Image Size dialog box. The term *resize* is intended to describe only the actual width and height dimensions of the image, not its file size or view setting.

FIGURE 4.7

You must resize a three-megapixel image to view it in a browser window.

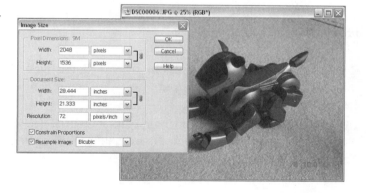

Choose the Zoom Tool (magnifying-glass icon) to zoom into or out of an image window. This tool enables you to change the view of the image without affecting the image itself. Click on the image to enlarge it, or hold down the (**Option**) [**Alt**] key and click to reduce or zoom away from the image.

You also can use the **Navigator** palette or choose a **Zoom** command from the **View** menu to set the magnification level of the viewable image in the document window. Click and drag the red rectangle to pan around the image window from the Navigator palette. The magnification level of the image appears in the lower-left corner of the Navigator palette and the work area (or image window for Macs). It also appears in the title bar of the image window.

If you want to change the width or height of the image, choose **Image Size** from the **Image**, **Resize** menu. The Image Size window opens. This window is divided into four general areas: pixel dimension, document size, check boxes, and buttons. On the right, the **OK**, **Cancel**, **Help**, and **Auto** buttons enable you to create a new window or exit the Image Size dialog box. You can adjust the Pixel Dimensions or Document Size, or choose a different method for Photoshop Elements to use to resample the resized image. The following list contains a brief description of each area of settings in the Image Size window:

- **Pixel Dimensions**—View the current dimensions of the image here. Enter a new width or height into the text boxes. The default behavior is to constrain the settings so that the proportions of the original image are preserved.

- **Document Size**—The Width and Height values indicate the actual printed size of the file. The default setting is in inches, and the width and height are constrained to preserve the original dimensions of the image.

- **Resolution**—This box shows the number of pixels per inch in the image. You can enter a new value into this text box to change the resolution of an image without changing the document size. Use 72 ppi for images you want to share on the Web or in email, 300 ppi or higher for printing images.

- **Constrain Proportions**—If this box is checked, the original proportion of the width to the height is preserved when you enter any new value in the Image Size dialog box.

- **Resample Image**—Choose the interpolation method you want Photoshop Elements to use on a resized image (see Figure 4.8). The interpolation method applies an algorithm to retain as much of the original image as possible.

FIGURE 4.8

A resized image will be resampled using the interpolation method selected from the Resample Image drop-down menu.

Converting Image Information

You might need to modify your images for several reasons. You might want to change the file type so that it matches another image with which you are going to combine it. After you open an image, you might find that you need to change the resolution, image mode, or size in order for it to fit your intended purpose. Whatever the reason, Photoshop Elements makes it fairly painless to accomplish just about any type of change you need to make.

Opening an Image in a Different File Format

When you open an image file using the (Open) [Open As] dialog box, you can convert it to a different file format (see Figure 4.9). When it's open, you can change its image mode or dimensions to more closely match the settings of another image file. For example, if you want to take a scanned image and combine it with an image created with a digital camera, you might need to work with the resolution and image sizes to scale both images until they match. Using the Image Size dialog box to adjust the settings, you can experiment with copying and pasting an image using different resolutions in multiple image windows. Then, pick the images you want to combine, and paste them into a single image window.

FIGURE 4.9

The (Open) [Open As] command enables you to convert a file to a specific file format when you open it.

Changing an Image to a Different Color Mode

The mode of an image determines the number of colors that can be used to display the image. Photoshop Elements enables you to work with an image in four image modes: RGB Color, Grayscale, Bitmap, and Indexed color. Most images will open in RGB Color mode. The following list matches up image modes with image files:

- Color photo—RGB Color
- Optimized color photo—Indexed Color

■ Black-and-white or monochrome image—Grayscale

■ Line art—Bitmap

Converting a File for Print Output

Printing a digital image can be either a pleasant or a frustrating experience. More precisely, it is a pleasant experience when you print an image that matches what you created on your computer screen. And it's frustrating when the printed image does not meet your expectations.

If the image originates from a digital camera, it was most likely created at a resolution of 72 dpi. You can adjust the width and height of the printed size of the image without changing its resolution to make the image match the dimensions of the paper on which it will be printed. Photoshop Elements will use an interpolation algorithm to resize the original so that it will retain as much color information and image detail when it is printed at 300, 600, or 1440 dpi. Interpolation uses a best-guess method to estimate how to adjust colors in the resized image to match its original. However, it's not capable of creating an exact match of the original because pixels will be either added or lost when the image size changes.

> **note**
>
> When you resize an image for the Web, Photoshop Elements uses the interpolation algorithm selected in the Resample Image option in the Image Size dialog box to determine which pixels to change. Bicubic interpolation, which is the default setting, usually offers the best and fastest method of resampling an image. However, you also can choose a bilinear or nearest neighbor algorithm when shrinking or growing an image.

If you've scanned an image, you might have captured a 300 or 600 dpi or higher resolution image. Save the file as a TIFF or JPEG file format to retain the image size and quality. If you print this image to a 600 dpi printer, it will print with a much higher quality than a resized digital picture because the original image consists of more dots packed into each inch of paper (see Figure 4.10).

CHOOSING A WEB FILE FORMAT

One of the great things about the Web is that you can easily download images from a Web page onto your hard drive. If you have access to a Web server, you can store a backup copy of your images on the Web, and easily download an original if you lose or remove it from your hard drive. Most images on the Web are stored as JPEG or GIF files. However, some browsers can display the PNG file format, too.

FIGURE 4.10

Both of these images are 72 ppi. The image on the left was scanned, and the one on the right was taken with a digital camera.

Converting PDF Files

You can convert the images stored in a multi-page PDF document, such as a PDF slideshow, into separate PSD (Photoshop) files. This command can come in handy if you want to share or edit a photo stored in a PDF file. You can also save the converted image in another file format, such as a JPEG or GIF, instead of as a Photoshop (PSD) file.

The following steps show you how to convert a photo from a PDF file into a Photoshop file:

1. Choose **Multi-Page PDF to PSD** from the **File**, **Automation Tools** menu. The Convert Multi-Page PDF to PSD dialog box will open.

2. Click **Choose** to select the PDF file. Set the number of pages you want to convert to PSD files.

3. Choose a resolution for the resulting images, and assign a common base name to each file.

4. Click the **Choose** button located at the bottom of the dialog box to select the destination folder for the PSD files.

When working with scanned images or images taken with a digital camera, it is necessary to preserve the original JPEG or TIFF image. Saving the original file enables you to archive the original state of the captured data so that you can easily go back to the original state if you find that the edits you are making don't achieve the result you want. As you work on an image, you might find that an image you captured can be more easily edited if you change some of the scanner or camera settings and bring the image back into Photoshop Elements again.

5. If the document contains text, or objects that Photoshop Elements won't recognize, check the **Suppress Warnings** check box—this will ignore any warnings that may otherwise stop the conversion process from completing.

6. Click **OK**, and Photoshop Elements will convert the images in the PDF file into PSD files.

5

SAVING AND SHARING FILES

The best thing about working with digital images is that you can preserve all the detail of an image as a file, and copy or back that file up as many times as you like. The quality of the digital image won't degenerate as the file is opened, copied, or closed, or while it is just biding its time on your computer's hard drive.

Saving a file also means you can share it with others. You can send an image file in an email or publish it on a Web page. This chapter shows you all the ins and outs of saving files, whether you want to print them or share them on the Web.

What's All the Fuss?

What can be so difficult about choosing the Save command from the File menu to save a file? Well, certain file formats retain image data better than others. For example, a JPEG file stored at a high compression rate will save a portion of the original image. A high compression rate usually results in a lower quality image, compared to the original image. However, if you choose the minimum compression rate, the quality of the image will be preserved; all the original image data will be stored in the compressed file.

When you save an image, you want to preserve all the image data so that you can edit the image with as much image and color data as possible. After you've created the final image, you can save a separate copy of the same image containing fewer colors, or only a portion of the original image. What I'm describing here is the general workflow for preparing digital camera images for printing or for posting on a Web page.

Using the Save Command

If you're working with a new document, the first time you choose the **Save** command and assign it a name, the Save As window will appear. If you've already chosen a file format for your image file, or are saving the same file as you gradually make changes, use the Save command. The **Save** command, located in the **File** menu, replaces the existing file with all the new information of the current image file, using the same file format. If you want to choose a different file format for an image, use the **Save As** command— it's chock-full of file-saving options (see Figure 5.1).

Heed these words of wisdom: Save, and save often. You can edit the images, undo a change, or copy and paste other images into multiple documents without ever saving them. But there's nothing more memorable than watching your computer crash after you've spent hours of work developing an image.

CHOOSING THE COLOR OF THE CANVAS

If the **Background Color** radio button is selected in the New dialog box, the color that appears in the background color square located in the Toolbox will be used as the background color for a new window. If the Web page you're working with uses a solid color background, you can work with images or graphics with the same color background. This can help you adjust transparency settings for each graphic object, and also choose colors that blend well with the background color of the page. To find out more about how to create a new document, go to Chapter 4, "Creating, Opening, and Converting Images."

FIGURE 5.1

The Save As window contains a treasure trove of file formats from which you can choose.

When you save an image, you can save a color profile along with it. The color profile contains color information that can help maintain the original captured colors as you work on the image with different applications, or on different computers (see Figure 5.2).

FIGURE 5.2

Save the color profile of an image so that you can preserve its color information if you copy the file to different computers, or work on it in more than one application.

You can access color management in one or more of the following ways:

- **File format**—Choose a file format that can preserve as many colors as possible (see Figure 5.3).

- **Color profile**—Choose a color profile to save along with the file.

- **Operating system**—Mac OS uses a color-management system called ColorSync. Check to see whether your computer has color-management software available for any connected devices.

FIGURE 5.3

Some file formats, such as JPEG and TIFF, have several file settings that enable you to control how much of the image data is saved to the file.

The options you choose when saving a file can affect how much data is saved. Some file formats, such as the JPEG format, shown in Figure 5.3, support compression, which reduces the file size of an image. You can adjust the compression options when you first save an image. A format options window will appear for a JPEG, GIF, or TIFF image after you click the **Save** button in the **Save** window. Although it's not the case for all file formats, more compression usually means that more image data is removed when the file is saved. Basically, the smaller the image, the less image data it contains.

If you're not sure which settings to use for a particular file format, your best bet is to use as little compression as possible. For example, if you're saving a JPEG file, choose an image quality setting of 12. TIFF images can also be saved with or without compression. However, some compression formats, such as LZW compression, might not work with different graphics editors or image viewer applications. Shareware programs are available that can view LZW-compressed TIFF files. You can use GraphiConverter or Preview for Macintosh computers or IrfanView for Windows.

note

Color management enables different output devices to translate color information to preserve color accuracy. To find out more about color management, go to Chapter 7, "Photoshop Elements and Color."

Saving a File for Any Occasion

Photoshop Elements supports a long list of file formats. Although you can use any of these file formats to save your image, Photoshop Elements' native PSD is the only file format that enables you to continue editing multilayered images time and time again. A PSD file can store any layers or other Photoshop Elements–specific settings. Other file formats will only be able to save a single, flat layer as an image file.

Flattening an image makes it much more difficult to edit later. It's better to preserve the layers of an image whenever possible, until you are positive you will no longer need to edit the file.

Supported File Formats

The following list contains all the possible file formats Photoshop Elements can open and save:

- **BMP**—The bitmap image file format used most frequently with Windows computers. This is the default format used when you create a screen capture in Windows.

- **PCX**—Another graphics file format used by many Windows and Macintosh graphics applications.

- **PICT**—The default file format used by Mac OS 9.x to store screen shots. (Mac OS X captures screen shots as TIFF files.) PICT also is referred to as a .PCT file or PICT Resource. A PICT Resource is a type of image stored in a Mac file.

- **Photo CD**—A file format created for image files stored on Kodak's Photo CD-ROMs. If you shoot a roll of 35mm film, many stores can create a Photo CD of that roll of film so that you can open the images on your computer. The Photo CD contains several sets of the 35mm images. Each set contains the images stored at different resolutions, such as 640×480 pixels or 1024×768 pixels. Photoshop Elements enables you to import Photo CD images into the work area. Photoshop Elements cannot save files in PCD format.

- **GIF**—Graphics Interchange Format. GIF images use LSW compression combined with a transparency layer and a color table to store an image. Choose CompuServe GIF to save an image as a GIF file.

- **JPEG**—Joint Photographic Experts Group. This format supports the widest range of colors of all the image file formats. It also offers file compression, but no transparency support. Also, the more compression you apply to a JPEG file, the more image data is lost.

- **JPEG 2000**—Joint Photographic Experts Group 2000. A new file format in Photoshop Elements 2. This file format enables you to adjust the amount of compression used in the JPEG file and choose from three different types of optimization. You can also adjust the quality of the image as well as its size and amount of compression applied to it. Most browsers do recognize this file format because it is different from a standard JPEG file. This is a file format unique to Photoshop Elements version 2.0.

- **PNG**—Portable Network Graphics. An alternative to GIF or JPEG image formats. The latest versions of Internet Explorer and Netscape Navigator can display PNG files. This file format was designed to replace the GIF file format; however, it does not support animation.

■ **TIFF**—Tag Image File Format. A common format used with Mac and Windows computers. You can save a TIFF file as a grayscale or color image, using no compression or JPEG, LZW, or ZIP compression. If the document contains layers, the default is to save layers with the TIFF file. You can also choose either PC or Mac byte order or apply options, such as **Save Image Pyramid** and **Save Transparency**. Layer compression options include **RLE**, **ZIP**, **Discard Layers**, and **Save a Copy**.

■ **(Photoshop EPS) [EPS]**—An acronym for Encapsulated PostScript. Sound like some sort of medicine? It's not. This file format was originally created by Adobe to preserve font and line art, or vector graphic data in a file. Opening an EPS file converts the vector graphics into pixels.

■ **PDD**—The native file format created by Adobe Photo Deluxe. This format is not available on the Macintosh version of Photoshop Elements.

■ **(Photoshop PDF) [PDF]**—An acronym for the Portable Document Format. It is the standard file format used by Adobe Acrobat and Acrobat Reader.

■ **(Photoshop) [PSD]**—The native file format for Photoshop and Photoshop Elements. This format enables you to preserve unique Photoshop Elements document information, such as layers, group layer information, and other settings. If you need to preserve an image that can be opened with Photoshop 2.0 (that's right, the second version of Photoshop), you'll need to have a Mac to choose and save a file in this file format.

■ **Raw**—This is not as much of a file format as it is a file that contains a stream of image information. This is a generic file format that can be used to transfer files between computers or applications. Compressed files, such as PICT or GIF files, cannot be opened using this format.

■ **Pixar**—Pixar is the 3D computer graphics company that makes feature films with computers. Pixar also is the name of the file format used to store the custom, high-end graphics required by their sophisticated computer systems. That's right, you can use Photoshop Elements to view image files created by Pixar graphics systems.

■ **Scitex**—Scitex is a type of computer used to process high-end images. The Scitex file format enables you to save your image in Photoshop Elements so that it can be viewed on a Scitex computer.

■ **Targa**—The TGA file format is designed for computers that have a Truevision video board. This file format is also supported by many MS-DOS color applications. You can choose a pixel depth of 16, 24, or 32 bits per pixel.

Choosing a File Format

There are so many different formats from which to choose that it can be difficult to decide which one to use. Your best bet will be to use a format that can be viewed on a Windows or Macintosh computer, regardless of whether that computer has Photoshop Elements installed. JPEG probably will be the best file format to save your digital images. It works well for both print and the Web.

Although there might be a few exceptions, most old and new computers will have a browser application already installed. Internet Explorer and Netscape Navigator are the most popular Web browsers currently in use. Plus, they're both free. You can visit Microsoft's Web site (www.microsoft.com) or Netscape's Web site (www.netscape.com) to download the software and install it on your computer.

The following file formats can be viewed in a browser, and are the most commonly chosen file formats for saving graphics and digital images for the Web or for printing:

- **GIF**—Graphics Interchange Format. Choose this format if your image has large areas of similar or solid color, or if you're creating a Web graphic, such as a button or menu graphic. This format supports transparency. Your image can be edited into an animation if the file is saved as an animated GIF in the Save for Web window.

- **JPEG**—Joint Photographic Experts Group. This format saves images of any size. However, this format won't save any transparency settings along with the image. Use this format to save scanned or digital images for the Web or print.

- **PNG**—Portable Network Graphics. Although not as commonly used as JPEG or GIF, this file format is supported by most browsers. It can create smaller file sizes and more colors than GIF. This file format supports transparency but does not support animation.

- **TIFF**—Tag Image File Format. The optimal file format for publishing. Choose this format if you want to submit an image to a book publisher, or for other professional-quality print jobs. You might need to install the QuickTime plug-in for your browser to view a TIFF file.

FILE INFORMATION

You can add copyright and caption information when you save an image. Choose **File**, **File Info**, and then choose either **Caption**, **Copyright & URL**, or **EXIF** from the **Section** drop-down menu. Type any caption information into the **Caption** window (see Figure 5.4). You can add the copyright notice or URL for the image into the **Copyright & URL** section of the **Caption** window.

Click the **Section** drop-down menu, and select **EXIF** to view any custom information saved along with the image by the digital camera. Some digital cameras store date, time, resolution in ppi, and exposure settings along with each image file. To find out more about EXIF annotations, read the documentation for your digital camera.

FIGURE 5.4

Choose **File Info** from the **File** menu to view or add copyright information to an image file. Choose the **Copyrighted Work** option and add a copyright notice to your photos.

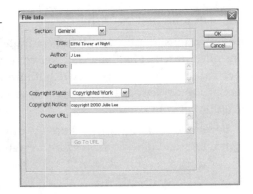

Optimizing Images

Depending on how you want to share your images, you might need to optimize an image before you print it or save it for the Web. For example, if you're working with a group of people, you might want to share your photos as-is without making any changes so that the team can decide how to proceed with each image. On the other hand, if you want to create custom images, correct portrait photos, or repair an old photo, you'll probably want to polish—or optimize—an image before you print it or share it on the Web.

Optimizing for the Web

Optimizing an image can involve several processes. The goal of optimizing an image is to minimize the file size of the image without sacrificing the quality of the image (see Figure 5.5). You can optimize an image based on a fixed file size, or enhance the quality of an image by choosing the best combination of settings for a particular file format. Photoshop Elements provides both kinds of tools that enable you to preview Web settings before you save the file.

FIGURE 5.5

A black-and-white image is significantly smaller than the original full-color image.

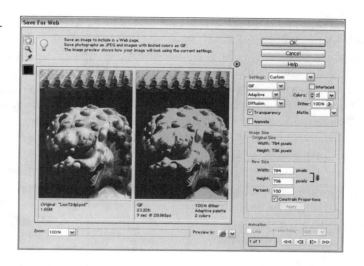

FILE SIZE AND DOWNLOAD TIME

With a growing base of broadband (fast Ethernet connections) Internet access, you might not need to worry about how long someone will have to wait to download your image to his or her browser. Broadband connections support anywhere from 144Kbps (kilobits per second) up to 1.5Mbps (megabits per second) connection rates—not too bad when you compare that to a 56Kbps modem, or a 10Mbps Ethernet data transfer rate.

Before you decide how to optimize an image, consider your audience, and then decide whether file size or image quality is more important for the image being optimized. If most of your visitors will have slow modem connections using traditional telephone lines, you should choose the smallest file size (around 50KB to 300KB) for your image. If the quality or colors in an image are more important to your visitors, you can ignore the size of each image and focus on creating a great-looking image. In some cases, you will be able to create a great-looking image with a relatively small file size.

Another alternative might be to reduce the width and height of the image, preserving its quality but reducing the overall dimensions of the file.

Choose the **Save for Web** command (**Command-Option-Shift-S**) [**Ctrl+Alt+Shift+S**] from the File menu to preview optimization settings. You will be able to optimize the image settings only for GIF, JPEG, and PNG file formats in the **Save for Web** window.

If you're working with a photo image, first view different compression settings for the JPEG version. Then, compare the quality and file size of the JPEG version to a GIF version. For most pictures, you'll find that JPEG creates the smaller, better-looking image. For example, the black-and-white GIF image shown in Figure 5.5 is just barely smaller than the low-resolution, highly compressed JPEG of the same image, shown in Figure 5.6.

If you want to create an image that blends in with the background color of a Web page, select the GIF format. The file size will be a little larger than the JPEG file, but if you don't think your Web page visitors will mind waiting a few more seconds for the GIF, save the image as a GIF. Figure 5.7 shows the previously shown JPEG file, this time as a GIF file. The GIF version has 128 colors, versus 2 colors as shown in Figure 5.5.

WHY SAVE A PHOTO AS A GIF?

In most instances, you will save a photo as a JPEG file. However, if you want to add transparency to an image, you need to use the GIF file format.

The GIF file format also supports animation. To convert the layers of a file into frames of animation, choose **Save for Web** from the **File** menu. The **Save for Web** window will open. Choose one of the GIF items from the Settings drop-down menu, and then check the Animate check box. To find out more about how to create animation with Photoshop Elements, go to Chapter 15, "Animating Images."

tip

If you want Photoshop Elements to remember your settings in the **Save for Web** window, open the **Save for Web** window, and then hold down the (**Option**) [**Alt**] key. The **OK** and **Cancel** buttons will change to **Remember** and **Reset**. Click the **Remember** button if you want to save the settings in the window. Click the **Reset** button to revert to the recommended settings of Photoshop Elements. The remembered settings will become the default settings the next time you open the **Save For Web** window, regardless of the image file you have open.

FIGURE 5.6

A low-resolution JPEG file isn't much larger than the black-and-white image, yet has much more image detail and color.

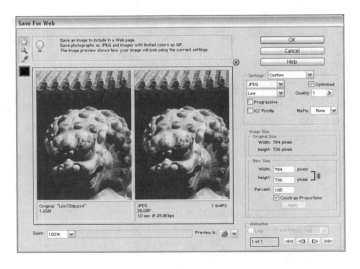

FIGURE 5.7

Increasing the number of colors in the GIF file also increases the file size and download time of the image.

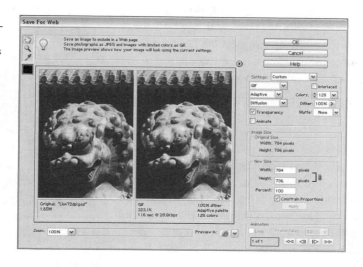

Comparing Web File Formats

There are actually three image file formats you should compare before picking one to save your file. PNG is an acronym for the Portable Network Graphics file format. Its biggest strength is that it can support more colors than GIF. Otherwise, it provides decent file compression compared to GIF. But JPEG tends to turn out the best image-quality-to-image-compression ratio. Figure 5.8 shows the image quality of a PNG-8 file. Compare the image quality and file size, as well as the download time with the JPEG and GIF files.

FIGURE 5.8

The same file saved as a PNG-8 file is slightly smaller than the GIF image with 128 colors.

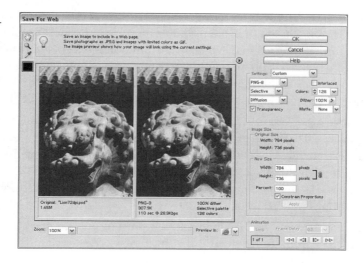

Consider these issues before saving a file for the Web:

■ Compare the optimized Web file format to the original. How close is the picture quality of the optimized image to the original?

■ Compare the file size of the original image to that of another file format. You can open the Save for Web window and compare a GIF, JPEG, or PNG file format to the original. You also can limit the number of colors available for any of these three file formats to try to reduce the file size of the image. How much smaller is the optimized file? If you don't see much of a difference, consider saving the original file as a JPEG and posting that to the Web.

■ Consider the download times for different optimized images. If the higher-quality, optimized file can download in less than 30 seconds, or a time that you consider acceptable, save the image and upload it to a Web site. If download time is not an issue for your Web visitors, you won't have to worry about file compression or loss of image quality.

> **note**
>
> The PNG file format does not support animation. It was originally intended to be a patent-free replacement for the GIF format. However, if you want to create animation for the Web, only the GIF format is capable of creating a single file containing animation.

Optimizing a TIFF Image File

Although you won't find the Tagged Image File Format (TIFF) as a format option in the Save for Web window, this file format is recognized by most graphics applications that run on Mac OS and Windows. A common file format ensures that the image quality will look the same on any computer or application that opens it. However, TIFF files are formatted a little differently for a PC and a Mac. Fortunately, Photoshop Elements enables you to open and save a TIFF image in either format.

You can save a TIFF image with or without layers and compression. If you want to save a master TIFF image, preserve layers; otherwise, remove them to create the smallest possible file. You can choose from three compression formats, and choose between a Mac or PC byte order for the saved image. When a TIFF file is compressed, the quality of the image is preserved. If that's not enough, you also can save transparency settings in a TIFF file.

Choose **Save As** from the **File** menu. If you want to save an open image as a TIFF file, select **TIFF** from the **Format** drop-down menu. Type a name for the file, and then click the **Save** button. The **TIFF Options** window opens. You will be able to choose compression options in this window if the **Enable Advanced TIFF Save** option is checked in the **Saving Files Preferences** window.

Click the IBM PC or Macintosh radio button to select the byte order of the TIFF file. The file will be formatted in a slightly different way depending on whether you choose IBM PC or Macintosh. The difference between Power PC and Intel processors apparently has some effect on the way TIFF files are processed. The good news is that most publishing applications, such as QuarkXPress and InDesign, can work with either TIFF format.

If the advanced TIFF option is selected in the **Saving Files Preferences** window, you will be able to choose from LZW, JPEG, or ZIP compression formats. Older TIFF-viewing applications will not be able to open JPEG- or ZIP-compressed TIFF files. You can use Adobe InDesign to work with these newer TIFF compression formats. LZW compression is the more common compression format applied to TIFF images.

WHEN TO EXPORT A FILE

Although there aren't any Export options installed, you can still export an image from Photoshop Elements. Like importing, exporting enables you to save an image in a specific file format, such as GIF89a, which is a variation of the GIF file format, or CompuServe GIF.

You can install an export plug-in with Photoshop Elements by placing the plug-in file in the (Import/Export) [Import-Export] folder, located in the Plug-ins folder of the Photoshop Elements folder. Unfortunately, there aren't any export plug-ins installed with Photoshop Elements, so I can't demonstrate the finer points of exporting. In case you're still wondering whether to export or save, it's always best to save, and save often. However, if you need to save a file in a specific format that's available only as a plug-in, it's better to export.

Sharing Files Electronically

When you save a file, you can copy that file to a file server, send it in an email, or print it. If you print your image, it's easy to show that printed picture to your friends and neighbors, or mail it to someone. Another way you can share the image is to post it on a Web site or send it attached to an email message. Email and Web sites are both great ways to share images immediately without sacrificing too many trees. Of course, your friends, family, and neighbors must have a computer to get to your Web page, too.

Before you can share files on the Web, you'll need the following items:

- An account on a Web server. You might have received a free Web site with your Internet service provider (ISP) when you signed up for Internet access. If you are a Mac OS X user, you have space available through iTools.

- Enough disk space to store the image files you want to share. This is probably the toughest issue to work around—especially if your Internet service provider can provide only 5MB or 10MB of disk space per Web site.

■ Software to connect to the Web server. Most Web servers support the File Transfer Protocol (FTP). You can upload or download image files to a Web server using an FTP application.

Sending an Image in Email

If you don't have access to a Web server that can accommodate all the images you want to share, you can use the **Attach to Email** button in the shortcuts bar and email files to others. You can use a browser or a dedicated email program to send or receive email. Yahoo! and Hotmail are a couple of the most popular Web sites that provide email services free. You can also download free email programs from Microsoft's or Netscape's Web sites. Microsoft's email application for Windows is Outlook or Outlook Express. Entourage is the latest email application available for Macs, although Outlook Express is also quite popular.

To send an image file with an email message, click on the **Attach to Email** shortcuts button. Choose **Convert** if you want to resize the image to roughly 12×9 inches. If the dimensions of an image are smaller than that, or if you don't want to resize the photo, choose **Send As Is**. Photoshop Elements will create a new email message and attach the photo.

> **tip**
>
> You can use the **Save for Web** window to estimate how long it might take someone to download an image attached to an email message. Choose **Save for Web** from the **File** menu to open the **Save for Web** window. Then compare the download times for different JPEG compression formats.

You can manually add any image file as an attachment to an email message, too. If you're using a browser to send email, log in to your email account, and then create or compose an email message. Click the **Attachments** button or link in the browser window. Navigate your hard drive and select the image file you want to attach to the email message. Type your message into the email, and then click the **Send** button.

If you're using Outlook or Outlook Express, click the **New** button in the toolbar to create a new email message. Click the **Attachments** button in the toolbar, or choose the **Attachments** command from the **Insert** menu. Then navigate to your hard drive and select the image file you want to attach to the email. Figure 5.9 shows an image attached to an email message in Outlook Express. After the image is attached, click the Send button, and away it will go!

EMAIL ATTACHMENTS AND FILE COMPRESSION

To help email attachments download faster, you might want to compress a file before you send it. For example, most computers can open files compressed in either a Zip or a StuffIt archive. WinZip is one of the more popular compression utilities available for Windows, and Aladdin provides free copies of StuffIt Expander for Macs and Windows computers on the Web. File formats that use compression, such as JPEG and PDF, will not shrink in size if you try to compress with WinZip or StuffIt. Other file formats, such as a Photoshop file, can be compressed to a smaller file size.

FIGURE 5.9

Saving a small file means faster sending and receiving times if you attach it and send it in an email. Outlook Express is one of several email programs available for both Windows and Macintosh computers.

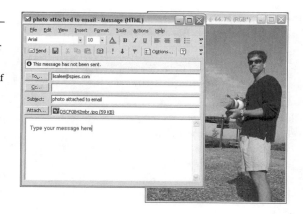

Using FTP Programs

Another way to share image files is to copy them to a file server or a Web server. If you have access to a Web site, you can use an FTP application to view and copy files to it. However, not all Web sites will require you to use an FTP application to post files to them. Some Web sites, such as www.kodak.com or www.shutterfly.com, enable you to post or remove files from your browser window.

The File Transfer Protocol (FTP) was first created as a networking tool for Unix, one of the first popular computer operating systems. Many FTP applications are available for Macintosh and Windows computers. One of the more popular FTP applications for the Mac is called Fetch. Many FTP applications are available for Windows. You might want to visit www.zdnet.com or another shareware collection Web site to review and try different FTP applications for Windows.

To share your files on a Web site, you'll need the account login and password information. You'll also need to know where the image files are located on your hard drive so that you can upload them to the Web site. If you have problems connecting or setting up your FTP application, you can try connecting to your Web site with a browser application. As with most Web pages, if you log in to an FTP site with a browser rather than FTP software, you'll be able only to view and download files from the FTP server.

Logging In and Uploading Files

Uploading files is the network term for copying files from a computer to a server. Start your FTP application, and then log in to your Web site. The interface will vary from one FTP program to the next. In general, you will be able to navigate the FTP server by clicking or double-clicking a folder in the FTP application's main window. Most FTP programs use the Put command to enable you to copy an image to the FTP server. Choose the Get command if you want to download a file from the FTP server to your local hard drive.

Figure 5.10 shows the application WS_FTP LE program. You can navigate to the files you want to upload in the local area of the FTP software. If you want to copy files to the FTP server, navigate to your Web server directory in the remote area of your software, and create a folder for your image files. Click on the file you want to copy from the Local System window list, and click the right-arrow button to copy it from your computer to the Web server. After the images have been copied to the server, type the URL (Universal Resource Locator), also known as Web address, such as www.flatfishfactory.com, in the browser window to view or download your image files. If you can open the downloaded image on your computer, you're ready to share the URL with friends and family.

note

If you're a Mac user, Apple's iTools Web site enables you to upload your files using iDisk, and share your photos online. You can use iPhoto to publish your photos as a hardcover book. AOL also provides similar features in version 7 of its online software.

FIGURE 5.10

Copy a file from your computer to a Web server to share it with other Web surfers.

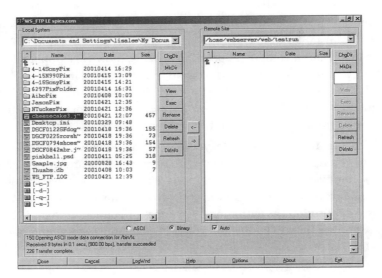

6

PRINTING IMAGES

If you have a color photo printer connected to your computer, you can use Photoshop Elements to print your photos. Photoshop Elements enables you to print photos straight to the printer, or lay out photos in a picture package or contact sheet. The Print Preview dialog box makes it super easy to scale a photo to fit on any size sheet of paper or assign a color profile for a print job. There are many options to choose from if you want to print a folder of photos as thumbnails onto a contact sheet or create a picture package.

Adobe enhanced the picture package dialog box in version 2. You can lay out a single photo in different sizes on a sheet of paper, or combine multiple photos into a picture package. This is great if you want to optimize the number of photos printed onto a page of premium glossy photo paper.

Printing Digital Images

Printing is printing—there's not a whole lot more to do other than click the Print button, right? Not necessarily. For example, when printing scanned images, you might need to do a little more preparation, especially if you scanned the white borders of a photo or captured the edges of a film negative along with the picture. Even if you've already performed some of these tasks before scanning the image, you might want to make additional adjustments to fit the image on the paper.

If you scanned a slightly larger area of an image than you need to print, you can use the Crop Tool (C) to remove the outer edges of the scanned image. Choose the **Crop Tool** from the **Toolbox** and click and drag the cursor around the area of the image you want to print. Then press the (**Return**) [**Enter**] key to resize the image.

Now that you have defined the image you want to print, you can see what the image's resolution is. Click the status bar to view the resolution of the active window. If the image is set to 72ppi, you will see 72 pixels/inch in the status bar. Next, click the status bar again and look at the height and width of the image. The printed size of the image will appear beside the height and width values in the status pop-up window. If the printed size is smaller than the paper size on which you want to print, you might have a tough time trying to grow the dimensions of the image without harming the quality of the image.

note

Photoshop Elements will print any image that appears in the image window. If you want to print the contents of a single layer, hide all other layers in the **Layers** palette and show the layer you want to print. This layer should be visible in the image window. Click the **Print** button in the toolbar to print the image layer.

Scaling a large image to a smaller size usually brings pleasant results. Taking a large image and making it smaller usually will improve the sharpness of an image, whereas resizing a smaller image to a larger one tends to expose blurriness or cause pixelation. If you choose to print an image that appears too small, consider keeping it at its original size. Don't enlarge it unless you don't mind viewing a photo that may contain squarish blocks, also known as pixelation. Table 6.1 shows how different image sizes at 72ppi match up with paper sizes. The Image and maximum paper size dimensions are displayed in width×height.

Table 6.1 Comparing Image Size to Print Size at 72ppi

Image Size	Maximum Paper Size
360×504 pixels	5×7 inches
640×480 pixels	8.89×6.67 inches
587×729 pixels	8×10 inches
800×600 pixels	11.11×8.33 inches
792×1,008 pixels	11×14 inches
1,024×768 pixels	14.22×10.667 inches
1,280×960 pixels	17.78×13.33 inches
2,048×1,536 pixels	28.44×21.33 inches
2,400×1,800 pixels	33×25 inches
2,560×1,900 pixels	35.56×26.67 inches

GETTING THE BEST PRINT

After you print a photo, compare it with the same photo open in Photoshop Elements and consider the following:

- **Sharpness of the image**—Are the brightness and contrast in the original image preserved? You may want to check the printer's color or print head calibration and ink levels (if the printer uses ink cartridges) and see whether adjusting these printer components improves the quality of the printed photo.

- **Paper**—Is the paper on which the image is printed capable of holding the color over time? Does the ink saturate the paper to the point of affecting the image quality? Consider using premium photo or premium glossy photo paper and comparing the color and print quality to the same photo printed on regular paper.

- **Consistency**—Can you print different images with the same printer without having to constantly change or tweak printer software settings? If the print quality varies dramatically from page to page, recalibrate the printer and check to see whether the ink cartridges need to be replaced. Listen for any odd noises and look for any paper jams or other things like dust that might block the path of the paper, and clean or repair the printer if necessary.

Photoshop Elements does not support CMYK color mode, only RGB, Indexed Color, Grayscale, and Bitmap color modes. You can print an RGB image to a grayscale or color printer. For best results, save the image with the Full Color Management color profile. Then, customize the print settings in the Print Preview dialog box, which you'll learn more about if you continue reading this chapter. To find out more about color management, go to Chapter 7, "Photoshop Elements and Color."

If you've opened an image that was scanned in at a resolution higher than 72ppi, you can scale it down in size to match the paper size on which you want to print. For example, if you scanned an image at 600ppi, you can either use the **Print Preview** window or the **Image Size** window to resize the image. Choose **Print Preview** if you do not want to alter the dimensions of the file to print the image. Otherwise, type new height and width values into the **Document Size** text boxes in the **Image Size** window if you want to resize the image.

> **tip**
>
> *Pixelation* is a squarish, blocky appearance that occurs when an image lacks enough color or image data to fill in those rough areas realistically. When an image is enlarged, the pixels from the original image are simply multiplied to fill in the new areas of the image. A pixelated image has the overall appearance of a low-resolution bitmap image.

If you want Photoshop Elements to scale the image to fit onto a specific paper size, perform the following steps. For best results, use a high-resolution image (such as a three- to five-megapixel image) and use the Scale to Fit Media check box to print to a 5×7 or 8×10 sheet of paper.

1. Choose **File**, **Print Preview** or press (**Command-P**) [**Ctrl+P**], or (**Command-Option-P**) [**Ctrl+Alt+P**] to open the Print Preview dialog box.

2. Check **Scale to Fit Media**. Type the height and width of the paper on which you want to print into the text boxes in the Print Preview dialog box.

3. Click **OK** to save your changes, or click the **Print** button to print the image.

If you want to permanently change the size of the image, perform the following steps:

1. Choose **Image Size** from the **Image**, **Resize** menu.

2. Change the resolution to match the resolution of your printer. Type a number into the **Resolution** text box—somewhere between 300ppi and 600ppi, or at least 170ppi.

3. Type the height and width of the paper size into the **Document Size** text boxes.

4. Click **OK** in the **Image Size** window.

5. Click the status bar for the resized image. The new dimensions should appear in the status bar pop-up window.

6. Click the **Print** button in the toolbar to send the image to the printer.

When your images are ready to print, you can set up the printer software. On a Mac, you can select the printer from the **Chooser**, located in the **Apple** menu. Choose **Page Setup** from the **File** menu. The **Page Setup** window will open. Click [**Properties**] (**Options**) button in the Page Setup dialog box to open the properties window of your printer, and choose the settings you want to use. For example, select the type of paper, resolution, and whether you want to print in color or grayscale (see Figure 6.1). You also can configure your computer to handle print jobs in the foreground, one at a time, or spooled in the background.

FIGURE 6.1

Print higher-quality images by choosing a different mode for the printer.

BACKGROUND PRINTING

Background printing enables you to send more than one print job to a printer simultaneously (see Figure 6.2). This can be helpful if you don't want to wait for each page to print. Windows and Macintosh computers have background printing built into the operating system. On a Mac, you can activate background printing from the Chooser. On a Windows computer, you can activate background printing from the printer's properties window from the Print Manager.

FIGURE 6.2

Set up the printer software to spool multiple print jobs.

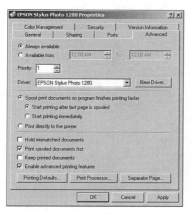

Printing Images from a Digital Camera

If you think about this in simple terms, your images either fit on the sheet of paper to which you want to print them, or they don't. A good example of an image that fits on an 8.5-×11-inch sheet of paper is a 640-×480-pixel image. You can open this image in the work area, set it to print in **Landscape** mode in the **Page Setup** window, and then print it to plain or glossy paper without having to worry about resizing or converting it.

SHOW AND TELL

Although you can queue several print jobs to a printer, it's a good idea to print a test photo before making multiple copies of an image. You can print a test photo at a lower resolution on less expensive paper if you want to find how the image will appear on a sheet of paper. After the test image has been printed, you might want to compare it to the onscreen image to determine the quality of the printout. Or, take a close look at the printed image to determine whether it meets your needs and expectations.

Creating a Contact Sheet

If you have a folder full of image files, you can print thumbnail images to a contact sheet to preview or catalog your photos. A contact sheet is a type of document generated by Photoshop Elements. A set of thumbnail images organized in columns and rows defines each document layout. You can use contact sheets to archive all your digital photos, and compare the composition of images without having to print each one on its own sheet of paper. Choose **Contact Sheet II** from the **File**, **Print Layouts** menu to open the fabulous dialog box shown in Figure 6.3.

FIGURE 6.3

Choose the set of images you want to place on the contact sheet. Select the document, layout, and caption settings for each picture from the Contact Sheet dialog box.

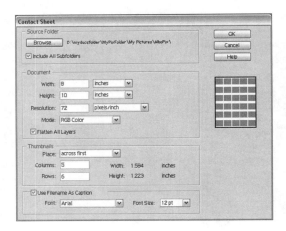

The Contact Sheet II dialog box has many bells and whistles. If you like all the default settings, select the folder containing the image files you want to put onto a contact sheet. Then, customize the page layout for the contact sheet. Click **OK** and wait for Photoshop Elements to create a new image window with the contact sheet images.

You can customize the size of the document, as well as the resolution and image mode of the pictures you want to print on the contact sheet by selecting a new value in the corresponding field in the Document area of the dialog box. For example, choose **Grayscale** from the **Mode** drop-down menu if you want to print all the images in Grayscale mode.

Several settings enable you to customize the layout of the contact sheet, too. On the right side of the Contact Sheet dialog box, you can preview the number of columns and rows selected in the Thumbnails text boxes that compose the layout. As you change the number of columns or rows for the contact sheet, preview the exact size of each thumbnail. Check the **Use Filename As Caption** check box to print the name of each file below each thumbnail image (see Figure 6.4). Unchecking this check box will enlarge each image to 1.8×1.8 inches.

tip

You can use a contact sheet to catalog image files saved to CD-ROM or removable media. Write the name of the Zip cartridge or CD-ROM on the contact sheet to enable you to quickly locate an image file.

When you click **OK**, Photoshop Elements runs a batch script that resizes each image to the settings you requested. The contact sheet, shown in Figure 6.4, will appear in a new document window, which you can save and print as you like. Choose **File**, **Print** to send the contact sheet to a printer.

FIGURE 6.4

You can catalog your images visually by printing them to contact sheets.

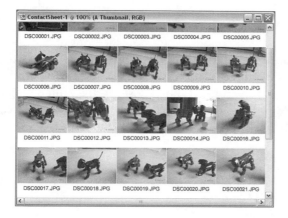

Printing a Fax

Although you probably won't find yourself faxing many images, Photoshop Elements won't hold you back. You can send your images to a fax instead of to a printer. On a Mac, open the **Chooser** and select the icon for the Fax software. On a Windows computer, choose **Fax** from the **Name** drop-down menu in the **Page Setup** window (**File**, **Page Setup**). When you choose the **Print** command, the active image will be converted to a 200×200dpi image. Then, the fax software will process the image, which can be sent over a modem or network connection to another fax machine.

Getting a Photo Printed

If you have several printers connected to a Windows computer, choose **File**, **Print Preview** to select a printer, size the image, and preview the image before you send it to the printer. The Print Preview or Print dialog box will open when you choose the **Print** command from the **File** menu. You can customize the **File** menu to show either dialog box from the **Print keys** drop-down menu in the **General Preferences** window (**Command-K**) [**Ctrl+K**].

note

You must have fax software installed on your computer to send a fax from your computer.

If you are using Mac OS X, both print dialog boxes will work only with the default printer. If you choose the **File**, **Print** command, the image will be sent directly to the printer unless you click the **Preview** button. On a Windows computer, you can click the **Page Setup** button to view and choose a printer. For best results on either Mac or Windows computers, open a high-resolution image and then choose **File**, **Print Preview**, and check the **Scale to Fit Media** check box. Scaling down a high-resolution image will send more data to the printer, resulting in a sharper printed image on paper.

If your Windows computer is configured to show the Print dialog box, the printer name will appear at the top of the Print dialog box. You can select the quality of the image generated by the printer, choose how many copies you want to print, or print the image to a file or to the printer. Figure 6.5 shows the Print dialog box for the Epson Stylus 740 color printer. Check each printer setting, and then click **OK** to print the contents of the image window.

FIGURE 6.5

Choosing the Print command opens the Print window of the default printer.

Printing More Than One Copy of an Image

Aspire to be a portrait photographer by printing multiple copies of an image on a single page. Choose from 20 layouts and 10 picture size combinations. To put together a picture package, choose **Picture Package** from the **File**, **Print Layouts** menu. The Picture Package dialog box will open, as shown in Figure 6.6. Select the file with which you want to work, and then pick a layout, or change the resolution or mode of the image.

FIGURE 6.6

Select the document layout and labeling options for a photo from the Picture Package dialog box.

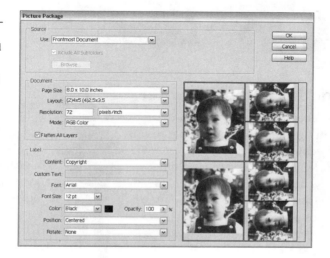

Choose the frontmost image window, or select a file by clicking on the Use drop-down menu. Choose the paper size from the **Page Size** drop-down menu (make sure it matches the paper size in your printer). Then choose a layout from the **Layout** drop-down menu. When you're ready to create a document with the picture package settings, click **OK**.

Photoshop Elements creates a picture package using a script to resize the selected image and apply any settings you chose in the Picture Package dialog box. Wait for the image to be processed. When the script completes, the picture layout will appear in a new document window, as shown in Figure 6.7. Now you can save or print the picture package.

tip

If you want to use the same picture package with more than one photo, choose **Picture Package** from the **File**, **Print Layouts** menu. Click on the **Use** drop-down menu and choose **Folder**. Click **Choose** to select the photos you want to include in the picture package. Click OK to print the multi-photo picture package. You can also copy and paste different photos from various picture packages to create your own custom picture package.

FIGURE 6.7

The **Picture Package** command creates a custom layout of an image in several different sizes and layouts.

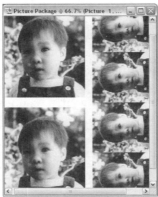

Preparing an Image for a Photo Printer

Take a contact sheet or picture package document and print the file to a photo printer to create, you guessed it, photos. Printing to a photo printer requires the same steps as most other printers. First, you must open the document you want to print. Then, choose the correct page orientation, such as portrait or landscape. Check your printer's color and resolution settings. Unfortunately, most photo printers don't allow you to use plain paper. If you have a photo printer, such as the Epson 1280 model, print a test page with plain paper before printing to the glossy paper.

Photoshop Elements has a **Print Preview** command (**Opt-Command-P**) [**Alt+Ctrl+P**] that enables you to modify the position or adjust the size of the image before printing it. Figure 6.8 shows the Print Preview dialog box. Click the appropriate setting to change it, and then click **OK** to exit the Print Preview dialog box. Choose **Print** from the **File** menu to send the image to the printer.

tip

The **Picture Package** command works with only a single image file. That is, you can't split a picture package across multiple image files. However, there is a workaround! If you want to split up a picture package, create a picture package for each photo. Use the **Edit**, **Copy** and **Edit**, **Paste** commands to move some of the photos from one picture package to the other image window. The resulting picture package will contain your multiple photos.

FIGURE 6.8

Open the **Print Preview** window to view the orientation and scale of the image with the target paper size.

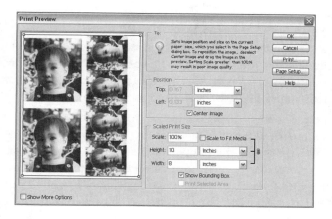

Considerations for Printing Images with Text

Adobe uses the term *type* for what you and I call *text*. The Horizontal and Vertical Type Tools (T) coexist in the Toolbox. Choose either tool from the Toolbox, and then type text into the image window. You can use the Type Tool to select text in the image window, too. Text formatting options are conveniently located in the options bar.

You can use two general kinds of fonts with Photoshop Elements: scalable or PostScript fonts. Scalable fonts are similar to vector graphics. Both use a software algorithm to re-create the image, large or small. PostScript fonts are more like bitmap images. Each font is a fixed size. If you don't have a specific font size for a PostScript font, its edges will appear aliased, or jagged, both onscreen and when printed.

The good news is that Photoshop Elements is smart. Text objects are created in their own layer. If you save an image, any layers will be flattened into one single layer. This means text objects are converted into bitmaps, which do not require the font to be installed on your computer for it to be printed. When you print an image with text, the text you see in the image window will appear exactly the same way on paper (see Figure 6.9).

FIGURE 6.9

You can add text to an image or graphics. The text will appear onscreen or in print.

Improving Printer Output

After you become familiar with the way a printer converts screen color on your computer into printed color, you probably will be able to print images faster and more accurately. Be sure to keep plenty of extra ink or toner cartridges nearby if you want to print different kinds of images or want to improve your images.

If you're looking for an easy way to improve printer output, look no further than your printer's [Properties] (Print) dialog box. If you're using Windows 2000, click the Start button, and then select the Printers menu item. The Printers window will open. Right-click the printer icon and choose **Properties** to open the Properties dialog box for your printer, and then try to locate the print quality settings. Print-quality settings for the Epson Stylus 1280 photo printer are shown in Figure 6.10. Higher-resolution settings for the printer (without changing the resolution of the image) will result in higher-quality printouts. Click **OK** to save your changes. Then print a test image to see whether you notice a difference. Compare a 600dpi-printed image with a 720ppi image.

FIGURE 6.10

Select a higher dpi to improve the quality of the printed image.

If you're using a Macintosh computer, first set up the printer for your computer. Open the Chooser application, and click the printer icon in the **Chooser** window. You might have to set up the printer if this is the first time you've printed to it. You might want to print a test page to make sure it is properly connected to your Mac. Next, go to Photoshop Elements and open an image you want to print. Then, select the **Print** command from the **File** menu. The Print dialog box will open. Look for the printer-quality settings for the selected printer. Adjust the printer settings, and print a test page at a lower and higher dpi setting. Compare the printer output and save or note the printer output settings for the printer.

Customizing Color Management Settings

Photoshop Elements enables you to save a color profile with an image when you save it to your hard drive. You can choose Limited color management if you want to attach a color profile for image files saved for the Web. Choose Full color management if you want to save a color profile for an image you want to print.

You also can customize the color management settings for a printer from the **Print Preview** window. First, open the Print Preview dialog box by choosing **Print Preview** from the **File** menu. Check the **Show More Options** check box. Then, choose **Color Management** from the first drop-down menu. The **Source Space** and **Print Space** options will appear at the bottom of the **Print Preview** window. Click the **Profile** drop-down menu to view a list of profiles for the printer. Choose **Same As Source** if you want the printer to use the color profile to determine the colors of the printed image. Choose **Print Color Management** (or **PostScript Color Management** if you're printing to a PostScript printer) if you want to use the print driver to manage color conversions. Otherwise, choose one of the predefined color profiles from the menu list.

> **note**
>
> You might not need to use a color profile to preserve color accuracy for a printed image. Print a test image to a color printer and compare it to the onscreen image. If the printed colors meet your expectations for matching the screen colors of the image, you won't have to worry about color management issues.

If you choose one of the color profiles from the Profile menu list, the Intent drop-down menu will become active. Choose a rendering intent to determine how colors are converted to the selected profile. Choose one of the following intents: **Perceptual**, **Saturation**, **Relative Colorimetric**, or **Absolute Colorimetric**. Perceptual preserves the visual relationship between colors based on the way the human eye perceives natural color. Saturation intent favors vivid colors over color accuracy. Absolute Colorimetric preserves color accuracy over and above preserving relationships between colors. Relative Colorimetric compares the white point of the color source to the white point of the destination color space and remaps all colors based on the new value of the white point.

Adjusting Page and Printer Settings

Many of the newer photo and color printers have the option to print the image so that it covers the full sheet of paper. That's right, no borders, just a page full of ink. Choose **File**, **Page Setup** to select the printer you want to use. Then, click the **[Properties]** (**Options**) button to view the printing options. The software options will vary depending on the type of printer you're using and the software options available for that printer. In Figure 6.11, I've selected the **Layout** tab in the **Properties** window for the Epson Stylus 740 color printer. Choose the **Fit to Page** radio button if you want the image to fill the page selected in the **Paper Size** drop-down menu.

FIGURE 6.11

Most newer printers have a **Fit to Page** option, which is an easy way to scale the image to fill the page.

Troubleshooting Printing Problems

Disappointed with the way your image printed? Not sure why the color isn't quite right, or why the printer output looks different from what's on your computer monitor? There are lots of things you can check. Finding a problem can take time and lots of patience. If you have Internet access, try checking the printer vendor's Web site to see whether newer software is available, or visit their support site to see whether there are any troubleshooting tips or known problems with your particular brand of computer.

The following list contains good starting points to check when you're unable to print:

- **Cables**—Be sure both ends of the printer cable are completely connected to each device.

- **Lights**—Check the lights on the printer. Most printers show a green light when power is on. If a print job is being processed, the green light should flash. If you send a print job and the light flashes, you might need to power the printer off and on, or restart your computer.

  Other lights let you know if the printer is out of ink or paper, if the paper jammed, or if a print job is in progress. If you don't see any lights, check the power adapter and be sure the printer is connected to a power-generating source.

■ **Printer Software**—If the printing software appears to be working but the printer is not responding when you try to print to it, be sure the printer software settings are set up correctly for that printer. You might need to restart your computer and try printing without running any other applications to be sure you have plenty of memory to print.

■ **Networks**—If you are unable to print to a printer that is connected to a network, try connecting the printer directly to your computer's USB, parallel, or serial port to see whether you can print to it. If you're able to print to it directly, check your network cables and try to see whether you can print using another computer on the same network. You might want to see whether a software upgrade is available for the printer or your computer's operating system.

■ **Paper**—Check the paper tray and paper-pushing mechanisms in the printer. If you're unable to print in Photoshop Elements, try printing from another application or from the desktop. If you have a second computer, determine whether you can print from it.

■ **Scale to Fit Media**—Check this option in the Print Preview window if you want the image to fill the printed page. Print a test page to see how the image fits the paper you want to print on. If you're trying to print a tall, thin image or a super-small image on a large sheet of paper, selecting this option will most likely distort the original image. Print a test page with this option turned on and off if you want to see the extent of any distortion that might result from scaling the image to fit on the printed page.

■ **Image Quality**—Uncheck the **Scale to Fit Media** check box, and print the image to view the image quality of the printer output. Depending on the type of printer you're using and the type of computer monitor, you might see some degradation of image quality between the printed image and the onscreen image. The image quality of the printed image should look similar to the image you see on your computer screen. If the printed image appears much smaller or larger than what you see on your computer screen, you might need to adjust the printer settings in the Print dialog box, or change the scale, orientation, or paper settings in the Page Setup dialog box.

■ **Printer Output**—Before printing, open the Print Preview dialog box and check the settings for the **Scaled Print Size** of the image. Use the preview area in the **Print Preview** window to scale the image you want to print. Select the **Show More Options** check box if you want to change color management or output settings for the printed image.

■ **Paper Size**—If the printed image is printed beyond the edges of the paper, or much smaller than expected, check the **Paper** option in the Page Setup dialog box. Choose **Page Setup** from the **Print** menu to select the paper size on which you want to print. If you're printing to an 8.5-×11-inch sheet of paper, choose letter for the paper size. If the printed image seems mismatched with the paper, check to see whether envelope, legal, or a different paper size is selected, and then choose the correct paper type for your print job. Also, check to see whether the **Scale to Fit Media** option is checked in the **Print Preview** window.

PART III

CORRECTING AND COMBINING IMAGES

7

PHOTOSHOP ELEMENTS AND COLOR

Whether you're working with grayscale or color images, Photoshop Elements enables you to work with both types of color modes. Before you start working with color, it's best to explore how color works outside and inside a computer. This chapter begins with a discussion of color theory, and then explains how computers and other output devices, such as printers, use numbers and color management technology to create colors.

Color Theory

This section reviews several color concepts that are essential to understanding how color correction works in Photoshop Elements. What exactly is color? First, color is what we perceive when light is refracted off or through different objects. Long, medium, and short wavelengths of light trigger red, green, or blue color recognition in our eyes. Our eyes convert light into neural data, which is interpreted by our brain.

Colors also can be mixed together. Blue and yellow make green, and red and blue make purple. However, you cannot create the three primary colors—red, yellow, and blue—by mixing other colors together. The three primary colors can be mixed together in different proportions to create the full spectrum of colors.

Representing color on a computer involves creating a numeric representation for each of the primary colors, and every combination of those colors, on a computer monitor. You can define color on a computer in several ways. Each method is referred to as a color space. For example, RGB is the name for the red, green, and blue color space used in Photoshop Elements.

COLOR AND THE TRISTIMULUS COLOR MODEL

In 1931, color scientists got together and developed a scientific model that defines color—CIE, Commission Internationale de l'Eclairage, or the International Commission on Illumination (www.cie.co.at/cie). They designed the *tristimulus* color model, which assigns hue angle, saturation, and value (or brightness) to define a color. Using this model, color can be mapped to an x, y, or z axis.

Primary Colors

Red, yellow, and blue are the three primary colors from which all other colors are made. Red, yellow, and blue cannot be created by mixing any other two colors together. White and black are colors, too, but they represent the maximum and minimum amount of reflectivity of all three colors combined. White absorbs no color and reflects all the light to our eyes, whereas black absorbs all the colors of the rainbow, so no light reaches our eyes. You can mix white with red to lighten the initial red color. Alternatively, you can mix black with red to darken the red.

In the real world, it's rare to find a pure red, yellow, or blue color. Many external factors affect the way we perceive color. The biggest factor is the medium that created the color. For example, a book probably will display different red, yellow, and blue colors than a blue ink pen, or than the blue color on a television or a computer screen. Computers, printers, scanners, and cameras each have their own way of identifying and reproducing color.

Despite the existence of primary colors, your chances of finding true red, yellow, or blue are slim to none. The more realistic approach is to use computers, scanners, printers, and cameras that support color models that can be converted from one device to the next, preserving as much of the original color as possible.

Viewing colors on the color wheel can help you understand different relationships between colors. Secondary colors are purple, green, and orange, the colors resulting from mixing red and blue, blue and yellow, or yellow and red. Tertiary colors are mixtures of secondary and primary colors, such as yellow-orange, yellow-green, blue-purple, or red-purple. Colors located on opposing sides of the color wheel are complementary colors.

In the physical world, the color of an object is defined by the way the object reflects and absorbs light. On a computer, you can choose a color arbitrarily from the Color Picker window, or use the color wheel to pick a primary, complementary, or tertiary color that you want to use in an image.

Light and Color

Color perception is the result of the way light is reflected off or through other surfaces. For example, when you look at a red ball, the ball absorbs all the color of the light except red, and reflects its own color, red, which is the color you see. The more light the ball is exposed to, the more color you'll see on the ball. However, there are limits; if you shine too much light on the ball, the light will bounce off it, hiding the red color and reflecting the light instead of the color. If you view the ball looking through glass, light will reflect off the ball in a different manner, and the red will be a slightly different hue when viewed through glass than when viewed without glass.

> **note**
>
> Hue and saturation define the purity of a color. Hue defines the specific attributes or intensity of a color.
>
> Saturation defines a color in the absence of white, using differences in gray values to adjust the saturation level of a color. A highly saturated color contains very little white.

Natural and artificial light can affect the appearance of a color. This is most obvious when you take a digital picture during the day in natural light, and then take a picture in the evening indoors. Tungsten and fluorescent light bulbs cast a unique shade of light. Tungsten bulbs usually cast a yellow-orangish *hue*. Fluorescent bulbs, besides having an annoying low-pitched hum, cast a greenish-yellowish hue. Hues cast by artificial light can be compounded if you use a flash or have another device, such as a television, in the picture.

When working with digital images, think about where the light source is originating from in the picture. Are there multiple light sources? Is the light bouncing off another object or color? Is the light passing through a window?

Next, try to determine the colors in the picture. Does the light wash out colors in the picture? Is the picture overexposed? Is there too little light? Experimenting with light and color in an image can be a time-consuming task. Consider saving multiple copies of an image as you're working on it so that you can experiment with different combinations of colors and lighting.

Computers and Color

Making a computer display what you see with your eyes is not an easy task. Several kinds of color spaces have been created as the result of different color scientists getting together to solve this task: How do you turn colors into numbers?

A color space defines the way colors can be reproduced so that a numerical set of values will always generate the same color. Different kinds of computer devices use different color spaces to define color. For example, a computer uses a red, green, and blue color space to determine how to display colors on a monitor. A printer, on the other hand, relies on cyan, magenta, and yellow and values corresponding to the amount of ink and the type of paper to create colors.

You're probably most familiar with the color space of your computer monitor. Some monitors enable you to use hardware buttons to adjust color settings. However, most monitors rely on operating-system software, such as a control panel, to allow you to set the way color appears onscreen. For example, the Display Calibrator Assistant in Mac OS X enables you to set the white point, gamma, and tristimuli values of the computer monitor (see "Calibrating Your Monitor," later in this chapter).

Introducing Color Space and Color Management

It's important to understand a slight clarification in color terminology. Correcting color can be associated with color-management systems, such as ColorSync. A color-management system is a specific software package designed to work with different input and output devices to produce consistent color. Color-management systems are designed to correct color, and rely on a particular color space, such as CIE, as a reference point for their color-matching engines to work with color profiles. Photoshop Elements can work with ICC color profiles. However, you must save a file with a color profile (see Figure 7.1), and select the color-management option in the Preference dialog box, to take advantage of color management in the work area.

FIGURE 7.1

Check the **ICC Profile** check box if you want to save the RGB color profile along with an image.

The terms *color space* and *color management* go hand in hand. A *color space* defines a color based on its relationship to light, or a particular form of color measurement. Photoshop Elements supports the HSB (hue, saturation, brightness), RGB, and hexadecimal color spaces in addition to bitmap, grayscale, and indexed color modes. You've already read about the RGB color space, which is the image mode you'll probably be using most (see Figure 7.2). Most scanners, digital cameras, and computers work well with red, green, and blue color space images. Hexadecimal color values, which commonly represent the 216 colors in a Web-safe color palette, are also important to be aware of if you'll be creating images in Photoshop Elements and using them on the Web.

ICC

ICC is an acronym for the International Color Consortium (www.color.org). This organization was founded in 1993 by six companies: Adobe, Agfa-Gevaert, Apple, Eastman Kodak, Microsoft, and Sun Microsystems. Since then the consortium has grown to consist of more than 50 companies. Its goal is to create standards for color management across computer platforms and imaging input and output devices. Find out more about ICC at www.color.org.

FIGURE 7.2

The Hue/ Saturation controls enable you to adjust color attributes, such as the hue, saturation, and lightness of an image.

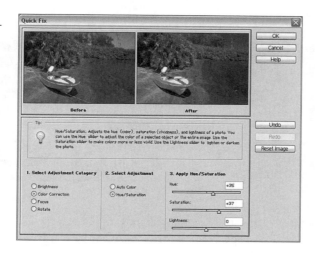

Each color space relies on both hardware and software to work properly. This is referred to as *device-dependent color*. Each computer monitor and printer has its own way of interpreting how to work with color. Some devices, such as a computer monitor, rely on an additive color process to create a full spectrum of colors, whereas other devices, such as printers, rely on a subtractive color process. A device-independent color space is a color space that can accurately reproduce color no matter which device is being used.

Photoshop Elements doesn't know whether it's displaying an accurate color. It's up to you to choose what you perceive to be the correct color for an image. Monitors create colors based on an additive color process (see Figure 7.3). Red, green, and blue are combined to create magenta, cyan, and yellow as secondary colors. First, you need to have a monitor that supports 24-bit or 32-bit color (thousands or millions of colors for you Mac folks). Plus, you'll need to configure your operating system to display 24- or 32-bit color.

Color management describes the software technology that translates a color space from one hardware output device to another, such as a monitor, printer, or scanner. ColorSync software on Macintosh computers performs this color management role. You can choose a color profile for the output device you want to use with the computer. When you print or view a color onscreen, ColorSync tries to make sure that the colors match.

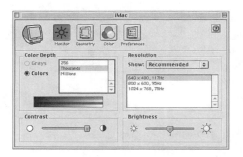

note

You can download many of the full-color photos shown in this book from Que Publishing's Web site (www.quepublishing.com). Search for your book on the site and you'll find a download link on the book's page.

FIGURE 7.3

Additive colors for the RGB color model are magenta, cyan, and yellow. Computer monitors use an additive color process to create colors on your computer screen.

Windows also supports color-management color profiles. Right-click on the desktop, and choose **Properties** to open the **Display control panel** window. Click the **Settings** tab, and then click the **Advanced** button. The **Multiple Monitors** window opens. Click the **Color Management** tab, and then click the **Add** button to choose a color profile for your computer monitor. The color profile files end with an .icm extension. These files are installed in the Windows operating system folder on your hard drive. You can choose the sRGB Color Space Profile or the AdobeRGB1998 color profile for your monitor; both profiles are common to Windows, Mac, and Photoshop Elements.

Every printer, monitor, scanner, or other equipment capable of producing color uses its own method for displaying a range of colors, also called a *color gamut*. For example, the colors you see on a monitor are created using an additive process, in which the phosphors in the monitor tube are excited by red, green, or blue colors. On the other hand, printers use a subtractive method based on cyan, magenta, and yellow to create colors. Color representation also varies among different monitor manufacturers. For instance, the colors on a Sony monitor look slightly brighter or bluer than the same colors on an Apple monitor.

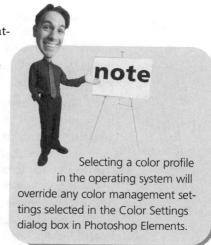

In the worst-case scenario, you might be creating an image with an orange color. At least your computer monitor shows the color orange in the picture. When you send that image to a color printer, the printer might need to mix yellow and cyan ink to create orange. The application displaying the image onscreen tells your computer that it needs the color orange. The computer sends this information to the printer. The printer gets the message for orange and tries to create that color. Here's how the exchange might go:

Selecting a color profile in the operating system will override any color management settings selected in the Color Settings dialog box in Photoshop Elements.

Application: Hey, I need some orange here!

Computer: Printer, make some orange, okay?

Printer: What's orange? Okay, let me mix some ink.

Printer: Okay, I'm printing orange.

Computer to the Application: Hey, the printer made orange.

Application: Okie dokie!

You: This isn't orange, it's pink ink covered with yellow ink!

GAMMA AND WEB COLORS

Recall that gamma affects the brightness of the image on a computer monitor. Although Windows and Macintosh computers share the same Web browser color palette, each computer system processes gamma using different hardware technologies.

The difference in gamma between Windows and Mac computers is most obvious when choosing colors for a Web page. A solid orange color created on a Windows computer might appear to have more red on a Mac.

The difference in gamma occurs because each computer system manages color differently. To compensate for the differences in gamma, try choosing colors that look more similar on both computer platforms.

To help hardware devices transform color more accurately from one device to another, the International Color Consortium (ICC) was formed in 1993. The ICC committee defined a workflow for color data to be translated from one device to another. This information was stored in a file, called a color profile.

An application that follows the ICC standards, such as Photoshop Elements, can store a color profile along with an image file. Before a printer uses its own color-management system to put ink on paper, it will load the color profile data (if you saved it with the image). The color profile contains the definition for the actual color data in the image.

If you have selected a ColorSync or color profile for Mac OS or Windows, you can skip this paragraph. If you haven't chosen a color profile for your Windows or Macintosh operating system, you can set the color profile in Photoshop Elements. Open the Color Settings dialog box with (**Command-Shift-K**) [**Ctrl+Shift+K**]. Choose **Limited Color** to save an SRGB IEC61966-2.1–compatible color profile with images intended for the Web. If **Full Color Management** is selected, the Adobe RGB Color Profile will generate a color profile for the image. For either color management option, choose **File**, **Save As**. Check the (**Embed Color Profile**) [**ICC Color Profile**] check box in the **Save As** window and Photoshop Elements will generate ICC color definitions when the image file is saved to disk.

DEVICES AND COLOR MANAGEMENT

Most printers use the CMYK color model to print an image. Some devices enable you to modify CMYK settings from your computer. Other devices have a translation system built into them. For instance, some standalone photo printers allow you to insert a CompactFlash or SmartMedia card directly into the printer, adjust the image, and print without using a computer. To print more accurate color, many printers include software that can translate an RGB image into a CMYK image. Printers that have this capability can produce printed images that match the colors of the onscreen image.

Calibrating Your Monitor

You need to calibrate your computer monitor in order to take full advantage of color management. Calibrating a monitor involves adjusting several video settings: brightness and contrast, gamma, phosphors, and white point. The settings you choose in the calibration software determine how other color spaces appear on your monitor, and, more important, how colors are translated to output devices.

If you have a Windows computer, you can use Adobe's Gamma control panel to calibrate your monitor. If you have Mac OS X, use the Display Calibrator application to calibrate your monitor. As an alternative, you can use a desktop colorimeter or spectrophotometer to measure and set its white point. There are also may third-party software products from companies such as Kodak that enable you to calibrate color on your Mac or Windows computer.

Photoshop Elements installs the Adobe Gamma control panel in the Control Panel folder on your hard drive. On a Windows 98 or NT computer, click on the Start menu, choose Settings, Control Panel, and then select Adobe Gamma from the

Control Panel list. If you're using Windows XP, click on the **Start** menu, choose **Control Panel**, and then select **Adobe Gamma**. Mac OS X folks can open the Display Calibrator program from the Applications, Utilities folder.

BEFORE CALIBRATING YOUR MONITOR...

To get the best calibration results, perform some of the following suggestions before changing any of your monitor's settings:

- Leave the monitor on for at least 30 minutes.
- Set the monitor to display at least thousands (16-bit) of colors.
- Set your desktop picture or pattern to a neutral color, such as a solid gray color.

The following list provides a brief explanation of the settings you need to adjust in order to calibrate your monitor and summarizes the settings available in the Adobe Gamma control panel. The Adobe Gamma control panel has two modes: manual and wizard modes. If you're not sure which settings to choose, use the wizard to help you choose the correct settings for your system.

- **Brightness/Contrast**—The **Brightness and Contrast** window for the Adobe Gamma control panel appears as a bar if you are adjusting settings manually, or as a black square surrounded by a white border. You can adjust the brightness and contrast settings of your computer monitor by changing the hardware or software settings. The controls will vary depending on the type of monitor and operating system installed with your computer.

  If you're using a Mac, you can adjust the monitor's brightness and contrast setting from the Monitors control panel. The brightness settings for a PC might be located directly on the computer monitor, or you might be able to open a control panel window or press the keyboard controls for brightness or contrast on the keyboard. Place the Mac or Windows control panel window beside the Adobe Gamma control panel window on your desktop. Set the monitor's contrast setting to its highest value, and then change the Brightness setting in the (**Monitors**) [**Display**] window so that the black square or bar in the Adobe Gamma control panel is as dark as it can be while keeping the brightness of the white bar as white as it can be.

- **Phosphors**—Monitors use phosphors to emit light and create the colors you can see onscreen. The red, green, and blue phosphors that create colors on your computer screen vary from one manufacturer to another. Select the phosphors for your monitor from the Phosphors drop-down menu. Select **EBU/ITU**, **HDTV (CCIR 709)**, **NTSC (1953)**, **P22-EBU**, **SMPTE-C (CCIR 501-1)**, or **Trinitron**, or create a custom phosphor setting. For most computer displays, Trinitron is the best setting. If you're using the Adobe Gamma (Assistant) [Wizard], it will choose a phosphor setting based on the color profile selected in the first step.

■ **Gamma**—Gamma settings define the brightness of the midtones on your monitor. Pick the Windows Default gamma setting (2.2) if you're using a PC, or the Macintosh Default (1.8) if you're using a Macintosh computer. Move the slider control below the square in the Gamma section of the Adobe Gamma window to select a custom gamma setting. Calibrate your monitor with a single gamma setting or view, or create custom gamma settings for red, green, and blue by deselecting the **View Single Gamma Only** check box.

■ **White Point**—There are two settings for calibrating the white point on your monitor. This will affect how color is translated for other output devices. First, choose a warm or cool white setting for the monitor's white point. 5000K is the equivalent of a white page. 6500K is the default white point for Windows. 9300K is the default white point for Macintosh computers. Next, choose an adjusted white point value that you might want to work with.

Lower values generate warmer, or yellowish, lighting. Colors might appear a little richer, or fuller, in low, or warmer, settings. As the value increases, the white point is cooler, or whiter. Cooler settings can reduce the range of visible colors in an image. The unit for measuring white point is in degrees Kelvin. Kelvin is a scale used to measure the color temperature, or the amount of color in a light source. Choose from 5000K (warm white), 5500K, 6500K, 7500K, 9300K, or a custom white point setting.

Some operating systems have calibration software settings enabling you to set the white point for the monitor. Figure 7.4 shows the white point settings in Mac OS X for an iMac monitor. Click on a radio button to select the white point of the

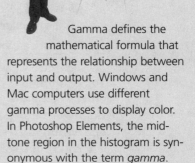

note

Gamma defines the mathematical formula that represents the relationship between input and output. Windows and Mac computers use different gamma processes to display color. In Photoshop Elements, the midtone region in the histogram is synonymous with the term *gamma*.

note

A color system made of three colors—such as RGB or CMY—is called a tristimulus. The white point is an achromatic value, meaning that it is colorless, and results when all three tristimuli are equal. Setting the white point defines the way other colors will be presented on the computer monitor. It also affects how accurately colors are translated from input devices, such as a scanner or camera, or to output devices, such as a printer.

monitor. Different white point settings will change the way white is displayed onscreen. This can have a significant impact on image editing, especially when you're relying on your computer monitor to determine the color accuracy of a photo. Configure each of the settings in the Display Calibrator program and then click **Create** to generate a custom Color Sync profile for your display.

FIGURE 7.4

The Display Calibrator program enables you to create a custom Color Sync profile for a display.

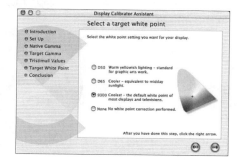

Choosing a Color Mode

Photoshop Elements uses two color spaces to enable you to view, select, and modify colors. The Hue, Saturation, and Brightness (HSB) color space is based on how people perceive color. The Red, Green, and Blue (RGB) color mode represents the color space for computer monitors. Each color space enables you to view and edit colors. However, the color mode of an image file determines how many colors can be displayed in an image.

The following list summarizes each of the color modes in Photoshop Elements:

- **RGB**—New image files opened in the work area are created in RGB mode, and chances are you'll be doing most of your work in this color mode. Most of the tools and commands in Photoshop Elements require an image to be in RGB mode before you can use them.

  RGB mode relies on the RGB color model to assign color values to each pixel. Values range from 0 (black) to 255 (white) for each red, green, and blue channel of the RGB image. To create black, each red, green, and blue value is set to zero (0). White is created when red, green, and blue are each set to 255. Any subsequent combination of equal RGB values results in gray. Each channel contains eight bits of color. When you work with an image in RGB mode, you can work with up to 24 bits of color.

note

Photoshop Elements uses the HSB color space in its **Color Picker** window and its Hue/Saturation Tool. However, no HSB color space is available for creating and editing images.

The RGB image file stores up to 32 bits of information. The data in an RGB image file is broken up into three 8-bit channels (red, green, and blue), and an 8-bit alpha channel that helps determine how the three layers are interpreted to create the final color image.

- **Indexed Color**—This mode supports up to 256 colors. Use this color mode if you want to preserve the quality of the image while reducing the number of colors and the file size of the image. Photoshop Elements creates a custom color table for the image when you choose this color mode. Any colors that do not map to one of the 256 colors in the color lookup table (also known as a CLUT) are mapped to the closest-matching color.

- **Grayscale**—In this color mode, 256 shades of gray are available. Zero represents black, and 255 represents white. Grayscale mode is optimal for viewing and editing black-and-white photographs.

- **Bitmap**—Only two colors, black and white, are available in this image mode. Images in bitmap mode are essentially one-bit images, with a color depth of one color. Bitmap mode can be used to view, edit, or save line art.

Adobe uses the term *color mode* to describe the RGB, Grayscale, Bitmap, or Indexed Color modes in Photoshop Elements. I frequently use the term *image mode* in this book. Image mode is synonymous with color mode.

Color and Photoshop Elements

It's time to get your feet wet. Photoshop Elements contains several tools that enable you to view and customize the color settings of an image. The primary tools you will use to select and change colors are the **Color Picker** window and the **Swatches** palette. In addition to these color-selection tools, you can also correct color using the commands located in the **Enhance** menu.

The following sections show you how to use the Color Picker, as well as the **Brightness/Contrast**, **Hue/Saturation**, and **Levels** commands to analyze color in an image. You will also learn how to create composite images.

Using the Color Picker

You can use Adobe's **Color Picker** window to select a foreground or background color for a tool, a command, or an effect. If you prefer to use a color space that's not available in the Adobe Color Picker, such as HSL, choose the Windows or Apple

Color Picker. Choose **Edit**, **Preferences**, **General**, and then choose (**Apple**) [**Windows**] from the **Color Picker** drop-down menu in the **General Preferences** window. Figure 7.5 shows the **Windows Color Picker** window.

FIGURE 7.5

Click the Define Custom Colors button if you cannot see the custom color selector on the right side of the Color Picker.

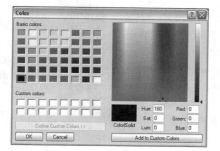

To change the color of an object in the image window, select the layer that contains the image. Then open the Color Picker dialog box by clicking on the **Set Foreground Color** square in the Toolbox, or options bar. Click within the boundaries of the large rainbow of colors on the right of the **Color Picker** window or click on a color square to choose a new color. You can also click on a color in an image window or type in values for **Hue**, **Sat**(uration), **Lum**(inosity), **Red**, **Green**, or **Blue** to select a color in the **Color Picker** window.

When you click on either color box, located at the bottom of the Toolbox, the default Color Picker dialog box will open. You can select the color space (such as RGB) that you want to use in the Color Picker dialog box. Figure 7.6 shows the Adobe Color Picker dialog box in Photoshop Elements.

FIGURE 7.6

If you don't want to guess at a color, use the Eyedropper Tool to click on the color you want in any image window.

The foreground color is the square on the upper-left at the bottom of the Toolbox. The foreground color appears when a brush, pencil, shape, filter, or image-editing tool is applied to the image window. The background color of the active image window is located in the lower-right square of the Toolbox. If the document was created with a background color, the background color appears if you apply the Eraser Tool or select part of an image and press the (**Delete**) [**Backspace**] key. Click on the two-headed arrow icon located just above the color squares in the Toolbox to swap the foreground and background colors.

The Apple Color Picker enables you to choose from **CMYK**, **HSV**, **HTML** (hexadecimal), **HLS**, and RGB color spaces. Apple's Color Picker window is divided into two main sections. On the left, you choose a color space. The color wheel settings for the color space appear on the right. The current color appears in the Original color swatch. Click and drag the slider controls, or type in a value, to select a new color.

If you don't want to think about color spaces, you can use the **Crayon Picker** to choose from 60 colors. The **Crayon Picker** is one of the color spaces located on the left portion of the Apple Color Picker window. Sorry, Windows folks— there's no equivalent to the **Crayon Picker** available in Windows. Regardless of whether you're using a Mac or Windows PC, Photoshop Elements enables you to work with HSB, RGB, or HTML color values in the work area.

Changing Colors with the Swatches Palette

The **Swatches** palette enables you to select a color, or load and save a swatch library of colors. You can add or remove a color square from the **Swatches** palette. If you have the **Info** palette open, you can also use the Swatches palette to "look up" a color value in your image (see Figure 7.7).

FIGURE 7.7

Add custom colors to the **Swatches** palette, and view any color in the image window from the Info palette.

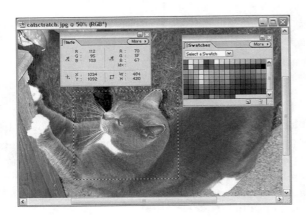

By default, 116 colors appear in the **Swatches** palette. You can load new swatch libraries by clicking on the arrow drop-down menu and choosing from the **Mac OS**, **VisiBone**, **VisiBone2**, **Web Hues**, **Web Safe Colors**, **Web Spectrum**, and **Windows** color palettes. Although your monitor might be set to display thousands or millions (16-bit or 24-bit color) of colors, the **Swatches** palette will usually not contain more than 256 colors.

You can use the **Swatches** palette to store particular colors from an image file, in addition to any Web-safe or OS-specific colors. Or you can create a custom palette for a series of color images. This can be helpful when you are creating an image using a specific set of colors, such as for a logo or Web site.

To add a color to the **Swatches** palette, do the following:

1. Click on the **Eyedropper Tool** in the Toolbox.

2. In one of the image windows, click on the color you want to add.

3. Click below the last row of color squares in the **Swatches** palette. When you place the cursor below the bottom row of color squares in the **Swatches** palette, its icon will change from an eyedropper to a Paint Bucket icon. After you click, the **Color Swatch Name** window appears.

4. Type in a name for the color square, and then click **OK**. The new color square will appear at the bottom of the **Swatches** palette.

To remove a color, click and drag the color to the Trash icon located in the lower-right corner of the **Swatches** palette.

CHOOSING A WEB-SAFE COLOR

A Web-safe color palette consists of 216 colors. These colors are the common colors Windows, Mac, and Linux computers share out of a total system color palette of 256 colors. If you choose a color on a Mac that isn't one of the 216 Web-safe colors, another computer platform might not have that color. If this is the case, the browser or operating system will convert the missing color to what it thinks is the closest matching color available.

Photoshop Elements Color-Correction Tools

The manual process of color correction in a digital photo is what most of this book is about. The complexity of a project depends on the quality and clarity of the original image. Photoshop Elements has a couple of tools that offer a quick-fix solution for certain kinds of pictures. However, although the automatic level and contrast tools can work great with some images, they might not be helpful with other images. Try out the **Auto Levels** or **Auto Contrast** commands to see whether they improve the image. If you like the change, save the image. Otherwise, you can choose **Undo** from the **Edit** menu to undo the automatic changes and make the improvements yourself.

Consider the following issues before taking a first step to correct color. First, determine whether this is the best image you can work with. Is there another image or photo that the image will need to match? Is there a set of colors or light conditions that might need to match each other if you plan to create a composite image?

Next, determine what types of media the image will be output to. Will the image be printed or posted to a Web page? Finally, be sure you have plenty of disk space, memory, and backup media for any projects you can't afford to lose. The following sections show you how some of the Enhance menu tools affect an image.

Hue and Saturation

A computer creates colors using primary colors. Of course, primary colors are the exception to this rule. Each color space defines it own unique primary colors. For example, red, green, and blue are the primary colors for the RGB color space, which is what your computer monitor uses. Cyan, magenta, and yellow are the primary colors for the CMYK color model, used in print output. When you change a color's hue, the computer adds or subtracts values from a color. When you move the hue slider control, it is similar to choosing a different color by moving around the color wheel.

Saturated colors are either primary or secondary colors. These colors are based on one or two primary colors with the third primary color set to zero. Choose **Hue/Saturation** from the **Enhance**, **Color** menu to open the **Hue/Saturation** window, shown in Figure 7.8.

When you adjust the saturation level from the Hue/Saturation dialog box, one of the primary colors is removed from the selected color, or from all colors in the image. When you move the Saturation control, you can increase or decrease the amount of gray mixed with the colors in the image. The Lightness slider control enables you to add a primary color back into the hue/saturation settings.

If you're using Mac OS X, you can use the Art Director's Toolkit to convert fractions to decimals, inches to centimeters, or points to picas. This handy utility program can also help you convert hexadecimal color values to RGB, as well as compare font point sizes to inches, centimeters, points, or picas.

The Hue slider control enables you to change a range of color values in the active image window. This method of changing colors creates a smoother color transition across all colors in the image, or in the selected area of the image. If you use the **Swatches** palette, you can easily change the color of a specific pixel. However, it's not quite as easy to tweak the colors of the surrounding pixels without spending a lot of time mixing and matching colors.

FIGURE 7.8

Adjust the mix-
ture of colors
using the Master
set of colors in the
Hue/Saturation
window. Or mod-
ify a specific range
of colors by choos-
ing one of the
options in the Edit
drop-down menu.

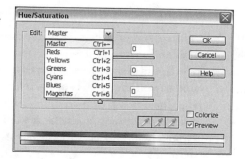

Color correction is usually a tedious task. Don't be surprised to find yourself experimenting with the **Hue/Saturation** command to correct colors, or change a color just to compare the results to another color-correction tool in Photoshop Elements. The following list describes situations in which you might want to use the Hue/Saturation command:

Color images consist of luminosity (light) and chrominance (gray level). By adjusting these levels in the **Hue/Saturation** window, you can change the brightness and intensity of a particular color or range of colors.

- **Color**—If you want to adjust a color in part of an image, you can use a selection tool to highlight the pixels you want to modify. Then open the **Hue/Saturation** command from the **Enhance**, **Color menu** (**Command-U**) [**Ctrl+U**] and slowly move the Hue control slider. If the **Preview** check box has been selected, you can watch the color of the selected pixels change as you move the slider.

- **Color Purity**—The Saturation control in the Hue/Saturation dialog box enables you to set the amount of gray level or *chroma* in a color. You might want to adjust this setting if a portion of an image needs a little less gray, and a little more color, than the rest of the image. You can adjust the satura-tion level of a specific color channel in an image, or of all the channels.

- **Color Brightness**—The Lightness slider control enables you to remove or add light to all or part of an image. This setting can help lighten or darken colors in an image, or help create more even lighting in part of an image.

Brightness and Contrast

The Brightness control enables you to increase or decrease the amount of light in an image, whereas the Contrast control enables you to increase or decrease the amount of dark and light pixels in an image. Choose **Brightness/Contrast** from the **Enhance** menu. This dialog box enables you to increase or decrease the overall tonal range of an image. Each slider control has a zero value at the midpoint of the slider, going from –100 to 100, or a range of 200 settings. Check the **Preview** check box to preview your changes in the image window. This tool provides a more general way to adjust the tonal range of an image.

The Brightness/Contrast settings in the Quick Fix dialog box are shown in Figure 7.9. Both the Brightness/Contrast dialog box and the Brightness/Contrast settings in the Quick Fix dialog box consist of one slider control to enable you to adjust the full range of brightness in a photo (see Figure 7.9). A higher brightness value increases the highlights in the image. A lower brightness value decreases the highlights, and increases the shadows in the image.

FIGURE 7.9

The Brightness/ Contrast controls enable you to adjust the ratio of dark and light pixels, as well as the amount of light exposed to the colors in an image.

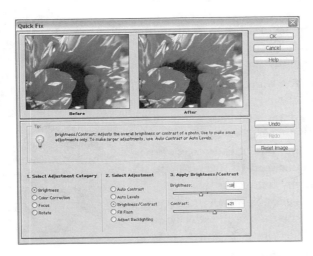

For broad, general adjustments to tonal range, use the Brightness/Contrast settings in the Quick Fix or Brightness/Contrast dialog box. For more precise adjustments to contrast or tonal range distribution, use the Levels dialog box. The **Levels** command enables you to more precisely modify the tonal range of pixels in an image. Choose **Levels** from the **Enhance**, **Brightness/Contrast** menu to open the Levels dialog box, or press (**Command-L**) [**Ctrl+L**]. Find out more about the Levels tool and customizing tonal range settings in the next chapter.

You can increase the shadows and highlights in an image by increasing the value of the Contrast slider control. Decreasing the contrast setting lowers the values of the shadows and highlights in the image.

The Levels dialog box contains three slider controls: one each for highlights (lighter grays), midtones (grays), and shadows (darker grays). You can adjust the tonal range for all three channels in an image, or customize each channel separately. The Levels command enables you to apply broad or precise changes that can affect some or all of the pixels in an image.

Adjusting Tonal Range Using the Levels Command

The **Levels** command enables you to adjust black (shadows), white (highlights), and middle tones (midtones). You can adjust pixels dynamically with the **Levels** command. For example, if you want to make the tonal range of highlights lighter, the midtone and shadow pixels will not be changed. You can use the Levels command to adjust the distribution of pixels in an image by either resetting the shadow/black, neutral gray/midpoint, or highlight/white point of an image (see Figure 7.10). When you adjust the settings in the histogram, you are changing the input levels of all the pixels in the image. You can also change the black and white output levels of the image by moving the arrow controls located at the bottom of the Levels dialog box.

FIGURE 7.10

A scanned image before adjusting its tonal range— note the relatively equal distribution of pixels across the tonal range.

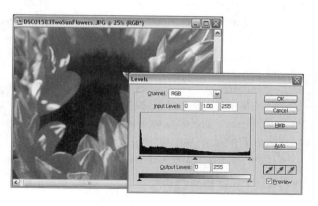

The histogram displays the tonal range of an RGB image. You can use the **Levels** command to modify all the pixels in an image by choosing the RGB option in the **Channel** menu. Choose **Enhance**, **Brightness/Contrast**, **Levels** to open the Levels dialog box. You can also view and edit the Red, Green, or Blue tonal ranges of the image in the Histogram or Levels dialog box. This enables you to customize a specific set of pixels in an image, reducing potential image data loss that can result from making broader tonal corrections with all three channels. If you've opened a grayscale image, a single window containing the distribution of grays will appear in the Levels dialog box (see Figure 7.11).

FIGURE 7.11
Changing the levels of the highlights and midtone can make the range of shadows in the photo stand out.

You can use the Levels dialog box to do more intensive tonal range correction, too. The three eyedroppers located in the lower-right corner of the Levels dialog box enable you to set custom black, gray, or white points for the image. The eyedropper tools will reset the input settings in the Levels dialog box. The eyedropper tools are not designed to make tonal corrections. You can use them to make small adjustments to correct the targeting of black, white, and grays in the image.

You can use the Levels eyedropper tools in two ways. First, you can choose an arbitrary color from the **Color Picker** window. Double-click on the eyedropper tool for which you want to set a target color, and then choose a color from the **Color Picker** window. Second, you can select one of the eyedropper tools from the Levels dialog box and then click in the image window to select the new black, gray, or white point for the image.

Color and Composite Images

You can apply any of the color or tonal correction commands to a single image, or to a combination of images. When you copy and paste one image into another, you create a composite image. The connecting edges of the composite image might not

A histogram is a visual representation of the number of pixels distributed in an image. Darker shades of pixels are located on the left side of the histogram, and lighter pixels on the right. Black vertical bars in the histogram indicate how many pixels share a common gray value in the image. View a histogram of an indexed color, RGB, or grayscale image. Choose **Histogram** from the **Image** menu to open the **Histogram** window. To find out more about how to read the data in the Histogram window, see Chapter 8.

blend in with the composite colors in the background image. Color mismatches and rough edges in composite images can result in a final image that lacks realism.

FEATHERING SELECTIONS

Blur the edges of a selected image before copying it. First, choose a selection tool and highlight an area of pixels in the image window. Then, choose the **Feather** command from the **Select** menu to feather the edges of the copied image to allow for better blending between the images.

The **Feather** command enables you to blend the color of the pixels located at the edge of the selected area. When you choose the **Feather** command, the Feather Selection dialog box opens. Type a number into the text box to adjust the number of pixels you want to blend with the edge pixels. The higher the number, the more pixels will be blurred at the edges of the selected image. Three to five pixels is a good value to apply with the **Feature** command. You can increase or decrease the number of pixels that will be feathered until you create the effect that works best with the image you're working with. Click **OK** to apply the command to the selected area. You should be able to see a slight blur at the edge of the selected image.

Choose the **Copy** command, and then paste the image into another image window. The pasted, feathered image should blend into the background image.

> **tip**
>
> If you want to apply the **Levels** command without altering any pixels in the original image, add a Levels adjustment layer. You can apply all the same great tools in the Levels dialog box in an adjustment layer except that the changes are stored in a separate layer until you're ready to merge them into the final image.

Figure 7.12 shows two images that have been added to a third image window. To create this image, I used the Magnetic Lasso Tool to select each image. Then I used the **Copy** and **Paste** commands to move the selected image to the middle window. Notice how the edges of the cat image are slightly blurred around the edges. The Feather command was not applied to the rabbit.

When you paste an image into an active document window, Photoshop Elements converts the color mode of the pasted image into the image mode of the active image window. To preserve all the color information of a composite image, open an image in RGB color mode, or create a new document window and choose **RGB Color** from the **Image**, **Mode** menu. RGB color mode supports up to 16.7 million colors. The 32 bits of information in

> Each time you apply any of the image-editing tools, you can change and delete a large number of pixels from the original image. As you apply multiple tools to an image, more and more data is lost. In contrast, if you create adjustment layers, and merge them together at the same time, you'll lose less image data than when applying each tool one by one.

an RGB image are broken up into three 8-bit channels (red, green, and blue), and an 8-bit alpha channel that helps determine how the three layers are interpreted to create the final color image. It's okay to paste an image in Indexed Color, Grayscale, or Bitmap color modes into an image window in RGB mode. The composite image will retain its resolution and color data.

FIGURE 7.12

Copy and paste images to create a composite. The **Feather** command was applied to the cat, but not to the rabbit.

Correcting the color between the two images might be an issue if you're combining images taken under different lighting conditions. For example, an image captured in daylight might not seem realistic if combined with another captured in low light. You can try to correct the highlights, midtones, or shadows of both images by adding an adjustment layer and applying it across layers in the image window. You also can apply the **Fill Flash**, **Adjust Backlighting**, **Brightness/Contrast**, or **Hue/Saturation** tools to an image before or after combining it with a second image. For best results, try to choose images that share similar lighting and image clarity. The greater the differences between the images, the more time you'll probably be spending trying to correct colors.

Another way to combine images is to select part of the background image and paste another image into it. Instead of choosing the standard Paste menu command, you can use a selection tool to highlight part of the image in the image window, and then choose the Paste Into command

note

You can apply color correction to RGB images using blending modes on multiple layers of the same image. For example, you can lighten the colors in a photo by applying the **Color Dodge** blending mode to a copy of the background layer that contains a photo. You can change the hue and saturation settings to a duplicate layer of an image and use the hue, saturation, or color blending modes to change the color cast of an image without changing any of the pixels in the original image.

from the Edit menu to create a masked composite image. Many of the same color matching and lighting issues apply to masked images. Be prepared to spend time correcting and blending colors to try to make the composite image appear more realistic.

A mask can also be used to isolate a particular area of an image where you might want to delete, replace, or correct the color. If you've pasted an image into the image window, you can (**Command-click**) [**Ctrl+click**] the composite image layer in the **Layers** palette. The image in the selected layer will automatically become selected. You can apply color correction tools to the selected image without affecting other images in the active image window.

A new layer is created for each new image pasted into the active image window. You can use the Move Tool to place the composite image in the image window, or apply the Erase Tool to delete any areas of the composite image that might not fit with the background image. You can use the Eraser, Magic Eraser, or Background Eraser tools to clean up a composite image or remove color from an area of the image.

Select the Eraser Tool (E) from the Toolbox. Click and drag it over an image to remove pixels from the image, and create transparent areas in the composite image, or across all layers in the image. A transparent color is actually an absence of color. Transparency is represented by a gray-and-white checkerboard pattern in the image window. If you see this pattern, no color will appear in the final printed or Web-published image. To find out more about the Eraser Tool, go to Chapter 11, "Adding Text and Shapes to Images."

note

A *mask* is a term used to describe a selected area of pixels in an image. A mask protects the unselected areas of an image from being edited, while enabling you to modify the selected area with commands and tools. You can create a simple mask by applying a selection tool to an image in the image window. When you apply the selection tool, the selected area is bordered with a flashing dashed line, or marquee. You can modify the pixels within the marquee. However, the pixels located outside the marquee cannot be edited.

Using selection tools to create masks is explained in more detail in Chapter 8.

8

TONAL RANGE AND COLOR CORRECTION

Photoshop Elements provides several color correction tools that enable you to perform an automatic color correction; experiment with quick fixes; or replace, adjust, brighten, darken, or remove color manually from an RGB image. Some tools, such as the Levels, Quick Fix and Brightness/Contrast tools, enable you to remap the dark and light pixels in an image. Grayscale and color images are created using a range of black, gray, and white pixels. These tools use the terms *shadows*, *midtones*, and *highlights* to define the range of dark to light colors.

The sections in this chapter show you how to use selection tools to choose pixels by shape, size, or color. You will find out how to use the histogram, which shows you how pixels are distributed in an image. The selection tools and histogram enable you to perform precise tonal range and color correction changes. You also will learn how to modify the tonal distribution of pixels using the Fill Flash, Adjust Backlighting, Levels, Brightness/Contrast, and other tools located in the Image and Enhance menus. These tools enable you to make darker areas lighter, or to add contrast to lighter areas of an image.

Several color-correction tools are also available in the Enhance menu. The Hue/Saturation, Color Cast, Replace Color, and Remove Color Tools enable you to customize the entire contents of the image window or focus on a specific selection of pixels. You can use a combination of tonal range and color-correction tools to make a blue sky bluer, remove red-eye, or correct brownish or greenish hues in scanned images of old photos.

Introducing Selection Tools

Although it's appropriate to apply any of the tonal range tools to an entire image, you also can apply them to selected areas. The selection tools reside in the Toolbox and in the **Select** menu. Each can be used with filters, effects, color correction, and transform tools in addition to the tonal range tools.

You can choose from two kinds of selection tools: ones that allow you to select an arbitrary set of pixels, and ones that help you select a group of pixels based on color or tonal variations. The Rectangular Marquee, Lasso, and Crop Tools fall into the former category, whereas the Magic Wand and Magnetic Lasso Tools fall into the latter category.

Selection tools primarily are used to select the pixels you want to modify, duplicate, or remove from an image. However, you also can use selection tools as a mask. A *mask* enables you to modify a specific area of an image, while all other areas are protected from change. You can apply filter, effect, drawing, eraser, or any number of other tools to the selected area without affecting the unselected pixels.

The following list describes the selection tools located in the Toolbox and the **Select** menu. Each of these selection tools can work with the Clipboard combined with the **Cut**, **Copy**, **Paste**, or **Paste Into** commands to bring other images into an image window.

You can use each selection tool one at a time or combine them. Hold down the Shift key to add another selected set of pixels to the current selection. Hold down the (Option) [Alt] key and click and drag the cursor over part of a selected area to remove those pixels from the selection area. You can use selection tools combined with the Info palette to view the size of a selected area. You'll find the following selection tools in the Toolbox:

> **note**
>
> Open the **Recipe** palette to see step-by-step instructions that explain how to adjust the tonal range, brightness and contrast, or hue and saturation of an image. You can also find out how to access tools to change an object's color, remove a color cast, or colorize a black-and-white photo.

- **Rectangular or Elliptical Marquee**—Create a rectangular or circular selection area in the image window. The marquee selection tools enable you to easily select an area of pixels in a particular shape. Click and drag the cursor in the image window to define the boundaries of the selected area.

- **Crop**—Apply this tool by clicking and dragging it in the image window. The Crop Tool grays the area surrounding the cropped image, enabling you to preview the cropped area. When you're ready to crop the selected area, press Enter. The image window is resized to the newly cropped image. You can use this tool to remove superfluous outer edges of an image you might want to use for a postcard or photo album.

- **Magic Wand**—Select, add, or subtract a range of colors with this magical selection tool. Click on a color in the image window to select all immediate occurrences of that color. Hold down the **Shift** key and click to add any other pixels to the selected area. Hold down the (**Option**) [**Alt**] key and click on a color to remove it from the selection. This tool is great for selecting or deselecting a range of colors you want to correct or replace. You can easily add or remove colors in different locations from the selection area.

- **Selection Brush**—Select pixels using a brush tool. View the selected areas in rubylith (unselected areas will appear with a red colored hue) or surrounded by marching ants. Adjust the brush's Size, Mode, and Hardness options.

- **Lasso, Polygonal Lasso**, or **Magnetic Lasso**—The Lasso and Polygonal Lasso tools enable you customize the shape of the selection area. Use this type of selection tool to choose odd-shaped areas, or to select pixels that you aren't able to select with the Marquee or Magic Wand. Click and drag the Lasso Tool to define the selection area. The Polygonal Lasso Tool enables you to click to define each side of a selection. Click on the first point again to close the selection area.

The Magnetic Lasso Tool is the smartest selection tool of them all. It will try to automatically select pixels based on previous clicks and pixel color information. Click in the image window to define the starting point of the pixels you want to select. Move the cursor around the image you want to select, and the Magnetic Lasso creates selection points. Unlike with the other lasso tools, you don't need to click to create each point of the selection area. As you move the cursor around, new selection points magically appear along the edge of the image based on previously created selection points. If you don't want a particular point, press the Backspace key once or several times to remove each successive point. Click to add a new point to the selection. Double-click or click on the first selection point to close the selection area.

Selection commands in the Select menu include the following:

- **All**—Select all pixels in the image window by choosing this command. You can use this command to select or deselect all pixels in a layer.

- **Deselect or Reselect**—After you've applied one of the selection tools, you might notice the marching ants or rubylith remain in the image window after you click outside the selected area. To remove the selection marquee from the image window, choose the **Deselect** command from the **Select** menu. Alternatively, you can press (**Command-D**) [**Ctrl+D**] or else (**Ctrl-click**) [**Right+click**] in the image window and choose the **Deselect** command. If you've deselected a selection, press (**Command-Shift-D**) [**Ctrl+Shift+D**] to reselect it, or (**Command-click**) [**Ctrl+click**] on the layer in the **Layers** palette. You can also (**Ctrl-click**) [**Right+click**] in the image window and choose the **Reselect** command from the shortcut menu.

- **Inverse**—Use this command to deselect a selection of pixels in the image window and instead select all the other pixels in the image window.

- **Feather**—Feathering helps reduce hard edges on images that are copied and pasted from one layer or image window to another by blurring the pixels on the perimeter of the selection. The **Feather** command can improve the way composite images blend together in an image. You can modify the Marquee and Lasso tools to automatically feather the edges of the selected area by typing a value in the Feather text box, which is located in the selection tool's options bar. To find out more about how to apply the Feather command, go to Chapter 13, "Experimenting with Composite Images."

- **Modify**—Four menu commands are stored in the Modify menu: **Border**, **Smooth**, **Expand**, and **Contract**. Each one adjusts the size and appearance of the selected area of pixels. Use one of these commands if you already have created a selection area but need to expand or contract the selection. These commands can be useful for creating photo-based animation.

- **Grow or Shrink**—These commands enable you to select pixels that share a similar color to those in the initial selection marquee. These commands work similarly to the Magic Wand Tool, selecting pixels by color value and not only by physical proximity.

- **Save/Load/Delete Selection**—These commands enable you to save a selected area of an image as a separate loadable or delete-able component.

> **tip**
>
> Hold down the (**Command**) [**Ctrl**] key and click on a layer containing an image object. This key combination automatically selects the image object in a layer. This is a great shortcut to use if you want to select an odd-shaped image that resides in its own layer in the **Layers** palette.

Applying the Rectangular Marquee Tool

The Rectangular and Elliptical Marquee tools are shape selection tools. Applying these selection tools to the image window is nearly identical to applying any of the shape tools—except, of course, you're using these tools to select pixels, not add them to the canvas. The marquee selection tools select an area of pixels in any rectangular or elliptical shape you want.

To select the Rectangular or Elliptical Marquee Tool, click its button in the Toolbox or press (**M**) [**Shift+M**] to toggle between the tools. The corresponding tool settings will appear in the options bar.

Hold down the mouse button and drag the cursor in the image window. A *marquee* (a broken white line, also called "marching ants," that appears in the image window) marks the boundary of the selected pixels. The marquee that appears when you select pixels in the image window looks similar to the tool's icon in the Toolbox. It also represents the selected pixels in the active layer in the **Layers** palette. The pixels will remain selected until you either choose and apply the selection tool again or press (**Command-D**) [**Ctrl+D**] to deselect the selection.

After you've selected a group of pixels, you can delete the selection, copy it to another image window, apply an effect to the selection, or make other changes that apply only to the selected pixels. If you have a problem copying text from the image window, be sure you have the correct layer selected in the Layers palette.

Applying the Magic Wand Tool

The icon for the Magic Wand shows a wand topped with a highlighted pixel. You can use the Magic Wand Tool to select a particular range of colors in an image. You can click on a color in the image window to select all pixels within its immediate proximity that share the selected color. The Magic Wand Tool works great if you want to select and change colors across different layers. You can use it to pick colors that need to be corrected, deleted, or merged with another image.

tip

You can use the selection tools and the **Paste Into** command to merge an image stored in the Clipboard into a selected image in the image window. First, open two images in the work area. Apply a selection tool to the first image. This selected area is where the second image will be pasted. Apply a selection tool to the second image. Choose the **Copy** command from the **Edit** menu. The selected image will be moved to the Clipboard. In the first image, click on the layer with the active selection (where you want to add the image).

Choose the **Paste Into** command located in the **Edit** menu. The second image is added to the layer in the first image.

Applying the Magnetic Lasso Tool

My favorite selection tool is the Magnetic Lasso Tool. The Rectangular Marquee Tool comes in as a close second. The Magnetic Lasso Tool is a lasso selection tool with smarts. It tries to determine which set of pixels you're trying to select based on the pixels that are not being selected in the image window.

To select pixels with this tool, first you must click in the image window. The first click creates an anchor point in the image. A single-pixel line appears as you move the cursor away from the anchor point. If you hold the cursor over the edge of the pixels you want to select, the Magnetic Lasso Tool creates additional anchor points automatically, although you can create each one manually, if you like. You don't need to click to define the selection area. To close the selection area, click on the first anchor point or double-click in the image window.

The selection area in Figure 8.1 was created with the Magnetic Lasso Tool. Making this type of selection "by hand" using the regular Lasso Tool would be a very slow, tedious process and probably wouldn't be nearly as accurate as the Magnetic Lasso Tool.

FIGURE 8.1

Click along the edge of an object in a picture. If you drag the Magnetic Lasso Tool along the edges of the image you want to outline, it will create anchor points for the selection.

Applying the Selection Brush

The Selection Brush enables you to select pixels using a brush tool. You can also use it to fine-tune a selection created by other selection tools. Choose the Selection Brush from the Toolbox and then adjust the brush size to match the number of pixels you want to work with. You can use the selection brush to add or subtract pixels from an existing selection area in the image window. Simply hold down the mouse button and drag the Selection Brush in the image window to add pixels to a selection. Press the (**Option**) [**Alt**] key to deselect pixels from a selection. Hold down the **Shift** key and click to add pixels to a selection.

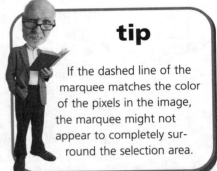

tip

If the dashed line of the marquee matches the color of the pixels in the image, the marquee might not appear to completely surround the selection area.

Correcting Tonal Range

The term *tonal range* defines how pixels are distributed across the black, gray, and white areas of an image. Many of the tonal range tools use a histogram to illustrate how pixels are distributed across an image. A *histogram* is a bar graph representing the pixel distribution of an image. The more pixels in the white or highlight areas of the histogram, the more light in the overall picture. The histogram shows a taller spike where more pixels are located in an area of an image, and a shorter spike, or no spike, if few or no pixels are present in that area of an image.

Some tools, such as the Levels and Threshold commands, use the histogram to display the tonal range of the image. Other tools, such as the **Fill Flash** and **Adjust Backlighting** commands, do not use a histogram to illustrate the tonal range of the image. Instead, these tools use slider controls to adjust the settings. Although the histogram is a very informative tool, and probably the most effective tool for viewing tonal distribution, most commands in Photoshop Elements rely on slider controls to enable you to view or change tonal or color settings.

HIGHLIGHTS, MIDTONES, AND SHADOWS

Although an image should not contain a huge spike of pixels in any one area of the histogram, it's also somewhat rare to view an image that has equal distribution of pixels across the full spectrum of black, gray, and white pixels.

You can take a look at how the histogram changes by creating a new window and viewing the histogram as you change the colors in the window. Choose **New** from the **File** menu. Type a width and height for the new window. Select **RGB** for the image mode, and then select the **White** radio button to get a new window with a white background. Next, choose **Image**, **Histogram** to open the Histogram dialog box. Be sure that the dialog box shows RGB in parentheses at the top. If it says Gray, go to **Image**, **Mode** and change the image mode to RGB. Choose any channel from the **Channel** drop-down list at the top of the Histogram dialog box and notice that there are no pixels in the histogram, although in a 200×200 pixel window, 40,000 white pixels are present.

Next, close the Histogram dialog box and choose black as the foreground color by clicking on the **Set Foreground Color** swatch at the bottom of the Toolbox. The Adobe **Color Picker** window opens. Click in the lower-left or lower-right corner of the **Color Picker** window to select black. Click **OK** to exit the **Color Picker** window. The foreground color in the Toolbox (the left color square) should be black. Next, select the Paint Bucket Tool, and click in the image window. The white background should turn to black. Next, choose **Histogram** from the **Image** menu to open the Histogram dialog box. You should see pixels on the left side of the histogram (Level 0) extending from the bottom to the top of the histogram.

For our next trick, choose the **Gradient Tool** from the Toolbox. Click on the **Linear Gradient** icon on the options bar, and then click and drag the cursor in the image window. The black background in the window changes into a white to black gradient. Next, open the Histogram dialog box and notice that the pixel distribution is spread somewhat evenly across the histogram (see Figure 8.2).

FIGURE 8.2

This black-and-white gradient generates a relatively flat histogram.

 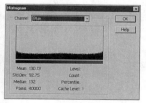

Balancing Foreground Light with Fill Flash

The Fill Flash, Adjust Backlighting, and Red-Eye Brush tools are designed to be quick fixes for some fairly easy, and commonly made, photographic errors. The Fill Flash Tool corrects photos in which the light source is behind the subject. This usually creates a dark foreground. The Fill Flash Tool lightens shadows in an image.

To apply the Fill Flash Tool, do the following:

1. Open an image file.

2. Choose **Fill Flash** from the **Enhance**, **Adjust Lighting** menu. The Fill Flash dialog box will open.

3. Click and drag the Lighter arrow slider to the right if you want to lighten the shadows in the image. The Fill Flash value can be adjusted to a value between 0 and 100.

4. Click and drag the Saturation slider control to the left or right to decrease or increase the saturation of colors in the image. You can choose a saturation setting between –100 and 100. Check the **Preview** check box if you want to see your changes applied to the image window before closing the Fill Flash dialog box.

5. Click **OK** to save your changes. View the changes in the image window.

The Lighter value will be set to zero the next time you open the Fill Flash dialog box.

note

Brightness is a separate attribute that can affect how we perceive color. The intensity of light on a color affects how brilliant or dull a color appears. Before modifying an image, note the differences in the way your monitor displays light and compare it to the original photograph, or to a reference image. Also, keep in mind that some monitors display all three colors equally well, whereas other monitors aren't as efficient at displaying colors equally well.

Figure 8.3 shows the original picture in which the foreground images are covered in shadows. Figure 8.4 shows the same image after the Fill Flash Tool has been applied to it. Notice that the foreground images, such as the chairs on the left, are more recognizable. The brighter images in the center and background area of the picture are also lighter.

FIGURE 8.3

The foreground images are much darker than the background images in this picture. The camera focused on the background light as the white point for this picture.

FIGURE 8.4

Lightening the foreground image with the Fill Flash Tool also lightens parts of the image's background.

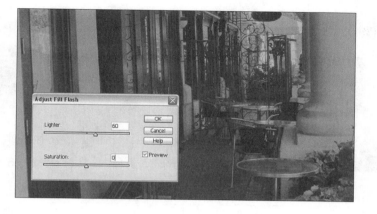

Bringing Out the Background with Backlighting

Another common flaw a camera can make when taking photographs is making the background area of the image too bright. You can darken the tonal range of an image by applying the Adjust Backlighting Tool. As with other tonal range tools, you can apply the Adjust Backlighting Tool to the entire image or to a selected area.

MONITOR SETTINGS, COLORS, AND TONAL RANGE

Although most monitors can display only 24 bits of color, most scanners can capture more data, in some cases up to or more than 48 bits of color. Even though you cannot see these additional colors on your computer screen, when you modify the tonal range or adjust color hues or brightness or contrast settings, the additional color information can bring out additional colors or details in the image. Keep in mind that you'll get the best results working with an image originally created with the highest resolution and sharpest, fullest color. Tonal range and color corrections are less effective with low-resolution images.

Choose **Adjust Backlighting** from the **Enhance, Adjust Lighting** menu to open the Adjust Backlighting dialog box. Figure 8.5 shows the image before the Adjust Backlighting Tool has been applied to it. In this image the sky is a little too bright. Figure 8.6 previews the same image with the Adjust Backlighting setting applied to it. Adjust the slider control and choose a value between 0 and 100. Then click **OK** to save your changes. View the modified image in the image window.

FIGURE 8.5
Bright background images can cause the foreground image to become underexposed.

FIGURE 8.6
Decreasing the amount of backlight dims the background image, neutralizing the overall image.

Using the Histogram with Tonal Range Tools

Each scanned or photographed image contains thousands of pixels, each capable of representing a million possible colors. You can modify an image by choosing a pixel's physical (x and y axis) location in an image, or by selecting and modifying colors. However, you can also modify an image's tonal range. The tonal range of an image represents how many pixels are distributed across each red, green, and blue channel in an image. Photoshop Elements provides the **Histogram** command to enable you to view how pixels share a particular tonal value in an image. You can use the Levels command to modify the tonal range settings in an image.

Tonal Range and the Histogram

A histogram shows you how many pixels exist in its y axis, with each possible shade between 0 and 255 represented along its x axis. Although it's possible for an image to look fine if true blacks or whites are missing from the histogram, images that appear over- or underexposed to the naked eye are usually missing pixels in the shadow or highlight regions of the histogram. You can find the black and white point in an image by locating the darkest and whitest areas of the image. The color that most closely matches black will be the black point for the image, and the closest white color will be the white point.

note

Most of the images you'll be working with in Photoshop Elements use the RGB color mode and color space. If an image is in RGB mode, you will see the letters RGB in parentheses following the name of the image in the title bar of the image window. Photoshop Elements opens an image file in RGB color mode by default.

Photoshop Elements enables you to view the red, green, blue, and luminosity information for an RGB image using a histogram. The histogram is also used as a part of the
Levels and Threshold color-correction commands. You can use these tools to view and
remap the tonal distribution of pixels in an image. Each red, green, and blue channel
stores different kinds of image information. For example, you are likely to find warmer
colors, such as red and orange, in the red channel of an RGB image (see Figure 8.7).
The single row of gray banding in Figure 8.7 indicates that pixels have been removed
from the image. The absence of pixels in the left and top-right parts of the image indicate that there are more pixels in the midtone and highlight range of the image.

FIGURE 8.7

Although there
are a couple of
spikes, pixels are
somewhat
evenly distrib-
uted across the
red area of the
histogram.

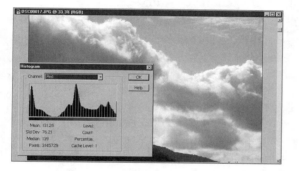

Open a color image in RGB color mode, and then choose **Histogram** from the
Image menu to open the Histogram dialog box. Select a channel from the
Channel drop-down menu if you want to view the histogram for a particular red,
green, blue, or luminosity channel in the image. The following list describes the various information you can get by looking at the image's histogram:

- The values representing the Mean (average intensity value), Standard
  Deviation (difference in variance of intensity values), Median (middle value
  for the range of intensity values), and total number of pixels in the image
  appear in the left column of the Histogram window.

- The Cache Level appears at the bottom of the right column of the dialog box.
  You can change this setting by checking the **Use Cache for Histograms**
  check box, located in the (Image Cache) [Memory & Image Cache]
  Preferences dialog box. If this check box is checked, the histogram information will sample the data using a faster algorithm. Instead of displaying
  actual pixel information, the cached histogram will display pixel values
  based on a representative sampling of pixels in the image.

- Move the cursor over the black areas of the histogram to view the level
  (intensity level), percentile (compares the number of pixels in the selected
  level with the rest of the pixels in the image), and pixel count (for the
  selected level) of the selected channel. The level, percentile, and pixels values
  change as you move the cursor over the histogram. The black areas of the
  histogram represent pixels in that tonal range.

Pixels that characterize the sharpness of an image, as well as pixels that contain contrast, tend to be stored in the green channel (see Figure 8.8). In a histogram, more pixels in a particular tonal range appear as a higher bar in the histogram window. Areas with more pixels represent the darker areas of the histogram. Areas of the histogram containing no pixels signify that no data exists for that tonal range in the image. Click and drag the cursor in the histogram if you want to view Count and Percentile data.

The blue channel tends to store blurrier, garbage aspects of an image (see Figure 8.9). Because the blurrier, distorted artifacts in an image tend to reside in the blue channel of an image, you might be able to more easily identify an area of an image that needs more work by viewing the contents of the blue channel in the image window. You may want to identify where most of the pixels are distributed in the image when you view the pixel distribution of the blue channel in the histogram. Cleaning up or removing blurry elements in an image may improve the overall picture.

Although the RGB channels combine to make a 24-bit image, a digital image actually consists of 32 bits of data. The remaining 8 bits of information define luminosity, or the tonal distribution of light in an image (see Figure 8.10). You can view the luminosity levels of an image in the Histogram dialog box. Zero represents black, and 255 represents white. The luminosity histogram represents the tonal range distribution of the pixels in an image as if it were in grayscale mode. When you modify colors or tonal ranges in an RGB image, the luminosity of the image also changes. You can use the luminosity histogram to see how many pixels are distributed in the shadows and highlights of an image and determine whether any true black or white image data exists. Luminosity is visible only in a color image.

note

If you're working with a grayscale image, the histogram window will display the tonal range for the gray channel: 254 shades of gray, plus white and black. The gray channel is the only channel in a grayscale image.

note

If you see regular intervals of missing pixels in the histogram window, this usually indicates that the image has been modified. Each time a tool, such as the **Brightness/Contrast Tool**, modifies an image, pixels are removed linearly from the image. For example, apply the **Auto Levels** or **Auto Contrast** commands to an image. Then open the histogram window. The banding that appears in the red, green, and blue histograms confirms that pixels have been removed from the image.

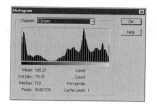

FIGURE 8.8

View the tonal distribution of grays by choosing the Green menu item in the Histogram window.

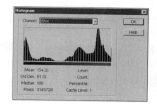

FIGURE 8.9

You can view the pixel distribution for the blue channel of an RGB image in the blue histogram window.

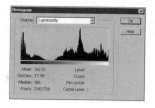

FIGURE 8.10

View the pixel distribution for light-related elements in the luminosity histogram.

Adjusting Tonal Range with the Levels Tool

You can make permanent changes to a layer by choosing **Levels** from the **Enhance**, **Brightness/ Contrast** menu. However, in most cases, it's more efficient to create a Levels adjustment layer so that you can adjust the tonal range of all or each channel in an RGB image without altering any of the original pixels in the image. Choose **Levels** from the **Layer**, **New Adjustment Layer** menu. The New Layer dialog box will open. Type a name for the new layer and click **OK**, and the Levels dialog box will open.

note

The **Auto Levels** command is a quickie version of the **Levels** command. It redistributes the midtone-range pixels for each channel in an RGB image.

FINDING BLACK AND WHITE POINTS

If you cannot visually identify black or white colors in an image, you can use the Levels dialog box to find them. Defining the black and white points in an image will help you adjust the tonal range settings for an image.

First, open an image in the work area. Adjust the size of the image so that the full image is viewable in the work area. Then choose **Levels** from the **Layer**, **New Adjustment Layer** menu. The **New Layer** window opens. Type a name for the Levels layer into the **Name** text box, and then click **OK**. The Levels dialog box will open. This new layer will affect only the layers below it. If you want the changes in the adjustment layer to affect all layers in the image, move it to the top of the **Layers** palette.

View the histogram of the tonal distribution of pixels for the image. Hold down the (**Option**) [**Alt**] key and then click and drag the left (black color) arrow-shaped slider control to the right until you see the first shades of black appear in the image. Note the number in the left **Input Levels** text box. This number represents the black point of the image. Observe the location of the black point in the image.

To find the white point of the image, hold down the (**Option**) [**Alt**] key and click on the arrow-shaped sliding control on the right, below the histogram. Move the slider control toward the left end of the histogram. Look for the first instance of the color white to appear as you move the slider from the right end of the histogram to the left. The first white pixels to appear represent the white point of the image. Note the number in the right Input Levels text box. The input levels will automatically change as you move the triangle slider controls located below the histogram.

You can use the black point and white point values to set, remap, and preview the shadow and highlight values for the image in the Levels dialog box. You can use the level controls to correct areas of an image that may be too light or too dark.

On first glance, the Levels dialog box looks like a treasure trove of slider controls, text boxes, eyedropper tools, and buttons. What it's really showing you is the input and output information of the selected pixels in the image window. You can perform tonal corrections to all channels by choosing RGB from the drop-down menu. Perform more precise contrast adjustment by modifying each red, green, or blue channel, one at a time. Choose the channel you want to view from the **Channel** drop-down menu.

The input and output level controls enable you to remap the way pixels are distributed in an image by increasing or decreasing the amount of contrast in the image. These controls can help you to correct over-exposed or under-exposed images. The input levels of the shadows, midtones, and highlights are shown in the Input Levels text boxes. The histogram displays how pixels are distributed across the tonal levels in the image. Notice the three triangle-shaped sliding controls located at the bottom of the histogram. As you move each control toward the middle of the histogram, the amount of contrast in the image increases. The following list describes each of the histogram controls in the Levels dialog box:

- The black triangle on the left, below the histogram, represents the shadow input slider. You can move the black triangle icon to change the zero value of the input level of the image.

- The white triangle on the right represents the highlight. You can move it to change the white, or 255, value of the input level of the image.

- The gray triangle in the middle of the histogram represents the midtone, or gamma, pixels in the image. You can adjust the lightness or darkness of the midtones without affecting the darkest or lightest tones in an image.

You can change the value of the shadows, midtones, and highlights independently. This means that if you change the pixels in the shadow tonal range of an image, the pixels in the midtones and highlights will not be modified or removed from the image. Moving the black and white slider controls toward the middle of the histogram will increase the contrast of the active image.

Figure 8.11 shows the selected image after the shadow and highlight input settings have been adjusted in the Levels dialog box. The selected image shows more contrast after the black and white points for the selected pixels are remapped to match the selection's pixel distribution. By decreasing the highlight input level from 255 to 169, the Levels command redistributes the pixels in the image so that all the pixels between 169 and 255 are changed to white, or 255, and the pixels between the midtone, or gamma, setting are redistributed using 169 as the new highlight value of 255.

FIGURE 8.11
Adjust the highlight and midpoints to lighten the selected item in the picture.

Output level information is located at the bottom of the Levels dialog box. A grayscale gradient represents the 0 to 255 range of output settings for the image. You can move the black or white slider toward the middle of the grayscale bar to change the output level settings.

Moving the left output slider toward the middle of the histogram will lighten, or neutralize, the darker pixels in the image. Conversely, moving the right output slider to the left will darken the highlight pixels in the image. The output level settings can be used to remap any adjustments to the input level settings made in the Levels dialog box.

You can set the target color for the highlights, midtones, and shadows using the eyedropper tools in the Levels dialog box. Use the eyedropper tools to manually set these values, or click on the Auto button to let

note

The **Auto Levels** and **Auto Contrast** commands redistribute tonal range values in between the shadow and highlight settings. They attempt to correct any extreme dark or light areas in an image.

Photoshop Elements reset these values. The following steps show you how to manually pick the black, white, and gray points in an image using the Levels dialog box controls:

1. Choose the Eyedropper Tool from the Toolbox. Then, choose a **Sample Size** from the options bar. Adjust the Eyedropper Tool in the Toolbox so that it can sample a portion of the image that's at least three-by-three pixels. Then set the image window to view the image at 100%.

2. Open the **Info** palette in the work area. Then open the Levels dialog box. Move the Eyedropper Tool around the image and try to identify x and y coordinates in the image that are good examples of highlights, midtones, and shadows in the image window. Note the RGB color values for the image areas you want to use to sample highlight, midtones, and shadow values for the image.

3. Double-click on the **Set White Point** eyedropper button in the Levels dialog box. The **Color Picker** window will open. Input the color values you want to use for the highlight color. For an RGB image, a good highlight color might consist of the RGB values of 244, 244, and 244.

4. Double-click on the **Set Gray Point** eyedropper button in the Levels dialog box. The **Color Picker** window will open. Type in the value for the midpoint color you want to use. Enter equal values for red, green, and blue to set the midtone values for an RGB image.

5. Follow the steps for setting the white and gray points, this time using the **Set Black Point** eyedropper button. Some sample RGB values for shadows might be 10, 10, and 10.

Changing Colors with Color Effect Tools

If you explore the Image menu, you'll find several commands in the **Image, Adjustments** menu. The **Equalize, Gradient Map, Invert, Posterize,** and **Threshold** commands each have a unique way of changing the brightness and color values in an image. These commands are most commonly used to create image effects, but occasionally they can help correct color in an image. Each of the examples in this section uses the image shown in Figure 8.12.

FIGURE 8.12

This purple orchid may have too much detail for some print media. Experiment with some of the tonal range tools to simplify the image.

Equalizing an Image

Adjust the brightness of an image using the **Equalize** command. This command uses the lightest and darkest levels in an image to define the white and black points of the image. All the in-between values are evenly distributed so that the brightness values of the overall image are, well, equalized. Figure 8.13 shows the results of applying the **Equalize** command to the image window.

FIGURE 8.13

FIGURE 8.13

Redistribute the brightness levels in an image by applying the Equalize Tool.

Changing an Image with Gradient Maps

You can apply the **Gradient Map** command to apply a map of colors to an image. Choose from a range of color or grayscale gradient maps from the **Gradient Map** window, or create your own in the **Gradient Editor** window. The Gradient Map command has controls similar to those of the **Gradient** command. You can select a gradient by clicking on the right edge of the gradient in the **Gradient Map** window. Double-click on the gradient to open the **Gradient Editor** window.

A Gradient consists of at least two colors. The Gradient Map connects highlights to one of the endpoints of the gradient, and the shadows to the opposing endpoint. Midtones are distributed across the in-between colors in the gradient. Figure 8.14 shows the Gradient Map dialog box, and the resulting grayscale image.

FIGURE 8.14

Map a grayscale gradient to an image by applying the Gradient Map Tool to an image.

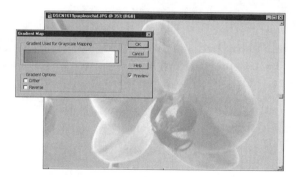

Inverting Colors

If you're working with a color image, the Invert command will replace the current color with its complementary color from the color wheel. If you could see Figure 8.14 in color, it shows that if you invert a purple orchid, it becomes green. Grayscale images invert black with white, and darker shades of gray with lighter shades of gray.

Posterizing Colors

The **Posterize** command enables you to reduce the number of colors in an image. The command remaps the image data in each channel of an RGB image to the number of levels of brightness input into the **Posterize** window. For example, if you define four levels for the image, 12 total colors—four each for red, green, and blue— will be used to create the posterized image. The resulting image probably will lack the clarity of the original. However, the hue and saturation settings are preserved.

Choose the **Posterize** command from the **Image, Adjustments** menu. The Posterize dialog box, shown in Figure 8.15, will open. Type a number into the **Levels** text box. This number represents the number of brightness levels, also called the tonal levels, of the resulting image. The number you type into the **Levels** text box is applied to each channel in the image to determine the total number of colors used in the final image.

FIGURE 8.15

Set the number of brightness levels with the Posterize Tool. This command remaps colors to the closest matching level, or reduces the number of gray levels in a grayscale image.

The **Posterize** command can help simplify an image for low-resolution printing. For example, if you have to print an image with a limited number of colors, you can experiment with different values in the Posterize dialog box until you find the right combination of colors that best matches the resolution of the printer.

Adjusting Threshold

The **Threshold** command remaps colors to black and white in an image. Colors that are lighter than the threshold setting change to white, and those that are darker change to black. That's probably why this command is great for finding the black-and-white points in an image. The histogram in the Threshold dialog box displays the pixel distribution of 255 grayscale shades in the overall image. The arrow control located at the bottom of the Threshold dialog box, shown in Figure 8.16, determines which pixels are changed to black or white. The numeric value for the Threshold appears in the text box at the top of the window.

FIGURE 8.16

FIGURE 8.16

The Threshold command enables you to adjust the black-and-white contrast in a grayscale or color image.

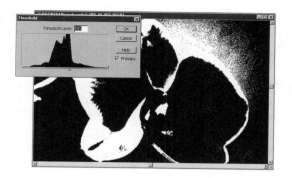

Replacing Colors

Most of the color-correction tools previously mentioned involve tools and commands based on the concept of a color wheel. These tools rely on the color wheel, or **Color Picker**, to change any colors. You can type in a color value or move a slider control to select a new color. The **Replace Color** command works similarly, but enables you to target specific pixels to change colors. You can add or subtract pixels to add or remove colors you might want to replace in the image window. The following sections show you how.

Preparing the Image

Before choosing the **Replace Color** command, open an image and adjust the **Levels and Brightness** and **Contrast** settings. Figure 8.17 shows the **Levels** command applied to the image that demonstrates how the **Replace Color** command works. As an alternative, you also can choose the **Auto Levels** and **Auto Contrast** commands to see whether any highlights or shadows become neutralized.

FIGURE 8.17

Before correcting the color, look at the highlights and shadows in the image to see whether it needs tonal range corrections.

Because the amount of visible color is dependent on light, you might want to adjust the highlights, shadows, or midtones in the Levels dialog box and see whether changing these settings reduces any extreme light or dark areas in the image.

Next, take a closer look at the image and look for any brightly lit areas that, for example, might be created due to reflected light from a flash or direct sunlight. Choose **Brightness/Contrast** from the **Enhance** menu to open the Brightness/Contrast dialog box. Move the Brightness slider control to the left to darken the image, or to the right to add more light. The contrast slider control will reduce highlight and shadows in an image as you move it to the left, and increase these levels as you move it to the right.

Replacing Colors

You can replace colors in an image. First, choose a selection tool and highlight part of the image in which you want to replace colors. Next, choose **Replace Colors** from the **Enhance**, **Colors** menu. The Replace Colors dialog box opens. Figure 8.18 shows a set of pixels that will interact with the Replace Colors settings. Click on the color square (where it says Sample), and then choose a color from the Color Picker dialog box to define the replacement color. Check the **Preview** check box to view the replacement color in the image window.

FIGURE 8.18
Use the Add to Sample and Subtract from Sample eyedropper tools to select or deselect the colors you want to replace.

To replace a color in the image, click on the Eyedropper Tool in the **Replace Color** window. Then, click on a color in the preview image located in the **Replace Color** window. Move the Hue, Saturation, and Lightness controls to choose the replacement color. The replacement color can replace more than one color in the image window. Check the **Preview** check box to preview your changes in the image window.

Choose the **Add to Sample** (with the plus [+] sign) Eyedropper Tool in the **Replace Color** window if you want to include an additional color to replace. Then, adjust the hue, saturation, or lightness settings to change the selected colors to the color of your choice.

tip

Double-click the Hand Tool in the Toolbox to view the full image within the image window.

If you select a color you don't want to include, choose the **Subtract** from Sample Eyedropper (the eyedropper tool with the [-] sign), and then click on the color you want to remove from the image window. Figure 8.18 shows how the colors in the image window are replaced after using the eyedropper tools to define which colors should be replaced. After you have replaced the colors in the image, choose **Deselect** from the **Select** menu, and then save the image to your hard drive.

REPLACE COLOR OPTIONS

After previewing the replacement color, you can click and drag the slider controls to change the hue, saturation, and lightness to choose the replacement color. Click and drag the Fuzziness slider to experiment with how the replacement color integrates with the other colors in the image window. The Fuzziness slider affects the range of colors that will be included in the color mask in the image. The higher the fuzziness value, the smoother the edges of the mask will become when the color change is applied to the image.

You can use the Eyedropper Tool or the Add to Sample (eyedropper-plus) Tool to select the colors you want to include in the color mask. Or choose the Remove from Sample (eyedropper-minus) Tool to deselect colors you do not want to include in the color mask. To find out more about masks, go to the first section of this chapter, "Introducing Selection Tools."

Correcting Color Cast

The **Color Cast** command is another color correction command located in the **Enhance**, **Color** menu. If you've scanned a photo that has an all-over color tint, you can use the **Color Cast** command to correct it. The **Color Cast** command uses an eyedropper tool to enable you to choose the gray, white, and black colors in an image. The Color Cast Correction dialog box appears as shown in Figure 8.19. The tough part is trying to determine which colors to use to define white, gray, and black.

FIGURE 8.19

Click on a gray, white, and black area of an image to adjust the color cast.

Click once on a black color. Then click on a white, and then gray color in the image window. You should see the tint of the image change after the third click of the eye-dropper in the image window. Don't be surprised if the color cast doesn't give you the results you expect. Click on the **Reset** button to revert the image to its original, incorrectly tinted state. Then, click on the white, gray, and black colors of the image to see whether the color cast changes provide more accurate results.

Removing Color from an Image

You can remove all the color from an image, or use a selection tool or layer to remove color from part of an image. The **Remove Color** command desaturates all color information in a layer into grayscale information.

Figure 8.20 shows a duplicate of the background layer that has had its color removed. To remove color from a layer, perform the following steps.

1. Drag and drop the background layer over the Create a New Layer icon in the **Layers** palette. A duplicate layer will appear in the **Layers** palette.

2. Click on the new layer to select it.

3. Choose **Remove Color** from the **Enhance**, **Adjust Color** menu or press (**Command-Shift-U**) [**Ctrl+Shift+U**] to remove the color from the selected layer. If you're working with a large image, or a relatively slow computer, you might see a progress bar appear at the bottom of the image window.

FIGURE 8.20

The **Remove Color** command can remove color from a layer.

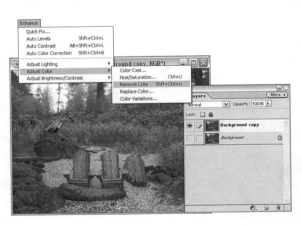

The **Remove Color** command will reset color saturation values to zero, leaving a grayscale-looking image in the layer and image window. However if you open the Color Variations dialog box, you can access and reapply color to the photo.

GRAYSCALE IMAGE MODE

An alternative way to remove color from an RGB or Indexed Color image is to choose **Grayscale** from the **Image**, **Mode** menu. A dialog box will appear, asking whether you want to discard color information. Click **OK** to remove the color, or choose **Cancel** if you do not want to remove it.

Changing the color mode from color to grayscale will remove all color information from the image. Don't worry; as long as you don't close the image window, you can press (**Command-Z**) [**Ctrl+Z**] to undo the color removal. If you close the image window and save the image file, you cannot restore any color information.

tip

Another way to change a color image to black and white is to add a gradient map. Click on the **Create New Fill** or **Adjustment Layer** icon in the **Layers** palette and choose **Gradient Map**. The default setting will add a black-and-white gradient map to the image.

Introducing Color-Correction Tools

The color correction tools located in the Toolbox are great for applying color correction to a specific, detailed set of pixels in an image. Use the Zoom Tool to magnify an area of the image you want to work on with the Red-Eye Brush, Dodge, or Burn tools. The **Quick Fix**, **Color Variations**, and **Hue/Saturation** commands enable you to access color correction tools that are great for wider scale changes.

The Red-Eye Brush Tool is probably the most obvious color-correction tool in the Toolbox. Of course, the Eyedropper, Paint Bucket, and Eraser tools can also technically be grouped with color-correction tools. However, these tools are explained in more detail in the preceding chapter. Most of the color-correction tools are found on the shortcuts bar and the **Enhance**, **Adjust Color** menu. The **Color Cast**, **Hue/Saturation**, **Replace Color**, and **Remove Color** commands enable you to correct your colors. The **Quick Fix** and **Color Variations** commands are perhaps the most versatile color-correction tools. You can use the Quick Fix Tool to correct brightness/contrast, fix color, or apply focus and blur. The Color Variations dialog box enables you to adjust red, green, and blue hues for a photo's highlights, midtones, and shadows, and saturation. The following list summarizes what each of these color-correction tools can do:

- **Red-Eye Brush**—Use this tool to remove red-eye from photos. Select a target and replacement color for this tool from the options bar. The target color will be the red-eye in the image, and the replacement color will be the natural eye color for the photo subject. Choose a brush size and apply it to the red-eye pixels in the image window to apply the correct color to the image. You can also use this tool to replace one color with another.

- **Dodge**—The icon for this tool looks like a lollipop. Use the settings in the options bar to work with highlight, midtone, or shadow tones of an image. Applying this tool to pixels will lighten their tone.

- **Burn**—Located with the Dodge Tool in the Toolbox, this tool will darken the highlight, midtone, or shadow tones of the pixels in an image. The hand icon for this tool appears to be pinching something.

■ **Quick Fix**—Preview and apply color, brightness/contrast, focus, and blur corrections from the Quick Fix dialog box.

■ **Color Variations**—Open the Variations dialog box to preview color correction options for the active image window. Click on a thumbnail image to change the highlights, midtones, shadows, and saturation of color in an image. Compare the original with the current, modified image and decide whether you want to keep the changes made to the image.

■ **Hue/Saturation**—Adjust the color, gray level mixture with color, and lightness values by moving the slider controls in the Hue/Saturation dialog box.

■ **Replace Color**—Select one or more colors to replace in an image window by choosing this command. Use the Eyedropper Tool to define the initial color to be replaced, and then modify your settings with the plus and minus eyedropper tools. Change the Hue, Saturation, and Lightness settings for the image to define the replacement color for the active image area.

■ **Remove Color**—Desaturates (minimizes color saturation levels) a color photo, although it appears to perform the same feat as choosing **Grayscale** from the **Image**, **Mode** menu. All color information remains in a layer despite the abundance of grays.

■ **Color Cast**—Change the black, white, and gray points of an image by clicking in gray, white, and black areas in an image. This tool enables you to remap the way colors are mapped to an image based on the colors you want to use to define black, white, or gray.

Adjusting Hue and Saturation Settings

The Hue, Saturation, and Brightness (HSB) or Hue, Lightness, and Saturation (HLS) color model uses three settings to define color. Hue represents one of 360 possible colors on a color wheel. The lightness, or brightness, level can be a value between 0%, or black, and 100%, which is white, or full illumination. The saturation level also ranges from 0% to 100%, with 0% representing the full gray, or midtones, of a color, and 100% representing the full nongray-containing color value.

You can customize the hue, saturation, and lightness of an image to intensify the color of an image (see Figure 8.21). Choose the **Hue/Saturation** command from the **Enhance**, **Colors** menu. The Hue/Saturation dialog box, shown in Figure 8.22, contains a slider control for hue, saturation, and lightness settings for all channels combined in an RGB image, or each individual channel in an image.

The Hue settings, shown in Figure 8.22, can change a green color into blue or turn orange to red. The Hue slider control represents the full spectrum of colors on the color wheel. You can change the color values in the image window by moving the slider control to the left or right. Click and drag the slider control and preview the colors in the image window. Wait until the colors in the image change to match another photo, or until the colors look accurate to your eyes.

FIGURE 8.21

This image contains reds, greens, and blues with both strong highlights and strong shadows.

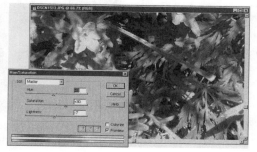

FIGURE 8.22

Use the master settings in the Hue/Saturation window to adjust the colors in the image window.

The Saturation and Lightness controls work similarly to the Hue control. Drag the slider control to change the setting. As you move the Saturation control to the left, the image should become grayer. As you move it to the right, the colors in the image should stand out, as any shades of gray dissipate. If you want to correct an image by bringing out the blue color in a sky, or a red color in a dress, select the item you want to work with in the image window. Then move the Saturation slider to the right to see whether the corrected color meets your needs.

The Lightness control adjusts the shadows and highlights in the image. Zero is the center-point value for this setting. Moving the slider control to the left darkens the image, whereas moving it to the right brightens it.

Customizing Channel Hue and Saturation

You can also adjust the color ranges for red, green, blue, cyan, yellow, and magenta. Notice the two color bars located at the bottom of the **Hue/Saturation** window. Choose one of the colors from the Edit drop-down menu to view the color range. Figure 8.23 shows a modified red color range.

tip

An alternative to choosing Hue/Saturation from the Enhance/Color menu is to create an adjustment layer. Choose **Hue/Saturation** from the **Layer**, **New Adjustment Layer** menu to add a modifiable Hue/Saturation layer to the image. You can hide or show the Hue/Saturation settings by clicking on the eye icon for this adjustment layer in the **Layers** palette.

FIGURE 8.23

FIGURE 8.23

Customize the range and falloff settings for a color in the Hue/Saturation window.

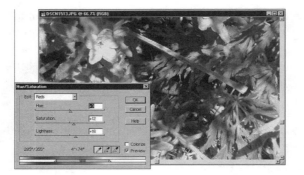

The range of the adjustment slider represents two settings for the selected color, as shown in Figure 8.18. The middle area of the slider represents the range of the color. The areas to the left and right of the middle represent the falloff range for that color. Although it's not likely you'll use this method to correct a color, you might want to experiment with these settings to see how color changes when the hue or saturation color ranges are changed.

Correcting Colors with the Red-Eye Brush Tool

Most digital cameras automatically activate a flash if the light levels are too low. If you're taking a picture of a person or pet, the brightness of the flash may bounce off the back of the person's eye before their eyes can adjust to the bright light. This causes the familiar red-eye you often see in photos.

> **tip**
>
> Hold down the (**Command**) [**Ctrl**] key, and then click and drag the cursor to the left or right in the color bar area of the color bars in the **Hue/Saturation** window. The cursor will change from an arrow to a hand icon when you click on either color bar in the **Hue/Saturation** window. The colors will scroll off the right and reappear on the left end of the color bar. You can use this shortcut to change the color that appears in the middle of the color bar.

Most digital cameras have a flash that reduces red-eye. These flashes actually flash twice or several times before capturing a photo. The flashes are brief, allowing the eye's iris to contract with each subsequent, brighter flash.

You can apply the Red-Eye Brush Tool to scanned photos or digital pictures to take care of any red-eye problems. The Red-Eye Brush Tool enables you to select the colors you want to replace, and then apply the brush to the red areas of the eye. Figure 8.24 shows how red-eye can add a spooky look to a photographed subject's eyes.

FIGURE 8.24
Red-eye occurs when the flash bounces off the retinas before the eyes can adjust to the brightness of the flash.

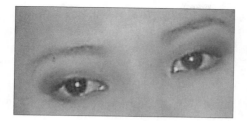

You can use the Red-Eye Brush Tool to remove red-eye, or to change one color in a photo to another. For example, you can change someone's eye color from brown to blue. The following steps show you how to correct red-eye by applying the Red-Eye Brush Tool:

> **tip**
>
> Choose **Image**, **Duplicate Image** to create a copy of an image window. This can come in handy if you want to zoom into one image window to fine-tune a photo and view the same image zoomed out to fit onscreen in the duplicate image window.

1. Open an image in the work area, and then select the Red-Eye Brush Tool from the Toolbox.

2. Click in the options bar, shown in Figure 8.25, to select a brush size. I recommend using a soft-edge brush, not a hard-edge one.

FIGURE 8.25
Choose a replacement color and apply the Red-Eye Brush Tool to change the red color.

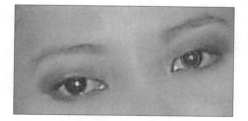

3. Select **First Click** from the **Sampling** drop-down menu (it's selected by default). Choose the color you want to remove by clicking in the red color of the eye in the image window. The target color appears on the right end of the options bar.

4. Choose a replacement color by clicking in the eye. You also can choose a different brush size from the options bar. Click on the **Brush** drop-down menu to view a list of brush options. You can load a new set of brushes by clicking on the right-arrow button located on the right side of the **Brush option** drop-down window. The number below each brush size indicates the number of pixels in that brush tip.

In the default set of brushes, the first row of brush sizes includes hard-edge brushes. These brushes will create a solid-color pixel edge when applied to the image window. The brush sizes in the second row are soft-edge brushes. The pixels on the edges of the soft-edge brushes will blend in with the colors of the surrounding pixels. Soft-edge brushes produce great results with the Red-Eye Brush and Clone Stamp tools. Choose a brush size that's about half to two-thirds the size of the eye. Select a smaller brush if you want to make fine-tuned changes. Use a larger brush if you want to make fewer brush strokes.

The tolerance setting, located in the options bar, enables you to define the range of the target color that's applied to the replacement color. A higher value replaces a wider range of colors. A lower value affects a limited range of colors.

The Sampling drop-down menu, located in the options bar, consists of two options: **First Click** and **Current Color**. The default setting is **First Click**. Simply click on the red-eye color in the image window to pick the target color. Choose **Current Color** if you want to select a custom target color. Click on the Current color square in the options bar to select a new target color.

5. Click once on the red color in the eye, and then drag the cursor over the red color in the eye area of the image window to replace any colors that match the red target color with the replacement color.

If you don't like the results, choose the **Undo** command from the **Edit** menu, or click on a previous action in the **History** palette to revert the document to a state before the Red-Eye Tool was applied to the image.

Color-Correction Variations

The color variations tools enable you to preview, point, and click to perform a color correction. You can adjust how much of a color change you want to apply to a photo and view thumbnails of each red, green, and blue change. Simply click on a thumbnail to change the color. A different set of options is available for grayscale images. However, both options enable you to preview and make changes without altering the original photo. The following sections show you how to correct color using the tools in the Color Variations dialog box.

> **tip**
>
> You can change a layer from color to grayscale by selecting a layer and choosing the **Remove Color** command from the **Enhance**, **Adjust Color** menu. Hide the color layers, and select the grayscale layer. Choose **Color Variations** from the shortcuts bar to apply color variation settings to the grayscale layer. You can add color to the grayscale layer because the image remains in RGB mode!

Grayscale Variations Options

Although you'll probably want to work with a color photo, you can work with a smaller group of settings in the Color Variations dialog box with a grayscale photo. You can either open a photo that's been saved in Grayscale mode, or choose

Grayscale from the **Image**, **Mode** menu to change all layers to grayscale. After the active image window is set to grayscale, click on the **Color Variations** button in the shortcuts bar or select the menu command from the **Enhance**, **Adjust Color** menu.

Click and drag the Amount slider control, shown in Figure 8.26, to adjust how much lighter or darker each variation will be. Select **Midtones**, **Shadows**, and **Highlights** radio buttons to pre-view the Lighter and Darker variations of the photo. For each radio button in section 1, click on the Lighter thumbnail to lighten the image, or click on the Darker thumbnail to darken the image. Compare your change to the original image located in the upper-left corner of the Color Variations dialog box. Click and drag the slider control to choose how fine or coarse you want the changes to be.

note

You can adjust the intensity of the color or grayscale variations in the Color Variations dialog box by moving the Amount slider control. Variations will be subtler as you move the slider control to the left. Colors or grays will change more dramatically as you move the slider control to the right.

FIGURE 8.26

You have only a few variations when tweaking grayscale images.

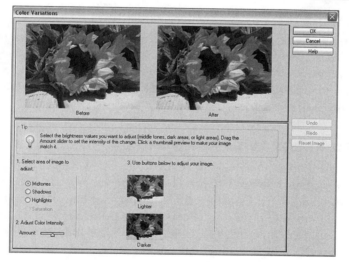

Color Variations Options

You can correct color for highlight, midtones, shadows, or saturation levels in an RGB image using the **Color Variations** command. Click on the **Color Variations** button in the shortcuts bar or select **Color Variations** from the **Enhance**, **Adjust Color** menu to open the Color Variations dialog box, shown in Figure 8.27. Click on a radio button to choose **Highlights**, **Midtones**, **Shadows**, or **Saturation**. The

Midtones radio button is selected by default. Next, click on one of the thumbnail images to increase or decrease the amount of red, green, or blue in the photo. Click on the Lighten or Darken thumbnail to increase or decrease the brightness level. Compare the changes by viewing the Before and After thumbnails.

FIGURE 8.27

You can adjust tonal range and color settings by clicking in a thumbnail setting in the Color Variations dialog box.

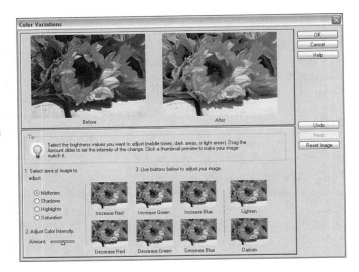

On the right side of the Color Variations dialog box are several buttons. At the top, click **OK** to save your changes, **Cancel** to exit without saving, or **Help** to view Adobe's HTML help pages. After you apply one or several color changes, click **Undo** to remove the previous change. Click **Redo** to reapply it. Choose **Reset Image** to remove all changes.

Warming Up an Image with Midtones

Highlights, midtones, and shadows thumbnails enable you to preview the image if red, green, or blue hues were applied to it, as shown in Figure 8.28. Click on a thumbnail image to change the color of the original image. Compare the change in the After thumbnail, located at the top-right of the window, to the Before thumbnail. Click and drag the Amount slider control to increase or decrease the amount of color applied to each of the thumbnail images.

On the bottom of the Color Variations dialog box, you can click on the Lighter thumbnail if you want to increase the brightness of the image. Alternatively, you can click on the Darker thumbnail image if you want to decrease the brightness of the image.

In Figure 8.29, I clicked on the **Increase Red** and then the **Increase Blue** thumbnails to add warmer colors to the image. You can click on any combination of thumbnails until you get the desired After image you want to keep. Click **OK** to save your changes.

FIGURE 8.28

Low-light shots can be taken indoors, or outdoors during dusk or evening hours. These images usually have a green or blue cast to them due to the light from a tungsten or fluorescent bulb.

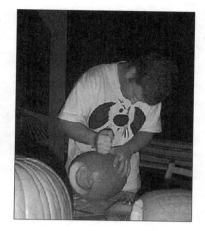

FIGURE 8.29

Adjust the colors in the midtones of the image. In this example, I chose the **Increase Red** and **Increase Blue** options to add warmer colors to the picture.

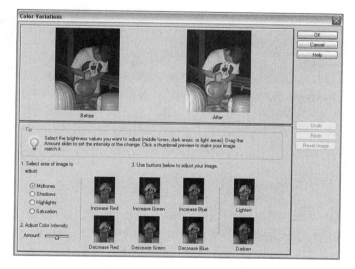

Modifying Saturation Variations

The **Saturation** radio button enables you to intensify or decrease the amount of color in the photo. Click on the **Saturation** radio button to adjust the gray levels within the Color Variations dialog box. Click on the **Less Saturation** thumbnail image to increase the amount of gray mixed with the colors in the image. Click on the **More Saturation** thumbnail to add more color to the image.

You can apply the **Undo** and **Redo** buttons to Saturation variations. You can undo one or several changes, and then selectively reapply each variation. If you're experimenting with color correction, you might want to make small changes to allow yourself to become familiar with how the colors in the image interact with different color-correction settings in the Color Variations dialog box. Then, save a copy of the different color variations to your hard drive if you want to compare them side-by-side on your desktop.

9

APPLYING FILTERS AND EFFECTS

Applying a filter or an effect to an RGB or Grayscale image is as easy as dragging and dropping the filter or effect into an image window. Filters and effects enable you to correct, deconstruct, or apply an artistic pattern to an image. You can view or choose filters from the Filter menu. Better yet, you can preview each filter and effect from the Filters or Effects palettes.

Previewing Filters and Effects

The **Filters** and **Effects** palettes enable you to view available filters or effects in List or Thumbnail view (see Figure 9.1). The **Thumbnail View** and **List View** buttons are located at the bottom of each palette. Each thumbnail image represents how the image might look if you apply that filter or effect to it. In List view, you can preview a filter in the palette if you click its name. The thumbnail image can be viewed for the original and the selected filter or effect in List view.

FIGURE 9.1

Click one of the view icons in the **Filters** or **Effects** palettes to view filters or effects in List or Thumbnail view.

Thumbnail view enables you to see how each filter would be applied to a sample image. The name of each filter or effect appears below each thumbnail, and an original thumbnail appears in the top corner of the palette. Filters can be organized in the palette windows as they appear in the **Filter** menu, or you can view all of them at once in the palette window. You can view or choose a group of filters or effects from the drop-down menu list, located at the top of the palette window. Choose **All** to view all groups in the palette window.

Introducing Filters

Filters enable you to apply special effects to images. For a filter to work, there must be a visible image in the image window, or the equivalent of an active layer in the Layers palette. The image must also be in RGB or Grayscale mode before you can apply a filter. You can preview or apply a filter from the **Filter** menu or **Filters** palette (see Figure 9.2). Some filters analyze the pixel color or tonal range of an image to manipulate the appearance of the image, whereas other filters apply an arbitrary change based on the proximity of each pixel in the image.

A dialog box might open when you choose a filter command from the **Filter** menu or **Filters** palette, enabling you to customize settings for that filter. The Filter dialog box contains a thumbnail-size preview window, enabling you to view the filter's effect on the image before you actually apply the selected settings. You must view or adjust these settings and choose **OK** before the filter can be applied to the image. After a filter has been applied to an image, that filter command becomes selectable from the top of the **Filter** menu, or by a press of (**Command-F**) [**Ctrl+F**].

FIGURE 9.2

Preview each
feature in the
Filters palette.
Drag and drop a
filter into the
image window
to apply it to an
image.

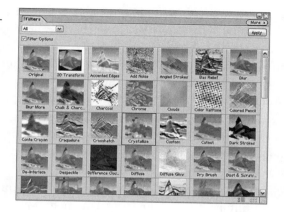

Adobe groups filters into categories, which you can
view in the **Filter** menu or the **Filters** palette. Click
on the drop-down menu located at the top of the
Filters palette to view or choose the way the filters
are grouped in the **Filters** palette. The **Filter** menu
displays all installed filter plug-in files on your
hard drive, grouped by category. The following list
contains a brief description of each category of filters. In general, filters can correct, deconstruct,
texturize, or add an artistic stroke to an image.

note

Adobe installs all fil-
ters into the Filters folder
and all effects into the Effects
folder of the Plug-Ins folder in the
Photoshop Elements folder on
your hard drive.

- **Liquify**—The Liquify Tool actually consists
  of seven effect tools. Each effect can be
  applied with a brush stroke. To find out
  more about this filter tool, go to
  Chapter 14, "Creating Complex Images."

- **Artistic**—Each of these filters opens a window of customizable settings.
  Choose from Colored Pencil, Cutout, Dry Brush, Film Grain, Fresco, Neon
  Glow, Paint Daubs, Palette Knife, Plastic Wrap, Poster Edges, Rough Pastels,
  Smudge Stick, Sponge, Underpainting, and Watercolor.

- **Blur**—Smooth hard edges with up to six blur filters. Select one or combine
  the Blur, Blur More, Gaussian Blur, Motion Blur, Radial Blur, and Smart Blur
  filters.

- **Brush Strokes**—Change a photo into a drawing by applying one of these
  stroke filters to an image. Experiment with Accented Edges, Angled Strokes,
  Crosshatch, Dark Strokes, Ink Outlines, Spatter, Spray Strokes, or Sunrise. If
  you like these filters, you might also want to experiment with the Sketch
  filters.

- **Distort**—The filters in this group fall into the destructive category. Pixels from the original image are removed to create exaggerated effects, such as Diffuse Glow, Glass, Ocean Ripple, Pinch, Polar Coordinates, Ripple, Shear, Spherize, Twirl, Wave, and ZigZag. If you choose the Distort group from the Filters palette, you can choose the Liquify filter. The Displace filter can be selected only from the Filter, Distort menu.

- **Noise**—Another group of destructive filters, these filters try to re-create many of the artifacts you'll try to remove from old, damaged photos in Chapter 12, "Repairing Images." Use Add Noise, Dust & Scratches, Despeckle, or the Median filter.

- **Pixelate**—This group of filters also removes pixels from the original image to create a Color Halftone, Crystallize, Facet, Fragment, Mezzotint, Mosaic, or Pointillize effect.

- **Render**—Most of the filters in this group replace the image in the image window. The 3D Transform effect has its own set of tools. It enables you to create a 3D object from some of the pixels in the image. The Clouds, Difference Clouds, and Lens Flare filters enable you to add custom elements to an image. If you click the Filter, Render menu, you can choose the Texture Fill filter. You can select a texture file on your hard drive that can be used to create a filter effect with the selected image in the active image window. The Lighting Effects filter enables you to change the lighting in an image. For more information about the Lighting Effects filter, go to Chapter 14.

- **Sharpen**—Sharpen filters try to create a clearer, crisper image by enhancing contrasting colors in an image. For most images, you might not notice a change in the image after applying the Sharpen, Sharpen Edges, or Sharpen More filters to an image. The Unsharp Mask filter is sort of an antisharpen filter. Although it is designed to add a slight blur to an image, it uses an algorithm designed to blend contrasting pixel colors closer together. This filter is commonly used to polish a multilayered or composite digital image.

- **Sketch**—Yet another group of strokelike filters, these can turn a photo into a drawing. Choose from Bas Relief, Chalk & Charcoal, Charcoal, Chrome, Conté Crayon, Graphic Pen, Halftone Pattern, Note Paper, Photocopy, Plaster, Reticulation, Stamp, Torn Edges, or Water Paper.

- **Stylize**—Diffuse, Emboss, Extrude, Find Edges, Solarize, or add Glowing Edges, Tiles, Wind, or Trace the Contours of an image with the filters in this group.

- **Texture**—Create special effects with a photo. Select from the Craquelure, Grain, Mosaic Tiles, Patchwork, Stained Glass, and Texturizer filters to turn a photo into a unique piece of art.

■ **Video**—The De-Interlace and NTSC Colors filters can convert the colors in an image for use with a television. Television broadcasts each successive image using odd and even horizontal lines of the television screen. The De-Interlace filter can replace missing lines of an image captured from video. The NTSC filter adjusts the colors in an image to match a set of colors that are acceptable for television broadcast. This set of colors is designed to prevent oversaturated colors from bleeding into television scan lines.

■ **Other**—Although the Dither Box, High Pass, Maximum, Minimum, and Offset filters are located in this menu, any third-party filters will also share this menu space.

■ **Digimarc**—Choose the Read Watermark filter to check an image for the presence of a watermark. Watermarks are sometimes used to copyright an image. This filter is available only in the Filter menu.

> **tip**
>
> You can install third-party Photoshop plug-ins and use them with Photoshop Elements. Installing filter plug-ins is similar to installing TWAIN plug-ins for Photoshop Elements. To find out more about how to install plug-in files, go to Chapter 3, "Acquiring Images from Scanners and Digital Cameras."

You can adjust the size of the **Filters** palette by clicking and dragging the lower-right corner of the palette window. If the palette is in thumbnail view, the number of viewable thumbnail images will increase or decrease to match the size of the palette window. The scroll controls along the right side of the window enable you to view or select any filter in the palette.

APPLYING MULTIPLE FILTERS

You can apply a filter more than once to an image. However, each filter alters the original pixels in an image. It is difficult to predict the resulting image after several filters have been applied to an image. The preview window can help you visualize how the current filter will change the image.

When you place the cursor over the Preview area of the filter window, the cursor icon will change from an arrow to a hand. You can click and drag the cursor to move the viewable area of the image that appears in the preview window. Click on the minus (−) button to zoom out from the image. Or click on the plus (+) button to zoom into the image in the preview window.

If you're experimenting, you can use the **Undo** command to view the image before and after applying a filter.

Introducing Effects

Effects are similar to filters and often are the equivalent of applying a combination of filters in a particular sequence to produce a complex special effect. As with filters, you can preview each effect from the **Effects** palette (see Figure 9.3). However, you cannot customize each effect. You can only choose whether to keep it. After applying an effect to an image, you'll also see a dialog box that asks, "Do you want to keep this effect?" Click **Yes** if you want to keep the effect. Click **No** if you want to return to the original image. If you check the **Don't Show Again** check box, the effect will be applied and the dialog box will stop appearing after any effects are applied.

FIGURE 9.3

Preview the result of each effect by viewing each thumbnail image in the **Effects** palette.

Although you can find filters in the **Filter** menu, effects are accessible only from the **Effects** palette. The following list describes the categories of effects available from the **Effects** palette:

- **Frames**—Each of these effects adds a custom picture frame to the image in the image window. Some frames, such as the Cut Out, Recessed Frame, Text Panel, and Vignette effects, require you to use a selection tool to select the part of the image window you want to apply the effect to. Choose from Brushed Aluminum Frame, Drop Shadow Frame, Foreground Color Frame, Photo Corners, Ripple Frame, Spatter Frame, Strokes Frame, Waves Frame, Wild Frame, or Wood Frame.

- **Textures**—Add a texture to an image. Select from Asphalt, Bricks, Cold Lava, Gold Sprinkles, Green Slime, Ink Blots (layer), Marbled Glass (layer), Molten Lead, Psychedelic Strings, Rusted Metal, Sandpaper, Sunset layer), Wood-Pine (layer), or Wood-Rosewood. Textures followed by (layer) indicate that a separate layer is created for that effect. You can adjust the transparency level of the layer to tweak the effect.

- **Text Effects**—Apply a special effect to a text object. Choose from Bold Outline, Brushed Metal, Cast Shadow, Clear Emboss, Confetti, Medium Outline, Running Water, Sprayed Stencil, Thin Outline, Water Reflection, or Wood Paneling.

- **Image Effects**—Each effect applies a set of filters to an image. Choose from Blizzard, Colorful Center, Fluorescent Chalk, Horizontal Color Fade, Lizard Skin, Neon Nights, Oil Pastel, Quadrant Colors, Soft Flat Color, Soft Focus, or Vertical Color Fade.

Different Ways to Apply Filters and Effects

Filters and effects can be applied to the entire image or to a selected area of pixels. You can apply a filter to an image in three primary ways. The easiest method is to drag and drop the thumbnail image of the filter or effect onto the image window. If there are multiple layers in the image window, a filter can be applied to an individual image layer. Figure 9.4 shows an image before a filter has been applied to it. Figure 9.5 shows the same image after the Gaussian Blur filter has been applied to selected areas of the image.

FIGURE 9.4

The first- and second-generation Aibo dogs before a filter is applied.

In Figure 9.5, he Magnetic Lasso Tool was used to select one of the dogs. Next, the Invert Selection command was applied to select everything except the dog. Then the Gaussian Blur filter was applied to the selected area of the image.

You can double-click a filter or an effect in the palette window, or click on a filter or an effect and then click the **Apply** button, to apply an effect. The active image window will be the target of the filter or effect. If the filter has a dialog box, view the settings, and then click **OK** to dismiss the dialog box. Wait for the filter or effect to process the image. Then view the resulting special effect. Figure 9.5 shows the result of applying the Gaussian Blur filter.

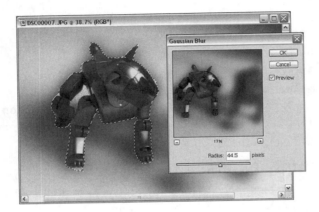

Yet one more way to apply a filter is to choose a filter command from the **Filter** menu. The **Filter** menu enables you to view each filter in its category. This can help you quickly navigate different groups of filters, although it won't give you any idea how any of these filters will change the image.

Introducing Blur Filters

The blur filters are helpful tools if you're trying to smooth rough areas of an image, reduce detail in an area of a picture, or hide information you don't want to share with your picture-viewing audience. The following list contains a brief description of each of the blur filters installed with Photoshop Elements:

- **Blur**—Smooths transitions between colors by averaging the color of the pixels beside hard edges of color, defined lines, or shaded areas.
- **Blur More**—Increases the degree of the blur by three or four times.
- **Gaussian**—In simple terms, this filter blurs an image by enabling you to customize the range of pixels affected by the blur. When the Blur filter is applied to an image, Photoshop Elements gives each pixel a weight value and applies a blur based on the average value of the pixels. This filter increases low-frequency detail combined with the adjustable settings you select in the filter settings window to create a hazy blur on the image.
- **Motion**—Blur an image from –360° to +360°. You can also adjust the intensity of the blur from 1 to 999. Try applying this filter to a moving object in a photo. This filter gives the illusion of motion.
- **Smart**—Enables you to create a specific kind of blur by setting the radius of the blur, quality, threshold, and difference between pixels.

- **Radial**—Creates a circular directional blur. Adjust the radius and number of pixels to be blurred with the Radial Blur settings. Create spin or zoom, or specify a degree of radial blur with the radial blur filter.

Introducing Filter Effects with Toolbox Tools

In addition to the **Filter** menu and the **Filters** and **Effects** palettes, you can apply a few filters as Toolbox tools. Being able to apply a filter as a tool enables you to focus on an area that might be difficult to select and then experiment with smudging, saturating, blurring, or sharpening it. Like menu or palette-based filters and effects, these Toolbox tools can be applied only if an image is in RGB or Grayscale color mode. The following list contains a brief description of the filter tools available in the Toolbox:

- **Smudge**—The Smudge Tool enables you to smear selected pixels in the direction of your brush stroke. You can customize the brush size, blending mode, pressure, and brush dynamics from the options bar. This tool can be applied across all layers of an image or to a single layer. Check the **Finger Painting** check box if you want to paint with the foreground color.

- **Sponge**—Choose desaturate or saturate blending mode, or a custom brush size, pressure, or brush dynamics for the tool from its options bar. Apply the Sponge Tool to adjust the saturation level of the pixels in an image.

- **Impressionist Brush**—This tool is co-located in the Toolbox with the Brush Tool (B). Select a brush size and adjust its settings in the options panel. Applying this brush to an image will enlarge, blur, and mix the pixels as you move the brush around.

- **Blur**—Apply the Blur filter to an image using a preset brush size chosen in the options bar. This is a great alternative if you don't want to use a selection tool combined with a filter command to change a small area of an image. You can adjust the brush size, blending mode, pressure, and brush dynamics from the options bar. Check the **Use All Layers** check box if you want to apply the Blur Tool across all layers of the active image window. Uncheck this check box if you want to apply it to the selected layer in the **Layers** palette.

- **Sharpen**—Choose this tool to intensify the colors wherever you apply this filter using a particular brush size chosen from the options bar. This is a handy tool if you're curious to see whether the Sharpen filter will have any impact on sharpening a slightly blurry area of an image. As with the Blur Tool, you can adjust the brush size, blending mode, pressure, affected layers, or brush dynamics from the options bar.

Variations with Blur Filters

Filters can subdue or bring out areas of an image. For example, if you're creating screen shots of your computer settings for a manual, you might want to blur some of your personal information from the captured images. If you're preparing a photo for publication, you might want to blur elements of the photo that might distract from the main subject. The example previously shown in Figure 9.3 and Figure 9.4 illustrated how the Gaussian Blur filter can highlight one element in a photo. The next example shows you how to selectively blur part of an image.

Using the Blur Filter to Emphasize Part of an Image

Choose one of the many selection tools available to select the area of the image you want to blur. In this example, I chose the Magnetic Lasso Tool to select the shoes on the right side of Figure 9.6.

tip

You can apply a selection tool by clicking and dragging the cursor in the image window. The selected area will appear with a flashing dashed line surrounding its border.

If you miss part of the image with the selection tool, hold down the Shift key and select the overlapping area using the same or a different selection tool. The original selection area will grow to include the overlapping selection area.

FIGURE 9.6
The before shot of the shoes.

Choose the **Blur More** filter from the **Filters** palette, or from the **Filter** menu. The selected area of the image should appear slightly blurry. The Blur More filter will then appear at the top of the Filter menu, as shown in Figure 9.7. Choose the filter once more if you want to make the selected area more blurry.

FIGURE 9.7

When a filter is applied to the image window, it appears at the top of the Filter menu.

You can apply more than one kind of Blur filter to the selected area to create blur special effects. The Gaussian, Motion (see Figure 9.8), and Radial filters enable you to create directional blurs, which can make the original image pattern unrecognizable. Blurring part of an image can hide sensitive information, such as a license number or password, without taking away too much from the bigger picture you want to share with your Web viewers or readers.

FIGURE 9.8

A motion blur applied to the selected area of the image makes the rest of the shoes in the picture stand out—no pun intended.

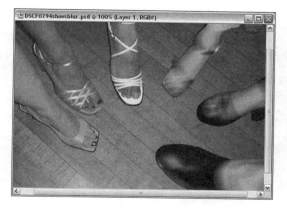

SHARPEN FILTERS

If you're impressed with the Blur filters, you might think the Sharpen filters can correct a blurry photo. Unfortunately, it's easier to blur an image than it is to sharpen it. The Sharpen filters interpret the pixels in an image and try to increase the amount of color based on the local neighborhood of pixels. Depending on how blurry the original image is, the Sharpen filters might not be able to improve the clarity of an image. They're actually more likely to make an image look flatter, or make the edge of something in the image look harder, rather than softer.

Polishing the Final Image with the Unsharp Mask

The Unsharp Mask filter is an unlikely but great tool for polishing an image before you save or print it. The Unsharp Mask filter looks for edge details in an image and makes the darker side of an edge darker, and the lighter side of an edge lighter. This filter can help sharpen an image as shown in the before and after shots in Figure 9.9.

FIGURE 9.9

The Unsharp Mask filter being applied to an image. The original image is on the left, and the motion-blurred, unsharp-masked image is on the right.

FIGURE 9.10

You can zoom out of the image in the filter dialog box to preview the full image or specific areas of the image before you apply a filter to it.

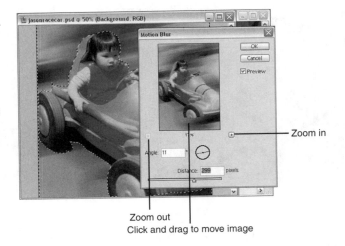

Zoom in

Zoom out
Click and drag to move image

Applying Artistic Filters

Although you'll find 15 groups of filters in the **Filter** menu, there are two general groups of filters: those that enhance (or degrade) an image, and those that apply some sort of effect, such as a brush stroke or stained-glass window effect. The blur and sharpen filters are image-enhancing filters. This section explores some of the more artsy filters.

Applying an Artistic Filter to a Selection

The artistic filters in Photoshop Elements enable you to apply fine-art or paint-related enhancements to all or part of an image. For example, you can apply the Dry Brush filter to change a photo into an image painted with a dry brush. Similarly, the watercolor artistic filter can help you visualize how an image might look if you painted it with watercolor paint. The Sketch and Brush Strokes filters can create paintlike filter effects similar to those in the Artistic group of filters.

You can apply an Artistic filter to an entire image or to a selected area of an image. If you choose a selected area, you can make part of an image stand out. For example, if a picture of flowers had one flower with the Colored Pencil filter applied to it, the colored-pencil flower would stand out from the others.

Conversely, you can apply a filter to everything except the selected item to make it stand out. First, use one of the selection tools to highlight an area of the image, such as the flower shown in Figure 9.11. You also can apply the **Select**, **Inverse** command to deselect the flower and select all the other pixels in the image. This command comes in handy when you want to apply the filter to everything in a picture except for a particular area of the image, or, as you'll discover in this chapter, when you want to apply more than one filter to different areas of an image. Figure 9.12 shows the same image after the Colored Pencil filter has been applied.

Applying the Accented Edges Filter

The Accented Edges filter is located in the **Brush Stroke** submenu of the **Filter** menu. This filter intensifies the edge colors in an image. You can increase the slider control, shown in Figure 9.13, to brighten the edge colors in the image to resemble white chalk. Lower Edge Brightness values darken the edge colors to resemble black ink.

FIGURE 9.11

The Inverse command enables you to exclude a particular part of an image so that you can apply a filter to only the selected portion or to everything but the selected portion.

FIGURE 9.12

The Colored Pencil filter is applied to all selected areas of the image window.

FIGURE 9.13

The Accented Edges filter softens the background images. You can adjust the settings before applying the filter to the selected areas of the image.

The Edge Width slider control enables you to determine how many pixels to use to define the edges in the image. This value is used with the Edge Brightness value to create the accented effect. Increasing the Smoothness value improves the smoothness of the color transitions between the original image and the accented edges. Click the **OK** button to apply the filter settings to the image. The resulting image is shown in Figure 9.14.

FIGURE 9.14

The realistic-looking flower stands out because the Accented Edges filter was applied to the rest of the flowers in this picture.

ARTISTIC FILTER VARIATIONS

You can see how filters interact with different kinds of images by applying different filters to the same image. Figure 9.15, for example, shows the previous picture of the irises with a Water Paper filter. The Water Paper filter belongs to the Sketch family of filters. It adds a pattern to the image so that the image appears to be printed on a wet, thick-fiber type of paper.

FIGURE 9.15

The Water Paper filter blends chunks of pixels together to create the illusion that the image is printed on wet, fibrous paper.

Applying the Conté Crayon Filter

The Conté Crayon filter creates a paper effect, as shown in Figure 9.16. Like the Water Paper filter, it is a Sketch filter. Conté Crayons consist of colors ranging from dark gray to bright white (black, sepia, and sanguine). The Conté Crayon filter takes the foreground color and uses it to create the darker areas of the image. The background color creates the light areas of the effect.

FIGURE 9.16

The Conté Crayon filter uses the foreground and background colors to create extreme dark and light crayon strokes.

Combining Filters in an Image

In a previous section of this chapter, you saw how the Inverse command could select everything except the pixels you want to preserve. This enables you to apply a filter to the area of the image that isn't the focal point. Figure 9.17 shows the ZigZag filter, one of the Distort filters, applied to the irises photo. Choose the **Inverse** command from the **Select** menu again to reselect the iris in the photo if you want to apply a different filter to it, such as the Plastic Wrap filter, also shown in Figure 9.17.

FIGURE 9.17

Two in one. The Plastic Wrap filter has been applied to the flower, and the ZigZag filter has been applied to the rest of the image.

Applying Halftone Filters

There are two halftone filters from which you can choose in Photoshop Elements: Color Halftone (choose **Filter**, **Pixelate**, **Color Halftone**) and Halftone Pattern (choose **Filter**, **Sketch**, **Halftone Pattern**). Both reduce the number of pixels in the image by breaking an image into rectangles and replacing each with a line, circle, or dot to simulate a halftone screen used in printing. The tonal range is preserved in the image, as shown in Figure 9.18, keeping the picture recognizable. However, a distinctive pattern is added to the image.

FIGURE 9.18

FIGURE 9.18

The Halftone Pattern filter reduces the resolution of an image without affecting the range of tones.

Exploring Effects

Effects can consist of adding a particular kind of gradient layer, or a combination of filters, to an image. Effect categories are Frames, Textures, Text Effects, and Image Effects. To apply these effects, the image must be in RGB or Grayscale mode and unlocked in the **Layers** palette. For some effects, a specific object must be in the image window, such as text for use with the Text Effects. Some other effects can require you to flatten all layers in an image so that the effect can be applied to all image elements.

Applying Effects

There are three ways you can apply effects to an image: double-click an effect, drag and drop one from the **Effects** palette into an image window, or click a thumbnail and then click the **Apply** button. Watch the progress bar at the bottom of the image window as the effect is applied to an image. Figure 9.19 shows the result of applying the Lizard Skin effect to an image.

Most of the Image Effects apply Artistic filters to an image. There might be one or two destructive effects, such as Blizzard and Fluorescent Chalk. However, most produce visually interesting effects, like the Soft Flat Color effect shown in Figure 9.20. Unlike with most filters, you cannot adjust settings for effects. If you like the preview image in the thumbnail, drag and drop the effect onto an image to see whether you like the resulting image.

FIGURE 9.19

Drag and drop the Lizard Skin thumbnail onto an image to apply this effect.

FIGURE 9.20

Another Image Effect, Soft Flat Color, makes this image look as if it were painted.

Applying Texture Effects

Most Texture Effects add a new layer to an image. When the effect is first applied, the new layer will cover the entire image window, blocking the background image. To combine the texture with a background image, you must decrease the opacity value for the texture effect layer. Select the texture effect from the Layers palette, and then type in a value less than 100, such as 60, in the Opacity text box. Figure 9.21 shows how the Sunset effect adds a gradient layer to the image. Notice that the texture effect is selected, and it has an Opacity setting of 56% in the Layers palette.

Applying Text Effects

Several effects can be applied only to text objects. The Water Reflection text effect appears on the text object in Figure 9.22. Before you can apply a text effect, you must first use the Horizontal or Vertical Type tool to add text to the image window.

You can use the Move Tool to select the text object from the image window or the Layers palette. Then, apply a text effect to the text object. Choose **Text Effects** from the **Effects** palette if you want to view only the text effects in the palette. A text effect changes only the text layer in the image window.

FIGURE 9.21

The Gradient Fill is a texture effect that adds a gradient fill layer to an image.

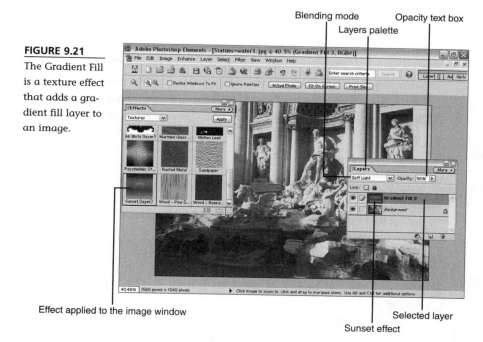

FIGURE 9.22

Apply a text effect to a text object. The Water Reflection text effect was applied to the Statue text in this image.

The Quadrant Color effect adds four big, light-colored squares to an image: red, green, blue, and brown. Figure 9.22 shows the Water Reflection text effect combined with the Quadrant Color effect. If you want to view the color image, visit Que Publishing's Web site at www.quepublishing.com.

Combining Effects

Several effects can be applied to individual image and text objects, or to the full image. You can apply a selection tool to part of an image to apply a Cut Out or Recessed Frame effect. Then, add a text object to the image. Select the text object, and choose an effect to customize the text in the image window. Texture effects enable you to blend a text layer with the rest of the image. A texture effect can help pull together different images and image effects by adding a common look to the picture. You can hide and show layers to create custom effects for images that have been copied or pasted into the image window. Then, flatten the layers together and apply one or more effects to the final image.

An original figure, as shown in Figure 9.23, can be changed into a picnic invitation, as shown in Figure 9.24. Some effects like the Recessed Frame effect can be applied only to a selected area of an image. Use one of the selection tools on an image layer before choosing this type of effect. Another kind of effect requires a text object to be created and selected before you can apply a text effect. For example, I had to type some text in order to apply the Sprayed Stencil text effect. Other effects, such as the Rusted Metal effect, add a new layer to the image. In this example, after the effect was created, the opacity level was set to 42 and the Linear Dodge blending mode was applied to the Rusted Metal effect layer.

FIGURE 9.23

The original image before any effects are applied to it.

FIGURE 9.24

The same image after the Recessed Frame, Sprayed Stencil, and Rusted Metal effects have been applied.

10

WORKING WITH LAYERS AND LAYER STYLES

Layers are a part of every document created by Photoshop Elements. For example, when you open an image file, the image is placed in the background layer of a document. A new layer is created whenever an image is pasted into the image window. You can also add fill and adjustment layers to correct colors in some or all layers in the document. Select, add, or remove layers from the Layers palette. The full capabilities of layers run deep and wide.

Layer styles enable you to customize the contents of a layer. You can add one or several layer styles, such as a drop shadow, bevel, or glow, to a layer that contains an image, text, or a graphic. You'll find eight groups of layer styles at your disposal in the Layer Styles palette.

Introducing the Layers Palette

If you're working with a photo, the first layer you'll see in the **Layers** palette is the Background layer. As you add shapes, add text, or copy and paste in the image window, new layers are added above the Background layer. Layers can be empty or can contain specific elements, such as an adjustment or fill layer. A layer can consist of text, vector graphic (shape), or bitmap (image, text, or graphic).

You can create, copy, move, or delete a layer in the **Layers** palette. Add fill or adjustment layers and position these layers to apply them to all or some of the other layers. The image window updates automatically as you make changes to the Layers palette.

Using layers makes it quick and easy to make changes or improvements to an image or text without affecting any other layers. Adding layers to an image window is like creating a stack of transparent pages, each with different colors, shapes, graphics, text, or effects. If at any point you don't want to use a particular layer, you can remove, change, or hide it without affecting any other layers in the image.

Layers also enable you to apply isolated changes to an image, such as image repair and color correction, without touching the original. You can make different corrections on various layers and hide and show them one at a time to see which combination provides the desired result. As you work on an image, or are ready to finalize it, you can merge the layers, thereby converting any text or vector graphics into bitmap graphics.

Each layer has a unique group of settings. By default, each layer has a blending mode, opacity, lock, and lock transparency setting. Select the **Layers** palette from the palette well in the work area to view any layers corresponding to the active image window. Click in the left column next to the layer to show or hide the contents of that layer in the image window. You can click on a layer in the **Layers** palette to select the contents of that layer.

Three shortcut buttons are located at the bottom of the **Layers** palette. These small buttons enable you to add a new fill or adjustment layer, create a new empty or duplicate layer, or delete the selected layer. You can drag a layer over the **Create a New Layer** button to create a copy of that layer. Drag and drop a layer over the Trash button to delete it.

If all this information about layers seems a bit overwhelming, it might be easier to understand all the possible kinds of layers by taking a peek at a file that's already chock-full of them. Figure 10.1 deconstructs each item in the Layers palette.

Each layer acts as a separate, transparent sheet, enabling you to combine images into the image window while keeping them separate. The order of layers in the Layers palette matches the order in which each layer is applied to the image window. The topmost layer affects all layers below it. You can click and drag a layer and place it above another layer in the Layers palette to make a layer visible in the image window. Move the selected layer below another if you want to exclude any fill or adjustment settings from affecting the layers above it. Conversely, you can move a layer below another if you want the layer above it to be the more visible layer.

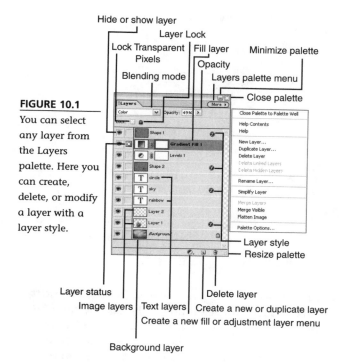

FIGURE 10.1

You can select any layer from the Layers palette. Here you can create, delete, or modify a layer with a layer style.

You can choose from any of the commands in the **Layer**, **Arrange** menu. The **Arrange** menu consists of the following commands:

- **Bring to Front**—Moves the layer to the top of the Layers palette.
- **Bring Forward**—Moves a layer up in the list of layers in the Layers palette.
- **Send Backward**—Moves a layer down in the list of layers in the Layers palette.
- **Send to Back**—Moves a layer to the bottom of the list, right above the background layer.

Click, drag and drop a layer to move it to a new location in the **Layers** palette. You can press (**Command**) [**Ctrl**] plus the left or right bracket ([]) to move a layer up or down a notch in the Layers palette. Press (**Command-Shift**) [**Ctrl+Shift**] plus the left or right bracket to bring a layer to the back or front of the image window. The background layer is locked at the bottom of the **Layers** palette (see Figure 10.2). Double-click the Background layer to convert it into a regular layer.

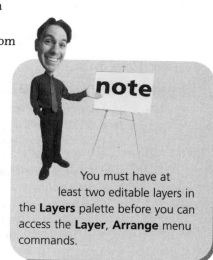

note

You must have at least two editable layers in the **Layers** palette before you can access the **Layer**, **Arrange** menu commands.

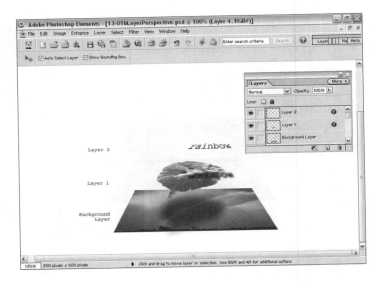

You can add layers to the active image window in several ways. You can choose the **New** command from the **Layer**, **New** menu, or select one of the **Layer**, **New Fill Layer**, or **Layer**, **New Adjustment Layer** menu commands. You can also copy and paste part of an image from any image window. Choose a selection tool from the Toolbox and select part of the background image. Then, use the **Copy** and **Paste** commands to add the selected image to a new layer in the Layers palette.

Create a new, empty layer if you want to add text or graphics to the image window. Click on the **Create a New Layer** button located at the bottom of the **Layers** palette to create a new, empty layer. You then can use a shape or brush tool to create an object in the new layer or copy and paste a selection from another layer. You can drag and drop a layer over the **Create a New Layer** button to duplicate the contents of a layer into a new layer. Click on the **Create a New Fill** or **Adjustment Layer** button in the **Layers** palette to quickly add a new fill, gradient, or pattern layer, as well as any of the adjustment layers.

Layers Palette Menu Options

Several menu commands can be accessed from the Layers palette menu. You can select this menu if the **Layers** palette is located in the palette well by clicking the right-arrow icon located immediately to the right of the palette tab. If the palette is open in the work area, click the right-arrow button located in the top-right corner of the **Layers** palette. The following list describes each menu item in the **Layers** palette menu:

■ **Help Contents/Help**—Choose Help Contents or Help to open a new browser window that shows the Photoshop Elements Help pages. Navigate the help content, find information in the index, or search for a help topic.

- **New Layer**—Select this command to create a new layer in the Layers palette.

- **Duplicate Layer**—Duplicate a layer that contains a bitmap or vector graphic object, such as images, text, or shapes.

- **Delete Layer**—Remove a layer from the Layers palette.

- **Delete Linked Layers**—Remove all layers containing a link from the Layers palette.

- **Delete Hidden Layers**—Remove all hidden layers from the Layers palette.

- **Rename Layer**—Select an editable layer to choose this menu item from the menu. The Layer Properties dialog box opens. Type a new name for the layer into the text box, and then click **OK** to save the new name to the Layers palette.

- **Simplify Layer**—Choose a shape tool from the Toolbox and add a shape to the image window. Select the shape layer from the Layers palette, and then choose **Simplify Layer** from the menu to combine the shape object with its linked color. The two thumbnails will merge into a single thumbnail image, and the vector shape will become a bitmap. You can apply the Paint Bucket Tool to the simplified shape if you want to change its color.

- **Merge Down**—Click on one of the middle layers in the **Layers** palette. Choose the **Merge Down** command to combine the selected layer with the one directly below it. Any layers above the selected layer will remain in the **Layers** palette.

- **Merge Visible**—Click on the left box for each layer to show or hide the layers you want to merge. Choose the **Merge Visible** command to merge all visible layers in the **Layers** palette. Hidden layers will not be merged and will remain in the **Layers** palette after the visible layers have been merged.

- **Flatten Image**—Select the **Flatten Image** command to merge all visible layers into a single layer in the **Layers** palette. Hidden layers will be permanently removed from the **Layers** palette.

- **Palette Options**—Choose **Palette Options** from the menu to open the Layers

note

You can lock all settings in a layer by checking the Lock check box for the selected layer in the **Layers** palette. Check the **Transparency Lock** check box if you do not want any pixels added to the transparent areas of an image. A lock icon will appear to the right of the layer name if either lock is applied to a layer. Uncheck the **Lock** check box to unlock a layer. Double-click the background layer to convert it to an editable layer.

Palette Options dialog box. You can select from three thumbnail image sizes, or click on the **None** radio button if you don't want to see a thumbnail image in each layer. Click **OK** to save your changes.

- **Close Palette to Palette Well**—If this menu option is not checked, when closed, the **Layers** palette will not appear in the palette well. Almost all the commands accessible from the **Layers** palette are also available in the **Layer** menu.

Introducing Blending Modes

A blending mode enables you to mix the color of the selected layer with the colors of the images in the layer directly below it. You might want to apply a blending mode to a layer if you want its colors to blend in with the colors or content in the layer below it. Choose one of 17 blending modes for any layer. Normal is the default blending mode for any newly created layer. The following list briefly defines each blending mode used in RGB images. The selected layer refers to the base, or original colors, whereas the term *blending color* refers to the colors in the layer directly below the selected layer. Blending and base colors are required in order to create the resulting color produced by choosing a particular blending mode.

- **Normal**—No blending is applied to pixels in this default mode. Colors are represented as-is. Referred to as Threshold mode if you're working with a bitmap or Indexed Color image.

- **Dissolve**—Pixel colors are randomly replaced with the base or blend color, using the opacity of any pixel in the image to set the color of the dissolved pixels. Try this blending mode with layers containing large Airbrush or Brush stroke graphics.

- **Darken**—Picks the darker of the base or blend color after checking each channel and replaces pixels lighter than the blend color.

- **Multiply**—Multiplies the base color of each channel with the blend color. The result is similar to applying overlapping strokes of a felt tip pen, which darkens the original color.

- **Color Burn**—Darkens the base color after checking each channel of the RGB image and reflects the blend color. Blending with white produces no change.

- **Linear Burn**—Darkens the base color, decreasing the brightness to reflect the blend color.

- **Lighten**—Chooses the lighter of the base or blend color after checking each channel color and replaces pixels that are darker than the blend color.

- **Screen**—Multiplies the opposite of the blend and base colors to create the resulting color, which is usually lighter than either of the original colors.

- **Color Dodge**—Lightens the base color after checking each channel in the RGB image and reflects the blend color. Blending with black produces no change.

- **Linear Dodge**—Lightens the base color and increases the brightness to reflect the blend color.

- **Overlay**—Preserves the lightness or darkness of the base color and multiplies or screens it before mixing it with the blend color.

- **Soft Light**—Darkens or lightens the base color depending on whether the blend color is lighter or darker than 50% gray. The result is lightened, which is similar to applying the Dodge Tool, if the blend color is lighter than 50%, or darkened, which is similar to using the Burn Tool, if it's 50% darker than the blend pixels.

- **Hard Light**—Screens or multiplies the base color depending on whether the blend color is lighter or darker than 50% gray. If the blend color is lighter than 50%, the result is a lighter color. Otherwise, the result is darker if the blend color is also darker than 50%. The resulting effect, if darkened, adds shadows to an image.

- **Vivid Light**—Increases or decreases contrast in order to lighten (dodge) or darken (burn) colors if the blend color is lighter or darker than 50% gray.

- **Linear Light**—Increases or decreases the brightness to lighten or darken colors based on whether the blend color is lighter or darker than 50% gray.

- **Pin Light**—Takes the blend color and determines whether to replace colors based on whether the blend color is lighter or darker than 50% gray. Darker pixels are replaced if the blend color is lighter than 50% gray. Lighter pixels are replaced if the blend color is darker than 50% gray.

- **Difference**—Subtracts the blend from the base color if the base color is darker than the blend color. The brighter of the two colors is subtracted from the other. Blending with black produces no change, whereas blending with white inverts the base color values.

- **Exclusion**—A lower-contrast color (compared to the preceding Difference blending mode) is created. This blending mode adds the blend or base color depending on the brightness values of the colors in each RGB channel.

- **Hue**—Combines the saturation and luminance of the base color and the hue of the blend color to produce the resulting color.

- **Saturation**—Combines the hue and luminance of the base color with the saturation of the blend color to produce the resulting color. The blend color must contain gray to produce a different color.

- **Color**—Mixes the luminance of the base color with the hue and saturation of the blend color to produce the resulting color. Can be used to colorize grayscale images or add tinted color to images.

- **Luminosity**—Creates a resulting color by mixing the hue and saturation of the base color with the luminance of the blend color, creating the opposite effect of the Color blending mode.

You can also simplify and combine layers as you complete all or part of an image. The Simplify Layer command enables you to combine linked components of a layer. You might apply this command to a fill or adjustment layer as you finalize each layer setting for an image.

When you create a fill or adjustment layer, a multi-part layer is created in the Layers palette. The linked color and shape elements enable you to easily change the color of the fill layer, or unlink the shape from the fill component. Choose the **Simplify Layer** command from the **Layer** menu if you want to merge the parts into a single bitmap layer. You will no longer be able to modify the fill or adjustment layer after it has been simplified.

CONVERT THE BACKGROUND LAYER INTO LAYER 0

If you want to modify or move the background layer up in the **Layers** palette, you can change it to a nonlocked, regular layer. Double-click on the background layer to open the Layer Properties dialog box. If you want to, you can type a new name for the layer. Photoshop Elements changes its name from the background layer to layer 0.

The background layer is a locked layer, but layer 0 is not locked and is fully editable just like any other layer in the Layers palette.

Modifying a Layer with Layer Styles

Pump up the content in a layer by applying one or more layer styles to it. Layer styles enable you to quickly add one or several effects to a layer that contains text or graphics. Choose from eight installed groups of layer styles. Each layer style modifies any previous layer styles applied to the selected image layer. The order in which you apply a series of layer styles affects the final look of the layer contents. Several layer style settings were used to create the yellow button shown in Figure 10.3:

- **Wow-Neon Yellow Off**—Drop Shadow is zero.
- **Simple Inner Bevel**—Bevel Size is 18 pixels. Bevel Direction is Up.
- **Simple Outer Glow**—Outer Glow size is 104 pixels.
- **Simple Inner Glow**—Inner Glow Size is 216 pixels.
- **Use Global Light**—Unchecked.

You can view and choose layer styles from the **Layer Styles** palette. As with the **Filters** and **Effects** palettes, you can preview thumbnail images of each layer style in the Layer Styles palette. Open the **Layer Styles** palette, select a set of styles from the drop-down menu, and click any one to add a drop shadow or a bevel layer style to a shape or image object in the active image window. You can add as many layer styles to a layer as you like. The following list briefly describes each set available in the Layer Styles palette:

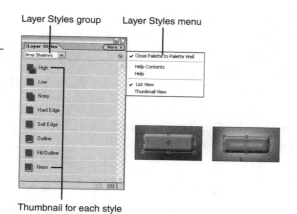

FIGURE 10.3

Preview a set of layer styles in the Layer Styles palette. Compare the gray button before and after a combination of layer styles with custom settings is applied to it.

■ **Bevels**—Adds a three-dimensional edge to the borders of text or a graphic. Great for creating Web graphics buttons.

■ **Drop Shadows**—Creates a drop shadow below the text or graphic object.

■ **Inner Glows**—Adds a custom pattern to the inside of the selected graphic object.

■ **Inner Shadows**—Applies a shadow effect inside the borders of the selected object.

■ **Outer Glows**—Creates a colored border effect around the selected object.

■ **Visibility**—Shows, hides, or creates a ghosting effect with a graphic object.

■ **Complex**—Adds a combined texture and color pattern to a graphic object. Choose layer styles with names such as Rainbow, Rivet, Star Glow, and Woodgrain.

■ **Glass Buttons**—Changes the selected object in a layer into a colored glass button shape.

■ **Image Effects**—Choose from 13 image effects, such as Circular Vignette, Color Burn, Color Fade Horizontal, Color Fade Vertical, Colorful Center, Fog, Night Vision, Puzzle, Rain, Snow, Sun Faded Photo, Tile Mosaic, and Water Reflection.

■ **Patterns**—Twenty-six Layer Style patterns come pre-installed with Photoshop Elements 2. Add a Dry Mud, Blanket, Brushed Metal, Abstract Fire, Diamond Plate, Stucco, Manhole, Denim, or Brick Wall pattern to a photo, graphic, or text.

■ **Photographic Effects**—Turn a photo into a negative, give it a beveled edge, or add a blue, red, gray, teal, or other-color tone with a single click.

■ **Wow Chrome**—Add one of nine cool chrome layer styles.

■ **Wow Neon**—Choose from three styles of red, orange, blue, purple, green, and yellow neon colors and of course, black.

■ **Wow Plastic**—Adds a cool plastic look to shapes and bitmaps.

Be sure you have more than one layer of images to work with in the image window. If this is your first time experimenting with layer styles, you might want to use the shape tools in the Toolbox to create a few graphic objects in an empty, new document window so that you can more easily see each layer style as you apply it to an object. You also might want to select a light foreground color for the graphic object. Black, for example, might make it difficult for you to see a bevel style that's been added to an object. To apply the layer style to your image, do the following:

1. Choose the Move Tool from the Toolbox. Click on the object you want the style applied to. You also can hold down the Shift key and click on several objects if you want to select a group of objects.

2. Choose a set of layer styles from the Layer Styles palette pop-up menu.

3. Click on the desired layer style to apply it to the selection in the image window. You also can drag and drop the layer style onto the image window. You will see an f icon appear in the selected layer if a layer style has been applied to it.

4. Apply additional layer styles as needed to get the desired result. Each additional style modifies any previous styles.

In addition to applying layer styles to your selections, most of the style sets have certain settings you can fine-tune to get exactly the effect you want. Double-click on the f icon in a layer that contains a layer style to open the Style Settings dialog box, shown in Figure 10.4. You also can choose Style Settings from the Layer, Layer Style menu. Each of the slider control settings becomes active if a layer style from the corresponding layer style group is applied to a layer.

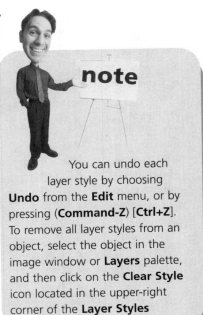

note

You can undo each layer style by choosing **Undo** from the **Edit** menu, or by pressing (**Command-Z**) [**Ctrl+Z**]. To remove all layer styles from an object, select the object in the image window or **Layers** palette, and then click on the **Clear Style** icon located in the upper-right corner of the **Layer Styles**

tip

You can adjust some of the layer style options from the Style Settings dialog box. Double-click the f icon located on the right side of a layer in the **Layers** palette to open the Style Settings dialog box.

If you applied a drop shadow, bevel, or glow layer style to an object, the corresponding slider control(s) will be selectable in the Style Settings dialog box.

FIGURE 10.4

Customize layer styles by changing settings in the Style Settings dialog box.

Renaming a Layer

As you add objects and create new layers, it's helpful to rename each one so that you can quickly hide, show, or select a layer as you need to work on it. In the Layers palette shown in Figure 10.5, you can see how easy it is to identify layers with custom names versus layers with generic names. Double-click on the name of a layer in the **Layers** palette to open the Layer Properties dialog box. Type a name for the layer into the Name text box. Then click on the **OK** button to view the newly named layer in the **Layers** palette.

FIGURE 10.5

Type a name for a layer in the Layer Properties dialog box.

Introducing Fill Layers

Adjustment and fill layers are yet two more kinds of layers you can add to a document. You can use solid, gradient, or pattern fill layers to correct colors, or enhance a graphic design. You can add a fill layer to an image to apply a color tint or color correction to any layer located directly below it in the **Layers** palette. This section shows you how to add a solid color fill layer to a selected area of an image.

If you want to make a blue sky bluer, you can apply the Magic Wand Tool to select a color in the image window. Then add a blue, solid color fill layer to it. Adjust the opacity level of the fill layer to adjust the blue color of the sky. Figure 10.6 shows the blue sky in a picture surrounded by a selection marquee, which was created by the Magic Wand Tool. If the sky consists of more than one shade of blue, you can hold down the Shift key to add other colors to the selected area. The solid color fill layer can be applied to a selected area or to the entire contents of the image window.

Adding a Solid Color Fill Layer

One way to enhance the color of the sky is to add a solid color fill layer to the picture. The following steps show you how:

1. Choose **Solid Color** from the **Layer**, **New Fill Layer** menu. The New Layer dialog box will open.

2. Type in a name for the fill layer and choose any custom settings you want to
   use (see Figure 10.7). Then click **OK**.

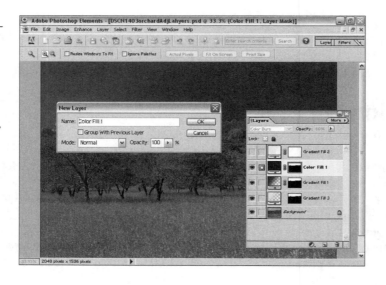

3. Next, the Color Picker dialog box will open. Pick a color for the fill layer.
   Then click **OK**.

A new fill layer will appear in the **Layers** palette. The contents of the image window will also change to show the color of the fill layer you just selected (see Figure
10.8). Reduce the opacity setting for the solid color fill layer to blend the fill layer
color with the layers located directly below it in the Layers palette.

Click on the fill layer in the **Layers** palette. Then click on the Opacity slider control
and decrease the value in the text box. As the fill layer becomes transparent, you'll
be able to see the graphics in the layers below the selected fill layer.

FIGURE 10.8

Adjust the opacity value for the solid color fill layer to blend the blue color of the fill layer with the other layers in the image. The solid color fill layer added a nighttime look to this daytime shot.

Fill Layer   Adjusted Color

Selected Area

Gradient Fill Layers

A gradient fill layer can be added to an image to create a controlled, but general, directional lighting effect, or a general background pattern. A gradient consists of at least two colors and is a gradation of tones changing from one color to the next. A gradient can add depth to an image. If applied correctly, it can imply a light source for other objects, or enhance a graphic composition.

A gradient fill layer consists of two linked components: the layer thumbnail and the layer mask thumbnail. Choose **Gradient** from the **Layer**, **New Fill Layer** menu to add a gradient fill layer to the **Layers** palette. Type a name for the gradient fill layer, and then click **OK**. The Gradient Fill dialog box opens. Click on the **Gradient** drop-down menu to choose the colors for the gradient. Select one of five kinds of gradients in the **Style** drop-down menu in the Gradient Fill dialog box, shown in Figure 10.9. Then, click **OK** to add the new gradient fill layer to the **Layers** palette.

Double-click the gradient fill layer to open the Gradient Fill dialog box. You can modify the gradient fill without affecting any of the pixels in the other layers in the image. Click and drag the radius in the circle graphic in the Angle area of the Gradient Fill dialog box if you want to change the angle of the gradient. You also can type an angle value into the Angle text box.

You can reverse the direction of the gradient by checking the **Reverse** check box. Select the **Dither** check box if you want to reduce color banding in the gradient. Check the **Align with Layer** check box if you want the gradient fill layer to align the gradient component with the graphic object in the gradient fill layer.

FIGURE 10.9

You can customize the gradient colors, style, angle, or scale from the Gradient Fill dialog box.

The following list briefly describes the five gradient styles you can choose from:

■ **Linear**—Creates a horizontal gradient from left to right in the image window.

■ **Radial**—Draws the gradient outward from the center of the selected area.

■ **Angle**—Applies a gradient at an angle in the selected area of the image.

■ **Reflected**—Adds a horizontal bar in the image window, and draws the gradient upward and downward in the image window.

■ **Diamond**—Creates a diamond out of one gradient color, and fades outward in all directions to the next color.

Modifying a Gradient

Click on the **Gradient** field in the Gradient Fill dialog box to open the Gradient Editor dialog box. Each square located in the Presets area of the dialog box represents a gradient you can choose. Click on a gradient square to select the colors for the gradient fill layer. Select a different group of gradients by clicking on the arrow pop-up menu. Each of the items at the bottom of the menu represents a group of gradients. Choose a custom group of gradients, such as Color Harmonies 1, Color Harmonies 2, Metals, Noise Samples, Pastels, Simple, Special Effects, and Spectrum. Choose **Reset Gradients** to show the original gradients' presets.

note

You can add more than one solid color, gradient, or pattern layer if you want to hide or show different effects and preview different combinations of colors without modifying the original image (see Figure 10.11). You can move each fill layer above or below other layers to change the color of specific layers, or preserve the colors of other layers. Try choosing a blending mode for a fill layer to experiment with different color effects between two layers.

Type a name for the gradient into the Name text box. Click on the **New** button to add the gradient settings to the Preset area of the Gradient Editor dialog box. Choose either **Solid** or **Noise** from the **Gradient Type** drop-down menu. Choose a percentage value from the **Smoothness** drop-down menu; a lower value produces a coarser blend of gradient colors.

The selected gradient's colors appear at the bottom of the Gradient Editor dialog box (see Figure 10.10). Click below the gradient bar to add a new color to the gradient. Click and drag the color slider control to customize each color in the gradient. Click in the **Color** box to choose a different color for the gradient. Click on the arrow on the right side of the **Color** box to access the **Color** drop-down menu, and select the **Foreground**, **Background**, or **User Color**. Click on one of the square controls located above the gradient bar, and customize the Opacity setting for that location of the gradient. Move the square along the gradient bar to change the location of that part of the gradient, or type a different percentage value into the **Location** text box. Move the diamond-shaped control in the center of the gradient bar to customize the Color Midpoint of the gradient. Click **OK** to save your changes and return to the Gradient Fill dialog box.

FIGURE 10.10

Pick a different gradient or customize your gradient colors in the Gradient Editor dialog box.

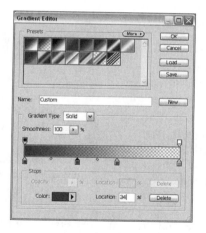

Pattern Fill Layers

You can create an adjustment fill layer that contains a pattern, too. Choose **Patterns** from the **Layer**, **New Fill Layer** menu. Type a name for the pattern fill layer, and then click **OK**. The Pattern Fill dialog box appears. Here you can choose a pattern from the Pattern drop-down menu. You can adjust the scale of the pattern file by choosing a percentage from the Scale drop-down list. You can choose from two groups of patterns.

Check the **Link with Layer** check box if you want the pattern to move along with the fill layer. Press the **Snap to Origin** button if you want to set the position of the pattern to match the grid or ruler settings for the image window. Finally, you can save your pattern settings by clicking on the New Document icon (white rectangle icon). Click on the **OK** button to add the pattern fill layer to the active image window.

FIGURE 10.11

Add more than one gradient fill layer to experiment with color changes in the image window. Modify a fill layer by removing the link between the fill and graphic components in a layer.

Introducing Adjustment Layers

Adjustment layers are similar to fill layers in that both create modifiable layers in the Layers palette. Adjustment layers enable you to customize Levels, Brightness/Contrast, Hue/Saturation, Gradient Map, Invert, Threshold, or Posterize effects with an image in RGB mode without sacrificing any of the original pixels in the image window.

If you plan to combine two images with disparate lighting, you can use adjustment layers to correct the color difference between the two images instead of using the same tonal range tools available in the Enhance menu. The tonal range tools permanently remove or remap the pixels of the original image. Using an adjustment layer enables you to experiment with tonal and color corrections without having to worry about degrading the quality of the image. Figure 10.12 shows a sample base image to which to apply adjustment layers. Figure 10.13 shows the secondary image, selected with the Magnetic Lasso Tool before it is placed into Figure 10.12.

tip

You can convert a photo, graphic, or text into a pattern. Open and resize the image and make it the active image window. Chose **Define Pattern** from the **Edit** menu. The Pattern Name dialog box will open. Type a name for your pattern, and click **OK**. Open another image window and add choose **Pattern** from the **Layer**, **New Fill Layer** menu. Choose your custom pattern from the drop-down menu in the Pattern Fill dialog box. Your pattern will appear in the image window.

The selected image in Figure 10.13 was copied to the Clipboard and then pasted into the background image shown in Figure 10.12. The pasted image appears in its own new layer in the **Layers** palette. You can click and drag the corner handles of the pasted image to scale it to fit with the background image. Choose the Move Tool from the Toolbox and place the pasted image in the image window.

FIGURE 10.12

Open an image file that needs tonal range corrections.

FIGURE 10.13

Select and copy the second image you want to combine with the first image. The Magnetic Lasso Tool marquee surrounds the selection. The bounding box appears if you select the marquee object with the Move Tool.

Making Changes with a Levels Adjustment Layer

For this example, the image needs help with a level adjustment to correct the tonal ranges and to bring out the detail in the image. Choose the **Levels** command from the **Layer**, **New Adjustment Layer** menu. The Levels dialog box shown in Figure 10.14 will open. Click and drag the slider controls to adjust the highlight, midtones, and shadow settings for the RGB image. Then preview the changes in the image window. Like any other layer, an adjustment layer will affect only the layers below it in the Layers palette. If you want an adjustment layer to affect all layers in the image, move the adjustment layer to the top of the Layers palette. Similarly, you can exclude layers from the adjustment layer by moving them up, positioned above the adjustment layer.

FIGURE 10.14

Adjust the tonal range in the Levels adjustment layer dialog box.

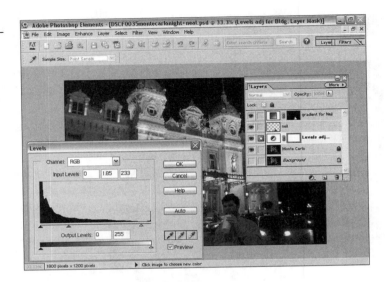

Each of the adjustment layer commands works exactly the same way as the matching menu commands located in the **Enhance** menu. Creating an adjustment layer brings the flexibility of being able to modify any of these settings before changing the original image. You can also click in the left column in the **Layers** palette to show or hide each of the adjustment layers. Compare different tonal range tools and pick the best combination of settings to create the best-looking image. The following list briefly describes each of the adjustment layer commands.

- **Levels**—View and change the tonal distribution of pixels in an image.
- **Brightness/Contrast**—Increase or decrease the highlights and shadows in an image by adjusting the brightness or contrast settings.
- **Hue/Saturation**—Add or decrease the intensity of color, the gray level in a color, or the intensity of light in an image.
- **Gradient Map**—Apply a grayscale gradient layer to the image window.
- **Invert**—Convert colors into their opposite values, for example, purple would be converted to green, and black to white.
- **Threshold**—Choose the black and white midpoints for an image. This command enables you to compare the midpoint results with the Levels adjustment layer. The Threshold commands enable you to adjust the threshold level for changing a color or grayscale image into a bitmap.
- **Posterize**—Reduce the number of colors by selecting the number of posterize levels in an image.

Blending Composites

When you copy an image and paste it into any other image window in the work area, one of the first things you might notice are the differences between the colors of the two images. You can use the Move Tool to adjust the scale and location of the composite image. However, because each image can have unique color and light characteristics, it would be difficult to apply a levels or color correction command to change both images at the same time. Fortunately, you can add a fill or adjustment layer to correct any subtle color differences between the two images.

When an image is pasted into an image window, Photoshop Elements creates a transparent layer containing the pasted or composite image. You can ignore the transparent areas in the image layer by holding down the (**Command**) [**Ctrl**] key while selecting the layer. The image will be surrounded by a selection marquee.

tip

Most of the adjustment layers can quickly be modified if you double-click on the adjustment layer from the **Layers** palette. You can also click on a layer and then choose the **Layer Content Options** command from the **Layer** menu to modify an adjustment layer.

Alternatively, you can select the layer and click on the Transparency Lock icon to prevent any of the transparent areas from being modified in that image layer.

Now, if you add a new fill or adjustment layer, it will be applied only to the selected area in the image window. Figure 10.15 shows the before and after image of adding a gradient fill layer to the secondary image. The gradient fill layer contains a few of the colors in the background image. In this particular example, the pasted image was taken under fluorescent light.

FIGURE 10.15

Select the object in a graphic layer by holding down the (**Command**) [**Ctrl**] key and clicking on the layer. Then choose the fill or adjustment layer you want to apply to the selected layer.

Adding the gradient fill layer, and reducing the opacity level of the gradient, enables the image to share some of the same colors of the background image, creating a very subtle color blending effect in the composite image. Figure 10.16 shows final blending mode and opacity settings for the gradient fill layer.

FIGURE 10.16
Adjust the opacity value for a gradient layer to match the colors between two images.

Correcting Images with Layers

You can use layers to temporarily store pixels as you correct an image. Figure 10.17 shows the before image that has several small dust and speck marks that need to be removed. If you look closely at the left and bottom areas of the image, you should see many small black specks. In this example, an empty layer is created to store corrections to the background layer.

FIGURE 10.17
The Clone Stamp Tool is used to sample the image across layers.

To apply the Clone Stamp Tool to an image, do the following:

1. Hold down the (**Option**) [**Alt**] key and drag the Clone Stamp Tool in the image window to capture the location where you want to sample pixels. Release the (**Option**) [**Alt**] key.

2. Click and drag the Clone Stamp Tool in the area where you want to apply the sampled pixels to the image.

   A circle will appear in the image window indicating the location of the pixels being replaced. A circle icon will appear over the area of pixels being sampled, as shown in Figure 10.18. The size of the circle will match the brush size selected for the Clone Stamp Tool in the options bar.

3. Click on the correction layer in the **Layers** palette. Sample and apply the Clone Stamp Tool in small areas of the image window until the dust and specks are cleared away from the image window as shown in Figure 10.19.

FIGURE 10.18

Zoom into the image and apply the Clone Stamp Tool to remove dirt or dust from the photo.

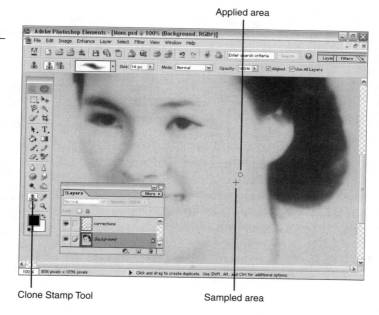

Applied area

Clone Stamp Tool   Sampled area

FIGURE 10.19

Choose the Overlay blending mode to preview your corrections over the original photo.

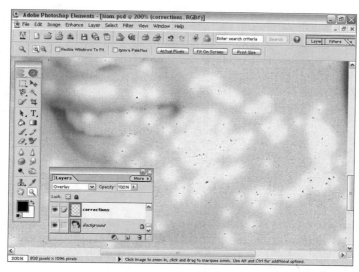

Although the **Layers** palette offers great image editing flexibility with fill and adjustment layers, try to work with the highest resolution possible to get the best results. If the image was scanned, you might want to consider rescanning the image at a higher resolution to capture more detail, or to work with a different image that has better tonal range, color, and detail.

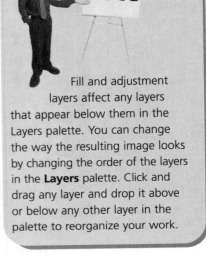

Merging Layers

As you make the final changes to each layer in the image window, you will want to simplify an image by merging some layers. Simplifying an image will not only reduce the size of the file, but also permanently merge two or more layers of images into one. Click on the eye icon to hide a layer you don't want to merge, or click to show a layer. Then choose the **Merge Visible** command, shown in Figure 10.20, to turn any visible layers into a single layer. Choose the **Merge Down** command from the **Layer** menu or **Layers** palette menu to merge the selected layer with the layer located directly below it.

> **note**
>
> Fill and adjustment layers affect any layers that appear below them in the Layers palette. You can change the way the resulting image looks by changing the order of the layers in the **Layers** palette. Click and drag any layer and drop it above or below any other layer in the palette to reorganize your work.

FIGURE 10.20

Use the Merge Visible command to flatten layers you want to finalize.

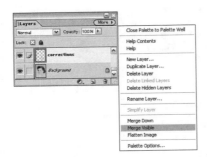

Flattening Layers

The **Flatten Layers** command combines all visible layers in an image into a single layer. Any hidden layers are permanently discarded. The before and after images are shown in Figure 10.21. If you've created an image file with multiple layers, you can preserve layers by saving the file as a PSD, the native Photoshop Elements file format. However, if you want to save the file in any other file format, such as JPEG, GIF, or PNG, you must first flatten all layers before you can save the image.

FIGURE 10.21

The **Flatten Layers** command merges all visible layers into a single layer.

REMOVING HIDDEN LAYERS

Click on the left column beside one of the layers in the **Layers** palette. The eye icon appears, indicating that the layer is visible. Its blending mode, lock check boxes, and opacity fields become selectable. You should be able to see the contents of the image layer in the image window.

Click in the box once more. The eye icon disappears, and the blending mode, opacity field, and lock layer settings are deselected.

Choose **Merge Layers**. All visible layers will be merged into a single layer. If any layers are hidden in the **Layers** palette, they will be permanently discarded from the image file when the **Flatten Layers** command is executed.

If you accidentally select this command before closing the image window, you can choose **Undo** from the **Edit** menu to restore any layers. Alternatively, you can open the **History** palette and click on a previous state to revert the document and show any layers you want to preserve.

tip

To preserve a layer in a file, hide a layer in the **Layers** palette, and then choose the **Merge Visible** command from the **Layer** menu. Only images appearing in the image window will be combined into a single layer. You can use the **Hide Layer** command to preserve changes you're not quite ready to save along with the rest of the image.

11

Adding Text and Shapes to Images

To most people, the terms *photos*, *images*, and *graphics* seem synonymous. However, some people use the term *graphics* to refer to text or hand-drawn vector or bitmap graphics. Photos created with a camera or scanner are considered images, not graphics. Whatever term you might prefer, Photoshop Elements enables you to create, edit, and delete graphics, images, and photos.

This chapter shows you how to create fabulous-looking horizontal and vertical text and create stunning text-shaped masks using the Horizontal or Vertical Type and Type Mask tools with, of course, your favorite photo. You'll also find out how to format text and create special effects with the Warp Text Tool. And you'll learn how to create and modify graphics with the Pencil, Brush, and Shape tools.

Introducing the Type Tool

Adobe uses the term *type* to describe what you and I call text. Type refers to a set of alpha, numeric, and symbolic characters that can be defined as a typeface, which is synonymous with the term *font family*, or *font*. The most commonly used formats for typefaces are PostScript and TrueType.

Photoshop Elements enables you to enter text horizontally or vertically in an image window. You can also create a type mask with the Horizontal and Vertical Type Mask tools. All four Type tools share one location in the Toolbox. You can press the letter T to select this tool, or hold down the Shift key and press T to cycle through each Type tool. You can also use the mouse to select any of the Type tools from the Toolbox.

Type tools create vector graphics—each character of text is drawn with a mathematical algorithm. The Type tools enable you to format text as vector graphics. You can customize the font family, font style, and font size, as well as choose from a small set of layout options and one or two special effects. I refer to these tools using the general term *Type Tool* or *Type Mask Tool*. You can use any of these tools to add text to a photo. You can convert vector type into a bitmap by choosing **Simplify Layer** from the **Layer** menu. This command rasterizes the vector into a bitmap. If you want to apply a filter or an effect to text, you must first simplify or rasterize the vector text into bitmap.

The Horizontal and Vertical Type Mask Tools enable you to create a text-shaped mask on an image layer. The marching ants or a rubylith color that borders a selection area defines the Type mask. The pixels within the marching ants or pixels that are not covered by the rubylith color can be modified, but the ones outside the marching ants cannot. To create a Horizontal or Vertical Type Mask, perform the following steps:

1. Choose the Vertical Type Mask Tool from the Toolbox. Select a font family, style, and size from the options bar.

2. Click in the image window and type one or two letters on the keyboard. Marching ants should appear around each letter thatVertical Type Mask Tools appears in the image window.

3. Click on the check button in the options bar to complete the mask. Then click on a selection such as the Rectangular Marquee Tool. If you like the selection the way it is, copy and paste it to place the masked text-shaped image into a new layer.

4. Use the Move tool if you want to transform, rotate, or move the mask in the image window. Select one of the selection tools, such as the Rectangular

Marquee Tool, if you want to move the text mask to a different location in Vertical Type Mask Tools the image window.

The Horizontal and Vertical Type tools create a separate Text layer when you type in the image window. You can modify any text layer as long as you don't rasterize it into a bitmap. To add text to an image, do the following:

1. Select the Horizontal or Vertical Type Tool from the Toolbox.

2. Click on the image window. Depending on which tool you chose, either a vertical or a horizontal line appears where you Vertical Type Mask Tools clicked, indicating where the text will appear.

3. Type a few characters to add text to the image window, as shown in Figure 11.1.

4. The text color is the foreground color selected in the Toolbox. You can use the Type Vertical Type Mask Tools Tool to select text, and then modify the text using any of the Type Tool settings in the options bar.

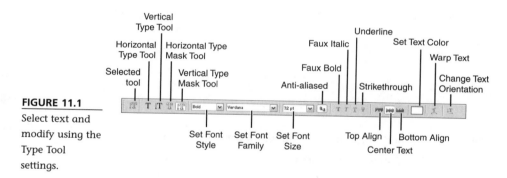

FIGURE 11.1
Select text and modify using the Type Tool settings.

Formatting Text

You can format text before or after applying the Type Tool to an image window. Formatting settings are located in the options bar. Select the Horizontal or Vertical Type Tool to modify the font family, size, or style. You can triple-click the text to select all characters (see Figure 11.2) in the image window. Select the Move Tool to move, transform, or rotate text.

The following list contains a brief description of each formatting setting located in the Type Tool options bar:

■ **Type Tool**—Choose the Horizontal or Vertical Type Tool or the Horizontal or Vertical Type Mask Tool from the options bar.

■ **Font Family**—Choose a font family from the drop-down menu. Any font installed with Windows or Mac OS will appear in the menu list.

FIGURE 11.2

Choose a font style from the drop-down menu in the Type Tool's options bar.

- **Font Size**—Font sizes appear in points. Smaller numbers represent a smaller size font; larger numbers represent larger fonts. You can also use the Transform and Move tools to enlarge text beyond the numbers in the menu list.

- **Font Style**—Add a bold, italicized, or bold italicized font style to a font, or remove styles by choosing Regular. The font style menu is shown in Figure 11.2.

- **Anti-aliased**—Smooth the edges of a font by checking this check box.

- **Faux Bold and Faux Italic**—If a font family doesn't have a bold or italic design, Photoshop Elements can create these font styles.

- **Underline, Strikethrough**—Add or remove underline or strikethrough styles to the selected type characters.

- **Align Text**—Align the text object to the left, center, or right of its location in the image window.

- **Text Color**—Click in this magical square to select the color for any of the Type tools.

- **Warp Text Tool**—Add special effects to the text by choosing or customizing settings in the Warp Text dialog box.

- **Text Orientation**—Draw the text horizontally or vertically in the image window.

tip

You can measure text by choosing View, Rulers (Command-R) [Ctrl+R]. Double-click a ruler to open the Units & Rulers preferences dialog box. (Ctrl-click) [Right+click] to change the measurement value of the rulers.

Choose different combinations of font settings to find the right text format to match the message and the photo. You can modify the contents of any text layer as often as you like. Duplicate a text layer and apply different combinations of text settings, and then hide and show layers to compare different text settings.

Modifying Type

You must select a Type layer and the Type Tool before you can modify text. The Move Tool only enables you to select and resize the text layer. You can select one character, a word, or all text in a text layer, and format a single character, word, or all words in a text layer. Figure 11.3 shows the first and last word in the text layer formatted with a larger font size, with a custom style setting.

TYPE AND LAYER ORDER

If you're working with several layers, you can create different effects with text depending on where the text layer is located in the **Layers** palette. Drag and drop the text layer to move it above or below other layers. The top layer in the **Layers** palette represents the most visible layer in the image window. If you can't see a particular text layer, you probably need to bump it up to a higher layer in the **Layers** palette.

FIGURE 11.3

The Type Tool enables you to add, modify, and select text. You can modify one or several characters with the formatting settings in the options bar.

Virtually all the text formatting settings in the options bar can be applied to individual characters. The Warp Text Tool, however, modifies all text in a text layer. If you want to customize a few characters in a text object, first choose the Type Tool. Next, highlight a specific character, word, or words in the image window. Then, choose a font, font style, or font size from the options bar. The highlighted text will change to match the settings you choose in the options bar.

Text objects are created as vector graphics. One way you can tell whether you're working with a vector graphic is to scale it up in size. If you don't see any jagged edges, you're working with a vector graphic. Vector graphics are great for generating crisp, concise graphics. However, they usually create a slightly larger file, and they can be customized only in the application in which they're created.

To use text in other ways, such as filling it with an image, you first must simplify the text into a bitmap. When a text object is converted into a bitmap, the mathematically calculated pixels are changed into a fixed set of pixels. You can apply filters, effects, and other tools and color-correction commands on the bitmap text as long as the image window is in the proper color mode for the tool you want to use. However, you cannot modify bitmap text with the Horizontal or Vertical Text tools.

note

You can format only text that's stored in a Type layer. After text has been simplified into a bitmap, you can no longer format it. However, you can apply filters, effects, and the **Paste Into** command to bitmap text.

The following steps show you how to convert vector text into bitmap text:

1. Press the (**Command**) [**Ctrl**] key and click on the text layer in the **Layers** palette. The outline of the text should be highlighted with a dashed line.

2. Choose the **Copy** command from the **Edit** menu, or press (**Command-C**) [**Ctrl+C**] to copy the selected text to the Clipboard.

3. Select the **Paste** command from the **Edit** menu, or press (**Command-V**) [**Ctrl+V**]. The vector text object will be pasted as a bitmap into the active image window, and a new layer will be created in the **Layers** palette.

Alternatively, you can (**Command-click**) [**Ctrl+click**] to select all text in a text layer, and then click the **Simplify** button in the options bar, or choose **Simplify Layer** from the **Layer** menu.

Vector graphics have many advantages over bitmap graphics. Text especially benefits from a long list of formatting options. The following list describes the benefits of working with vector text:

- **Scalable**—Text will look crisp and clear whether you increase or decrease its size.

- **Editable**—You can select the Type Tool and modify the Text object layer at any time.

■ **Filters and effects**—You can drag and drop a filter or an effect onto the text object to blur, sharpen, or texturize it, or give it an artistic look. When a filter or an effect is applied to a text object, that text is permanently converted into a bitmap.

■ **Layer Styles**—You can drag and drop a layer style onto a text object to give it a three-dimensional look, or to add other spiffy effects. Layer styles can turn two-dimensional text into professional-looking, Web-ready graphics. If you drag and drop a layer style onto a text object, the text is converted into a bitmap graphic.

> **tip**
>
> Drag and drop a Bevel layer style onto a text object to give it a three-dimensional look. When a layer style is added to a layer, an f icon appears on the right side of the layer. Double-click on the f icon in the text layer to customize the bevel settings in the Style Settings dialog box.

BITMAP TEXT AND THE PASTE INTO COMMAND

Convert a vector text object, which is the default state of a text object, into a bitmap by copying and pasting the vector text into the image window. First (**Command-click**) [**Ctrl+click**] on the text layer to select each character in the text layer. The highlight should surround each letter in the text layer. Then choose **Copy** from the **Edit** menu, or press (**Command-C**) [**Ctrl+C**] to copy the image to the Clipboard. Then choose the **Paste** command from the **Edit** menu to create a new layer containing the bitmap text.

The letter T will appear as the thumbnail image for a vector text layer, regardless of the text in the layer. A tiny image of the bitmap text object will appear as the thumbnail image for a bitmap text layer. After you create the bitmap text layer, you might want to hide the vector text layer so that only the bitmap text appears in the image window. Click in the left box beside the vector layer. The eye icon should disappear from the box, indicating that the layer is hidden from the image window.

After you've converted the text object to a bitmap, you can copy an image onto the Clipboard. Open a new image file, and then use a selection tool to select all or part of the image in the image window. Then choose the **Copy** command from the **Edit** menu, or press (**Command-C**) [**Ctrl+C**] to copy the selected image to the Clipboard.

Next, select the bitmap text by (**Command-clicking**) [**Ctrl+clicking**] on the bitmap text layer in the **Layers** palette. Then choose the **Paste Into** command from the **Edit** menu to paste the image from the Clipboard into the bitmap text object. The image will appear in each character of the selected text object.

Warping Type

When a piece of text is highlighted with the Type Tool, the Warp Text button appears to the right of the text color well in the options bar. The icon for the Warp tool resembles the letter T with an arched line below it. Click on the **Warp Text** button to open the Warp Text dialog box, shown in Figure 11.4.

FIGURE 11.4

Apply special effects to text by choosing one of many styles from the Warp Text dialog box.

Click on the **Style** drop-down menu to view a menu list of 15 warp styles you can apply to the selected text object. The following list briefly describes each of the four groups of Warp Text effects. Choose **None** if you want to remove a previously applied effect, or if you do not want to apply a Warp Text effect to the selected text object.

- **Arc**—Raise the top or bottom area of the text object by choosing **Arc Lower** or **Arc Upper**. Make the entire text object arc by choosing Arc.

- **Arch**—Arch or bulge the midsection of the text object. Choose **Shell Lower** or **Shell Upper** to push out the upper or lower midsection of the selected text object.

- **Flag**—Makes the text object take the shape of a waving flag. Choose the **Flag**, **Wave**, **Fish**, or **Rise** style.

- **Miscellaneous**—The styles located at the bottom of the menu list are a collection of miscellaneous effects. The Fisheye effect bloats the middle area of the image, Inflate bloats the entire text object, Squeeze puckers the entire image, and Twist twirls the text object.

The settings in the Warp Text dialog box will remain unselectable until you choose one of the warp text styles from the **Style** drop-down menu, shown in Figure 11.4. You can apply only one style to each text object. Each style changes the entire text object. You cannot apply a warp text effect to individual characters or words in a text object.

After you choose a style, you can customize the Horizontal or Vertical direction, Bend, Horizontal Distortion, and Vertical Distortion of the warp text style. Figure 11.5 shows the settings for the Fish style in the Warp Text dialog box. Drag the sliders to control the warp effect. You can preview your changes in the image window. Click on **OK** to apply the Warp Text settings to the text object.

FIGURE 11.5

Customize warp text effects by moving the slider controls in the **Warp Text** window.

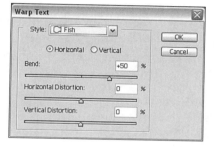

The letter T appears in the text object thumbnail box in the **Layers** palette. The T icon indicates that the text object is editable with either the Horizontal or Vertical Type Tool. If you apply the Warp Text Tool to a text object, the letter T in the **Layers** palette will change into the Warp Text icon (the letter T with an arc line below it), as shown in Figure 11.6.

FIGURE 11.6

The Type icon in the **Layers** palette changes if the Warp Text Tool is applied to a text layer.

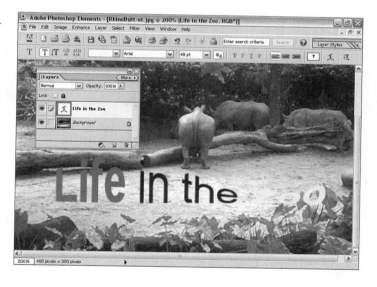

The Warp Tool will affect every character in the text layer. However, you can continue to modify the formatting and style settings of any character in a warped text layer. Select the Horizontal or Vertical Type Tool and click on the warped text in the image window to highlight the characters or words you want to modify.

Adding Graphics to an Image

In addition to all the fabulous bitmap-editing tools, Photoshop Elements enables you to create custom graphics with brush and shape tools. Brush tools, such as the Brush and Airbrush tools, enable you to apply a custom brush type, size, and customize options, such as spacing, color jitter, hardness, scatter, roundness, and angle, and also toggle tablet support. The shape tools enable you to add vector-based geometric shapes to the image window.

Introducing Brush Tools

The Brush, Impressionist Brush, and Pencil tools are the three kinds of brush tools available in the Toolbox (see Figure 11.7). Each of these tools enables you to draw freeform in the image window. Click on a tool to view its option settings on the options bar. The Brush and Pencil have custom brush settings, blending modes, and opacity settings. The Airbrush is available as a custom setting on the Brush Tool options bar. The Sponge, Smudge, Dodge, and Burn tools have brush, blending mode, and pressure settings, but no opacity setting, in the options bar. Click and drag the cursor in the image window to apply the foreground color to the selected layer in the **Layers** palette.

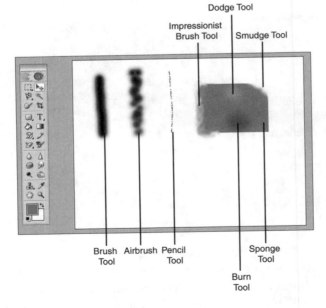

FIGURE 11.7

Each brush tool applies color in a slightly different way.

The Brush Tool has a wide selection of brushes available. Experiment with different brush sizes in addition to different types of brushes, such as hard-edge and soft-edge brushes. The following list summarizes how each of the paint tools and the Eraser Tool work:

- **Impressionist Brush**—Blend pixels using Style, Area, and Tolerance brush options to customize the impressionist effect in this tool. Choose from 10 styles. Type the number of pixels you want the brush to affect, and set the tolerance to determine the range of colors.

- **Airbrush**—A spray effect is created with this paint tool. The longer you leave this tool over the image window, the darker the foreground color will become in the image window. Click the **Airbrush** button and adjust the Color Jitter and Scatter settings in the **More Options** drop-down menu in the Brush Tool options bar to bring the Airbrush to life.

- **Brush**—Creates a pressure-sensitive stroke of color to the selected layer. Set spacing to 25% and roundness to 100% (all other settings to zero in the More Options drop-down window) to create a standard brush stroke. Choose a soft-edge brush.

- **Pencil**—Creates a hard-edge, single-pixel stroke by default. Choose from a full range of brush types and sizes.

- **Eraser**—Applies the background color to the image window. The Magic Eraser deletes the first color you click on in the image window. You also can use the Magic Erase Tool to change pixels to the background color, erase to transparency, or erase contiguous or all similar pixels in a layer. The Background Eraser removes all color from the layer or layers.

Each paint tool has several settings you can customize in the options bar. Select one of the paint tools from the Toolbox. Then view each of the settings in the options bar. The following list briefly describes each paint tool setting:

- **Brush**—Choose a brush size and style from the drop-down menu. The number below each brush indicates the number of pixels that are in that brush tip. You can customize the hardness, angle, spacing,

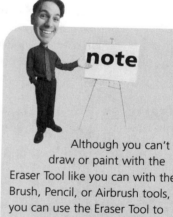

note

Although you can't draw or paint with the Eraser Tool like you can with the Brush, Pencil, or Airbrush tools, you can use the Eraser Tool to remove any strokes created by the brush and drawing tools. In fact, you can customize the mode of the Eraser Tool to match the settings in the Brush, Airbrush, or Pencil tools by choosing one of these tools from the Eraser Tool's Mode drop-down menu, located in the options bar.

and roundness of each brush. Click on the arrow button to choose a different set of brushes.

■ **Mode**—Select a Blending mode for the foreground color applied by the paint tool.

■ **Opacity**—Set the transparency level of the color. This setting is not available for the Airbrush Tool.

■ **Auto Erase**—The Auto Erase check box enables the Pencil Tool to erase the foreground colored pixels with the background color.

■ **Brush Options**—Customize the Spacing, Fade, Color Jitter, Hardness, and Scatter setting for the Brush. Adjust the Angle and Roundness of the brush. Check the **Table Support** check box if you want to use a USB pen and tablet with the Brush Tool.

note

The Smudge, Blur, Sponge, and Sharpen tools in the Toolbox also enable you to customize the Pressure setting in each tool's options bar.

The Eraser Tool can remove any strokes created by the Brush, Airbrush, and Pencil tools. It can also erase strokes created by other bitmap-editing tools, such as the Clone Stamp Tool. You can use three eraser tools from the Toolbox: Eraser, Background Eraser, and Magic Eraser. Figure 11.8 shows how each type of eraser affects a set of paint strokes created in the same layer.

FIGURE 11.8

Use the Eraser Tool to remove pixels from an image.

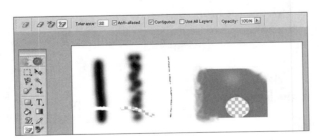

Each eraser tool has a unique group of settings. The Eraser Tool can share many of the same settings as the Brush, Airbrush, or Pencil tools. For example, if you select **Brush** from the **Mode** window of the Eraser Tool's options bar, you will see the following options appear along with the Brush setting: Brush, Mode, Opacity, Wet Edges, and Brush options. The Airbrush option enables you to adjust the pressure of the Eraser Tool in Airbrush mode. The Pencil mode enables you to adjust the opacity of the Eraser. You can choose Block mode if you want to use the Eraser Tool without any special Painting Tool options.

The following list briefly describes each of the settings of the Background Eraser Tool:

- ■ **Brush**—Select a brush size from the drop-down menu.
- ■ **Limits**—Choose either Discontiguous to erase the sampled color only, or Contiguous to erase connected areas of sampled color.
- ■ **Tolerance**—Drag the slider control or type a value into the text box to adjust how much color is erased from the path of the tool.
- ■ **Brush Options**—Set the Size and Tolerance settings for the selected brush.

The following list briefly describes the Magic Eraser Tool's settings:

- ■ **Tolerance**—Enables you to customize the amount of color removed from the selected layer.
- ■ **Anti-aliased**—Smoothes the edges of the erased colors.
- ■ **Contiguous**—Erases only pixels similar to the color you initially sample.
- ■ **Use All Layers**—Deletes colors and pixels across layers in the image window.
- ■ **Opacity**—Enables you to set the transparency level of the erased color, by moving the slider control or by typing in a value into the Opacity text box.

BITMAP VERSUS VECTOR GRAPHICS

Paint tools create bitmap patterns of color in a layer. These images will not scale well if increased in size. If you plan to use a paint tool, try to draw the image to scale, or larger than the actual size you need.

Drawing tools, on the other hand, create vector graphics. Vector graphics use a mathematical algorithm to retain their original shape if increased or decreased in size. If you want to create dynamic graphics, use the drawing tools, such as the shape tools, to create your graphics.

Introducing Shape Tools

Shape tools enable you to create a precise shape, whereas brush tools enable you to draw freeform lines. You'll find seven shape tools sharing one location in the Toolbox. You can select any shape tool from the options bar, regardless of which one is selected in the Toolbox.

You can create rectangles, circles, lines, and custom shapes with the shape tools, as shown in Figure 11.9. Each shape tool creates a shape layer in the **Layers** palette. Select a shape layer to select a shape in the image window and apply a layer style. Simplify a shape into a bitmap to apply a filter or an effect.

FIGURE 11.9

Master the shape tools by adding and changing shapes in the image window.

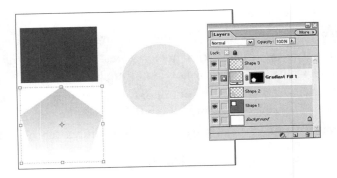

The following list briefly describes each shape drawing tool:

- **Rectangle**—Draw a square or rectangle with this tool.
- **Rounded Rectangle**—Identical to the Rectangle Tool, except each corner is rounded. Great for creating signs and buttons.
- **Ellipse**—Click and drag this tool to create a circle, an oval, or an ellipse.
- **Polygon**—Draw a multisided graphic.
- **Line**—Draw a straight line. Click on the **Shape** drop-down menu, located on the right end of the shape selection window in the options bar. Click on the **Start** or **End** check boxes if you want to add arrowheads to either end of the line.
- **Custom Shape**—Choose a custom shape from one of more than a dozen custom shape libraries. Click on the **Shape** drop-down menu to choose custom shape options.
- **Shape Selection**—Pick a shape that has been added to the image window. Check the **Show Bounding Box** check box if you want to view the selected shape's bounding box.

Each shape can have unique settings. For example, you can apply a gradient or an effect to a shape to create great-looking graphics, as shown in Figure 11.10. The following list briefly describes each setting in the shape options bar:

- **Shape**—Click on a shape icon to choose the shape you want to create in the image window.
- **Radius**—This option enables you to set how many pixels each corner is rounded if the Rounded Rectangle shape is the selected shape.
- **Create New Shape Layer**—Creates a new layer in the Layers palette for the shape that will be drawn in the image window. This icon is located in the middle of the options bar when a shape tool is selected. It is grouped with the Add/Subtract, Intersect, and Exclude Shape icons.

FIGURE 11.10
Simplify a shape
and then apply
layer styles, fil-
ters, or effects to
create custom
graphics.

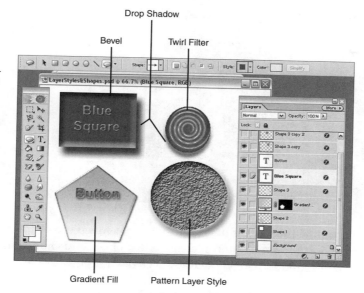

Drop Shadow

Bevel   Twirl Filter

Gradient Fill   Pattern Layer Style

- **Add/Subtract from Shape**—Choose the **Add** setting to add a new shape
  to an existing shape. Or use the **Subtract** setting to subtract a shape from
  an existing shape in the image window.
- **Intersect Shape Areas**—Preserves the overlapped area of two overlapping
  shapes.
- **Exclude Overlapping Shape Areas**—Preserves the non-overlapping area
  of two overlapping shapes.
- **Layer Style**—Add a Bevel, Drop Shadow, Glow, or other effect to the shape
  by choosing a layer style from the drop-down menu.
- **Color**—Select a color for the shape or line.
- **Simplify**—Merge the color and shape components in a shape layer into one
  component. This button converts a vector graphic into a bitmap graphic.

Variations—Creating Signs with Drawing and Painting Tools

You can enhance your photos by combining painting and drawing tools to design
custom graphics. For example, you can use the paint tools to add graffiti to the wall
or sidewalk of the storefront shown in Figure 11.11. In this example, two kinds of
signs will be created with shape and text tools.

You can combine shape tools and layer styles to create a three-dimensional sign, as shown in Figure 11.12. Or you can create a text object and change the Opacity, Blending mode, and Layer Style settings to create a sign.

To create a sign using the drawing and painting tools, do the following:

1. Select the Rounded Rectangle shape to create the sign. A separate layer will be created in the Layers palette for the rounded rectangle. You can change its color or shape by selecting either component in the Shape 1 layer.

2. Next, choose a custom shape to place in the center of the sign (see Figure 11.13). In this example, I chose a symbol shape from the People library. You can choose a library from the drop-down menu located in the **Shape** window of the **Symbol Shape Tool** options bar. Use the Move Tool to place the custom shape on the rounded rectangle.

3. Place the cursor between the two shape layers in the **Layers** palette.

4. Hold down the (**Option**) [**Alt**] key. The cursor icon changes from an arrow to a small arrow with two overlapping circles. Click on the line between the two layers. Then release the (**Option**) [**Alt**] key. A down-pointing arrow, as shown in Figure 11.14, will appear in the top layer, indicating that the two layers are grouped together. You can group two layers together to preserve their order in the **Layers** palette.

FIGURE 11.13
Use the shape tools and layer styles to create a sign.

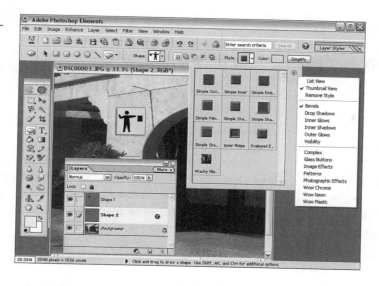

FIGURE 11.14
(Option-click) [Alt+click] between layers to group the two shape layers in the Layers palette.

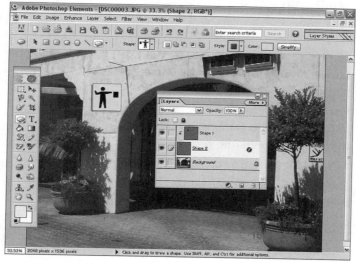

5. Select the Horizontal Type Tool and type some text into the image window. Use the Move Tool to line up the text object with the background image.

6. You can apply the **Transform** commands to add perspective, or scale the text to fit with the rest of the image. If you want the text object to blend in with the background image, choose a **Blending** mode and decrease the **Opacity** value in the **Layers** palette.

LINKING IS NOT GROUPING

Grouping two layers together is different from linking layers together. Linking two or more layers together preserves the location of each object relative to the others in the image window. Whenever you move the primary object in the link, all other linked objects will adjust to the new location.

You can link together two or more layers in the Layers palette. First, select the layer to which you want to link other layers. Then, click in the right check box beside a second or third layer to link those layers to the selected layer.

When you select a custom shape, a Shape selection window appears in the options bar. Click on the shape window to view its drop-down menu. You can choose from five views to navigate through the 14 custom shape libraries. The following list briefly describes each view:

- **Text Only**—Lists each shape without any visual aids.
- **Small Thumbnail**—Probably the ideal view for custom shapes. Enables you to view all images in a library without scrolling.
- **Large Thumbnail**—Doubles the size of the small thumbnail images.
- **Small List**—Organizes the library items in list view with a small icon in the left side of each item name.
- **Large List**—Same as the small list, except it uses larger icons.

note

When two or more layers are grouped together, the bottom layer defines the boundary of any layers that are a part of the group. The name of the bottom layer of the group will become underlined in the **Layers** palette. You can ungroup two layers by holding down the (**Option**) [**Alt**] key and clicking on the group icon (two overlapping circles), which is located between the two grouped layers in the **Layers** palette.

Designing Bitmap and Vector Graphics

Because most of the tools in Photoshop Elements are bitmap tools, you won't be creating vector graphics unless you're working with the type or shape tools. Nevertheless, you can combine bitmap and vector graphics in the same file or image window.

Combining these two kinds of graphics isn't really the big issue. The big concern is usually whether you should create a graphic as a bitmap or a vector graphic. As mentioned previously, vector graphics are great because they keep their sharpness whether you grow or shrink them. However, bitmap graphics are made up of a fixed set of pixels.

Growing a bitmap image generally results in creating a bigger bitmap, with chunkier, squarish-looking pixels.

Because vector graphics are so flexible and dynamic, they carry more information along with them, which usually increases the overall file size. In general, a bitmap graphic will be smaller than, and possibly not as crisp as, a vector graphic of equal shape and color.

Drawing Bitmap Graphics

Open an image file, such as the one shown in Figure 11.15. In this example, bitmap and vector graphics will be added to this image. Follow these steps to add a bitmap graphic to an image:

FIGURE 11.15

The background layer stores the locked image of a newly opened image file.

1. Choose **Layer** from the **Layer**, **New** menu, or click on the **Create a New Layer** button at the bottom of the **Layers** palette to create a new layer. Select the new layer in the **Layers** palette. Choose the **Brush Tool** from the Toolbox.

2. Choose a brush type and size, as shown in Figure 11.16. Specify the blending mode and opacity of the brush. Set the **More Options** settings to 0, except for **Spacing**, which should be set to 25%. Both fish shown in Figure 11.17 were created with a 38-pixel, soft-edged brush using the Brush Tool.

FIGURE 11.16

Choose a brush type from the options bar for the Brush Tool.

3. Click and hold down the mouse as you drag the cursor in the image window to draw on the image.

4. Select the Move Tool and click and drag a corner of the selection to resize the graphic. You can experiment with different compositions, such as the one shown in Figure 11.17. Apply the Eraser Tool to remove pixels from the layer that contains the bitmap graphics.

FIGURE 11.17

You can enlarge the shape of each graphic or move each one around in the image window.

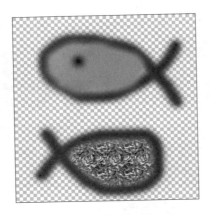

Creating Transparent Text

Because text is a vector graphic, you can reselect it by choosing the Type layer or Type object in the image window, as shown in Figure 11.18. Then type a value between 0 and 99 to change its opacity setting from the **Layers** palette. Lowering the text layer's opacity setting can help it blend in with the image layer located directly below it in the Layers palette. The Opacity setting in the **Layers** palette enables you to add transparency to an object as you decrease the value in the Opacity text box. You can create transparent text or graphics that blend in with the background image like the text object shown in Figure 11.19.

FIGURE 11.18

You can adjust the opacity setting of text before or after applying an effect to it. The Warp Text Tool can add instant special effects to a photo.

The following steps show you how to add text to an image, apply the Warp Tool, and then adjust the text object's opacity settings (shown in Figure 11.18):

1. First, select the Text Tool and type some text into the image window.

2. Click on the tools in the options bar to format the text. Click the **Warp Text** button to open the **Warp Text** window.

3. Choose a warp style and adjust the warp text effect.

4. Click on **OK** to save your changes.

5. Select the text layer in the **Layers** palette. Click on the drop-down arrow to move the slider control for the Opacity setting.

6. Set the opacity to roughly 50% to 70%, as shown in Figure 11.19. The background should show through the solid regions of the text.

FIGURE 11.19
Decrease the opacity level of the image to increase its transparency with the background image.

You can place the text anywhere in the image window. Use the Move Tool to select and move the text object. Place it over a part of the background image that might show a pattern or an object through the letters of text.

Modifying Custom Shapes

Shapes are also vector graphics. You can choose a shape tool from the Toolbox to add a simple geometric shape to a photo. When you apply the shape tool—or any other vector graphic tool—to the image window, Photoshop Elements creates a new layer to store the new graphics. This new layer is usually created above the selected or active layer in the **Layers** palette, enabling you to overlap the graphic with the picture.

If shape tools don't do the trick for you, try adding text or applying a brush to a photo. You may be able to create a cool-looking graphic by applying the brush tools freehand or combining bitmap text with graphics. Text layers can be combined with or overlap graphics layers. Organize the order in which text and graphic objects appear in the image window by changing their order in the Layers palette. For instance, you can place a particular text or graphic in front of or behind other objects by placing it above or below other layers in the Layers palette.

To add a drop shadow or reflection to a text object, select the layer you want to copy and drop it over the **Create New Layer** icon in the **Layers** palette. Photoshop Elements will create a new layer containing the contents of the original layer. The following steps show you how to add a new shape to an image window:

1. Select the **Shape Tool** from the **Toolbox**.
2. Click on the custom shape in the options bar.
3. Click on the **Shape** drop-down menu to view the shapes loaded from the currently selected library, as shown in Figure 11.20.
4. Click on the right-arrow button in the drop-down menu to view or select a different shape library. In this example, I chose a fish from the Animals library.

FIGURE 11.20

Choose a custom shape from the built-in library of shapes.

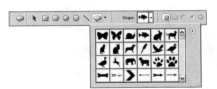

To add a color or layer style to the custom shape, perform the following steps:

1. After the shape is added to the image window, the Add, Subtract, Intersect, and Exclude icons will become selectable beside the **Layer Style** drop-down menu in the options bar.
2. Click on the **Layer Style** menu button, shown in Figure 11.20, to view and select a layer style. You can drag and drop the layer style onto any object in the image window to enhance the target object.
3. Click on the right-arrow menu, also shown in Figure 11.21, to choose a different layer style library. Choose **Remove Style** from the drop-down menu to remove all styles from the shape layer.

You can change the color of the custom shape by clicking on the **Color** swatch in the options bar. The **Color Picker** window will open. Choose a color for the graphic in the **Color Picker** window, and then click **OK**. The new color will appear in the left thumbnail beside the shape thumbnail in the shape layer of the **Layers** palette.

You can change the shape color as often as you like, as long as you do not simplify the shape layer.

FIGURE 11.21

Access any layer style from the Style drop-down menu. Drag and drop a layer style onto the custom shape.

The Transform commands enable you to grow, shrink, skew, distort, apply perspective, and rotate a shape in the image window. Click on the **Image**, **Transform** menu to view the Transform commands. You can also press (**Command-T**) [**Ctrl+T**] to enable the **Free Transform** command for the selected layer.

If you want to experiment with the Transform commands, create a copy of a custom shape. Select the shape layer of the graphic, and then drag and drop it over the Create a New Layer icon in the **Layers** palette. The copied layer will appear in the **Layers** palette, and the copied shape will appear over the selected shape in the image window. Select the Move Tool to move it to a new location in the image window.

Select the Move Tool and drag the copy of the shape to a new location in the image window. Select a custom layer style and color for the shape. In this example, I reduced the size of the copied shape, and then flipped it horizontally, as shown in Figure 11.22. If you want to permanently keep the shape settings and prevent the shape from being edited, select it, and then choose **Simplify Layer** from the **Layer** menu. The color and shape thumbnails will merge into a single thumbnail image.

Merging Completed Layers

As you put together different graphics and images, you might want to merge some layers together to make those changes permanent. You can combine two or more layers by hiding all layers except for the ones you want to merge. Then choose the

Merge Visible command from the **Layer** menu. Photoshop Elements will convert the layers that appear in the image window into a single layer in the Layers palette.

FIGURE 11.22
Click the
Simplify button
in the options
bar to combine
layer styles and
linked elements
in a layer.

If you want to make the shape part of the background image, first show the two layers in the **Layers** palette. Then choose the **Merge Visible** command from the **Layer** menu. You can also press (**Shift-Command-E**) [**Shift+Ctrl+E**] to merge any visible images in the image window. The two layers will be merged into a single layer.

Applying Effects with the Impressionist Brush

If you want to apply an impressionist effect to a specific graphic, or to an area of a bitmap image, you can merge two layers, and then choose the **Impressionist Brush**, shown in Figure 11.23, to paint with stylized strokes. The Impressionist Brush applies a unique look by blending the colors of a particular layer together. Choose a large brush size and select a layer that contains a photo. Apply the tool to the image window to see how it affects the pixels in the photo.

You can adjust the brush settings to experiment with different kinds of impressionist effects and different types of images. Select the **Impressionist Brush** from the Toolbox to view its settings in the options bar. The brush settings are located on the left side of the options bar. If you're working with an image that consists of more than one layer, select the layer to which you want to apply this tool from the **Layers** palette. Then click and drag the brush over the image window to texturize the pixels in the image window.

FIGURE 11.23

You can use the Impressionist Brush to blend a bitmap graphic with pixels from the same image layer. The Impressionist Brush was applied to the bottom half of the fish graphic.

In addition to the Mode and Opacity settings, which are also available with the Brush and Airbrush tools, there are several other settings you can customize when using the Impressionist Brush. The following list briefly describes each setting:

- **Brush**—Pick a brush tip for the Impressionist Brush.
- **Mode**—Select a blending mode from the drop-down menu.
- **Style**—Control the shape of the painted strokes. Choose a Tight Short, Tight Medium, Tight Long, Loose Medium, Loose Long, Dab, Tight Curl, Tight Curl Long, Loose Curl, or Loose Curl Long style from the menu list.
- **Fidelity**—Decide how much the paint color changes between the new and old colors in the image window. A lower percent adds more color to the resulting stroke.
- **Area**—Type the number of pixels you want the brush to affect.
- **Spacing**—Enter a percentage to restrict the way the paint stroke is applied. A lower value enables you to paint anywhere in the image window. A higher value limits the colors the brush can change.
- **Brush Options**—Adjust the size and opacity settings of the brush stroke.

Previewing the Final Image

Show each layer in the image window and view the final image before saving it for the Web or printing it. If you are going to use the image on the Web or send it via email, you can optimize the final image by choosing **Flattԉen Image** from the **Layer** menu. Then adjust the color palette in the Save for Web dialog box to a Web-safe palette, or just convert the image to Indexed Color mode. With the exception of

Photoshop native and TIFF formats, most file formats will automatically flatten all layers into one in order to create the final image. Figure 11.24 shows the final text and graphics photo. If you have the hard drive space available, save a copy of the image as a PSD file to preserve its layer information.

FIGURE 11.24

The final photo. Save a copy of the photo as a PSD file to preserve its layer information.

12

REPAIRING IMAGES

Restoring damaged photos is a challenge that usually requires lots of patience, skill, and time. It's no picnic trying to re-create missing portions of an image, or trying to determine the original colors of a worn, faded photo. However, the reward can be extraordinarily worthwhile in sentimental value alone. Repairing a worn or torn image helps preserve the look and feel of earlier photography, as well as family history and heritage.

Repairing Folds and Tears

It would be nice if we all kept two copies of important photos: one in pristine condition locked away in a safe place, and another one in our wallet, photo album, or picture frame. Unfortunately, this usually isn't the case. Sometimes photos are accidentally folded or torn as they are shuffled from album to album, or from home to home over the years. Figure 12.1 shows a color photo that has been folded and has gathered dust and stains over the years.

FIGURE 12.1

The before photo with torn, folded paper.

My mother asked me to repair the photo shown in Figure 12.1. She didn't have the negative, and she requested any size print I could muster up, expecting me to repair any wear and tear accrued over the years. Before I started to work on this image, I tried to assess the different kinds of work and tools I might need to use for this project.

The Clone Stamp Tool was my tool of choice. It enables me to sample from the selected layer, or across all layers, and then apply the sampled pixels to the active layer. This is helpful for using undamaged areas of an image to repair missing, torn, or worn areas of an image.

I also wanted to keep my repairs on separate layers so that I could undo any area I incorrectly tried to fix. Several tools, such as the Clone Stamp, Blur, Smudge, and Eraser tools, can be applied either to a single layer or across all layers in an image. Working with these tools and keeping my corrections on separate layers enables me to experiment with different repair techniques without altering the original image.

In addition to the torn, folded edges that create x and y axes in the photo, the white areas of the photo had dust, stains, and coloring imperfections. There also were several speck marks in various places in the image, probably created when the original print was made. I decided to experiment with different soft-edge brush sizes with the Clone Stamp Tool to repair these smaller areas of the image. I created a correction layer in the **Layers** palette to store the dust and speck corrections.

Eliminating Wrinkles and Torn Areas

You can apply tools directly to the background layer of an image to repair damaged areas, and save different copies of the image file to your hard drive until you create a repaired image you want to publish or print. However, it's best to create one or several new layers in the **Layers** palette, as shown in Figure 12.2, to store any corrections. Click in the left column on the eye icon in the **Layers** palette to hide a layer, or click on the empty box to make the eye icon appear and show the selected layer in the image window. You can hide or show the corrected areas of the image and quickly compare them to the original. You can apply the Erase Tool to the correction layer to remove any corrected areas you're not happy with.

FIGURE 12.2

Create a new layer for the corrections.

You might want to keep different kinds of corrections in different layers so that you can keep track of what is changing. You can also compare different corrections, or experiment with different methods of repairing the image, without altering the actual pixels of the scanned or photographed image. The following list highlights a few of the common kinds of image damage and suggestions for repairing or correcting each one. You can create a separate layer for each type of correction you want to perform on an image that you want to repair.

- **Heavily damaged areas**—Removing torn or folded paper and replacing it with an image can be a cumbersome task. You can create a new layer and apply the Clone Stamp Tool to sample an undamaged portion of the original image and apply that to a correction layer. If you like the changes, you can replace the torn image in the lower layer with a reconstructed image in the correction layer.

- **Color-correction areas**—You might want to create a fill or gradient layer to correct aged photos or color casts created by flash or internal lighting.

- **Changes in color**—Consider creating separate layers for skin tones versus clothes, furniture, or other items in the photo.

- **Dust and specks**—Sometimes it's difficult to discern a dust spec from actual image details. Keeping these corrections on a separate layer can help restore detailed elements in an image.

- **Mold and stains**—Tiny areas of color distortion might be difficult to correct. You can adjust the brush size of the Clone Stamp, Smudge, or Blur tools to try to remove small sets of pixels that need to be repaired.

You can repair an image with the image window set to any view. However, in most cases, it will be easier to repair an image if you use the Zoom Tool to magnify the area on which you want to work. Click on the **Zoom Tool**, and click on the area you want to magnify. Press the (**Option**) [**Alt**] key and click on the image if you want to zoom out from the image. You also can set the image window view to 200% or 300%. Click in the text box located in the lower-left corner of the (image window) [work area] and type 200 or 300, or choose the **Zoom In** command from the **View** menu until the text box shows 200 or 300, or type in any other number to increase the magnification of the photo. Adjust the view so that you can see all or part of the image you want to repair in the active image window.

When you're ready to begin repairing the image, select the layer in which you want to store the corrected pixels. Then, magnify the image in the image window. Figure 12.3 shows the torn area of the image before and after the Clone Stamp Tool has been applied to the image. If you select the **Clone Stamp Tool** from the **Toolbox**, check the **Use All Layers** check box. This setting enables you to sample pixels from any layers located below the active layer in the **Layers** palette. Select the correction layer from the **Layers** palette. Then, sample and apply the Clone Stamp Tool in the image window, and repair areas close to the damaged area without altering the original image.

FIGURE 12.3

Create a new layer for different repair areas of the image. Compare the image before and after applying corrections by hiding and showing the correction layer in the **Layers** palette.

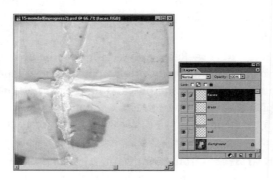
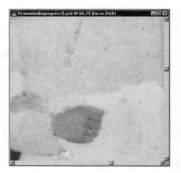

Keep these issues in mind when making image repairs with the Clone Stamp Tool:

- Choose a brush with a soft edge so that the edges of the brush strokes blend into the surrounding pixels.

- Pick a brush size that covers part of the torn area of the image. You can compare the torn area with the repaired pixels in the image. If the repair looks like it matches the rest of the image, you might want to repair the remaining torn area, or resample pixels close to each area of the torn image before applying the replacement pixels. Don't try to use a brush that's too large or too small to repair damaged areas in the image.

- Try to avoid sampling discolored or shaded areas of the image. If you sample damaged or worn areas of the image, they will be applied to the correction layer in other areas of the image. If you can't avoid sampling part of the damaged image, try choosing a smaller brush and reconstructing smaller portions of the damaged area.

- Avoid creating long strokes. Make a few small corrections, and then zoom out to a wide view to see whether the corrections match the surrounding image, as shown in Figure 12.4.

FIGURE 12.4
Zoom out to view the repaired portion of the image and compare it to the rest of the photo.

Removing Aged Color, Dust, and Stains

Although you can remove dust and stains before or after repairing an image, you might find that it is easier to make small corrections to an image after fixing the bigger problems. For example, Figure 12.5 shows how it is a little easier to identify the stains and dust after the folds and tears have been removed.

Again, you can apply the Clone Stamp Tool to remove dust, stains, or discoloration in an image. Use the following steps to correct a damaged image:

1. Click on the **Clone Stamp Tool** in the **Toolbox**, and then choose a soft-edge brush from the options bar. Be sure to use a brush size that roughly covers part of the size of each stain. Also, check the **Use All Layers** check box. This setting enables you to sample pixels in any layer below the selected layer. Then, apply the sample pixels to only the selected layer.

FIGURE 12.5

Stains and dust cover most of the scanned photo. This is a close-up of the white jacket shown in Figure 12.4. You might need to look closely to find the faint hues of the stains.

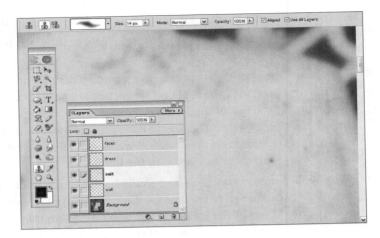

2. Look for an area of pixels near the stained pixels.

3. Sample a set of pixels about half the size of the stained area by holding down the (**Option**) [**Alt**] key while moving the cursor over the area to be sampled. The tool will sample the image from the background layer.

4. Select the correction layer in the **Layers** palette. Apply the Clone Stamp Tool to the correction layer. Remove a small portion of the stain, and hide and show the correction layer to see whether your correction matches the unstained areas of the image.

5. Repeat these steps until the dust or stain is removed. Then, clean up the area in the image window, as shown in Figure 12.6. The Clone Stamp Tool is the most commonly used tool for removing dust and scratches. However, you might want to experiment with the Smudge, Blur, or Magic Eraser tools to see whether they are easier to use or provide better results for the image you're working with.

You can apply the **Undo** command to remove any corrections added to the image window. If you like part of a correction, try applying the Eraser Tool to the corrections layer. Remove any undesired pixels from the correction layer to restore the original pixels.

You can choose from three kinds of eraser tools in the Toolbox. In addition to the standard Eraser Tool, you can remove a range of colors with the Magic Eraser Tool. It works similarly to the Magic Wand Tool, except it removes any color you click on in

tip

Hold down the **Shift** key and press the letter **E** to cycle through each eraser tool in the Toolbox.

Select the **Eraser**, **Magic Eraser**, or **Background Eraser Tool**. Hold down the (**Command**) [**Ctrl**] key to change the cursor to the Move Tool.

the image window. The Eraser and Magic Eraser Tools can be used to remove specific-colored pixels, or pixels in a certain location in a correction layer.

FIGURE 12.6

After applying the Clone Stamp Tool, the stains and dust are no longer visible in the photo.

You also can use the Background Eraser Tool to remove the pixels in a correction layer, thus exposing transparency. It can override the Lock Transparency setting if it has been applied to a layer. The Background Eraser Tool can show the previous layer through the layer where this tool has been applied.

Fine-Tuning the Image

To fine-tune an image, you have to move to different parts of the image and gradually repair small areas of the image. Compare the before and after areas by hiding and showing the layer that contains the corrections as you progress to see whether the corrected image resembles the original. This part of the restoration process can take quite a bit of time. Patience plays a big role, especially if you want to preserve as much of the original picture as possible.

After you've corrected most of the problems in the image, you might want to add fill or adjustment layers to pull together any disparately lit areas of the picture. Figure 12.7 shows fill and adjustment layers added to the repaired image to warm the colors in the photo. Adjust the settings in the fill or adjustment layers if needed, and then merge any visible layers you want to keep in the final picture.

You can add adjustment layers to correct any areas of the image that are too light or too dark.

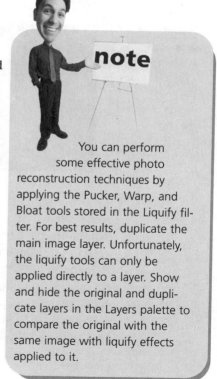

note

You can perform some effective photo reconstruction techniques by applying the Pucker, Warp, and Bloat tools stored in the Liquify filter. For best results, duplicate the main image layer. Unfortunately, the liquify tools can only be applied directly to a layer. Show and hide the original and duplicate layers in the Layers palette to compare the original with the same image with liquify effects applied to it.

Apply a fill layer and adjust its opacity level to add color to the image. You can create adjustment or fill layers for a selected area of the image, and then merge the correction layer and the fill or adjustment layer to make those changes permanent.

FIGURE 12.7

Merge layers together as corrections are made. Apply adjustment and gradient fill layers to pull the final image together.

Comparing Images

Before saving the final image, compare it to the original, damaged photo. You might want to keep one or two visual defects in the digitally retouched photo if you want to preserve the look and feel of the original photo. Figure 12.8 shows the final, flattened image.

FIGURE 12.8

After you've repaired folds, tears, and stains, the image should resemble the original.

If you want to post the image to a Web site, you can resize it after the layers have been flattened into a JPEG file. You might want to choose the Save for Web command from the File menu to optimize the file size of the Web file. However, if you want to print the image, it's best not to remove any pixel information by shrinking it.

Save the final image to your hard drive. Compare the original, damaged photo with the restored photo by zooming into both images. In Figure 12.9, notice that the original image has a little more detail than the restored image. However, it is difficult to tell where the damaged areas were upon examining the restored image.

FIGURE 12.9

Zoom into the original and compare it to the final image.

Rebuilding a Damaged Photo

Worn photos might also be missing portions of the original image. You can use the Clone Stamp Tool and, if needed, additional photos, to reconstruct missing areas of a scanned image. Figure 12.10 shows the before and after pictures of a photo of my great-grandmother. Wear and tear removed most of the left side of the photo. The following sections show you how to restore the missing areas of the image and then re-create the tattered, frayed areas of the photo.

FIGURE 12.10

A photo of my great-grandmother before and after the image was repaired.

Sorting Out Tasks by Layer

First, create a separate layer for each area of the photo that you want to correct or repair, as shown in Figure 12.11. In addition to the damaged areas on the left side of the picture, there are a few small scratches on the right. Apply the Clone Stamp Tool to sample and correct the scratches in a correction layer.

FIGURE 12.11

Create a
separate layer
for each area of
the image that
needs to be
repaired.

Assess the different kinds of damage before applying any tools to the image window
after selecting the appropriate correction layer in the **Layers** palette. You might
want to save a copy of the image as you work on it if you want to experiment with
different techniques for repairing the image. You also can duplicate and show or
hide different correction layers. You can delete a layer if it turns out you don't need
it as you repair the image with other correction layers.

Removing Scratches and Dirt

It can't hurt to remove any scratches or dirt from an image before you start to
rebuild the missing areas of the image. For example, if you plan to sample from an
area of an image that contains scratches, it will be easier to reconstruct the missing
areas after you remove any specks, dust, or scratches from the image. Then the
reconstructed image will not inherit these defects.

Before you begin to sample or repair the scratches or dirt, first zoom into a damaged
portion of the image, as shown in Figure 12.12. Try to identify the original color or
tonal range of the image. Also try to differentiate the paper and backdrop in the
photo from the subject of the photo.

The following steps show you how to remove scratches or dust from the photo:

1. Click on the **Create a New Layer** button at the bottom of the **Layers** palette.
   A new layer with a transparent background will appear in the **Layers** palette.

2. Select this new layer in the **Layers** palette. Click on the **Zoom Tool** (Z) in
   the **Toolbox**, and magnify the area of the image you want to rebuild (see
   Figure 12.12).

3. Choose the **Clone Stamp Tool** from the **Toolbox**. Check the **Use All
   Layers** check box. Select a brush size to match the thickness of the scratch.
   Then, use the Clone Stamp Tool to sample undamaged pixels and replace the
   scratches and specks with the sampled pixels. In this example, the Clone
   Stamp Tool will sample pixels from the background layer and apply them to
   the new layer to repair the scratches and dust in the image.

FIGURE 12.12

Zoom into the image and try to identify as much detail from the original photo as possible.

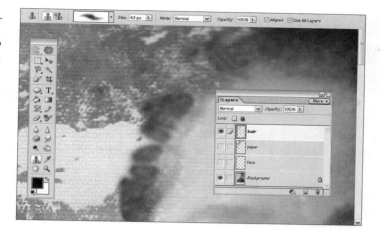

Replacing Missing Pieces of the Image

There are a couple of different ways you can replace a missing piece of an image. One way is to sample small portions from the existing image and reconstruct the missing area. The second way is to copy and paste part of an image from a different image file. This second method works well for replacing unique images, or images that are missing larger portions of an image. The first method is effective for reconstructing images missing small sections of an image.

The general process for replacing a missing portion of an area is fairly straightforward. First, select a correction layer in the Layers palette. Then, apply a tool, such as the Clone Stamp Tool, to the image window. Check the **Use All Layers** check box, and then sample a whole, undamaged area in the image. Apply the Clone Stamp Tool to fill in a missing chunk of the image with the sampled pixels. Zoom out to see whether the repaired area visually matches the rest of the picture.

Repeat these steps until the missing areas of the image are reconstructed. Try to use other photos of the subject to restore hairstyle or clothing patterns, if you have them. Figure 12.13 shows the repaired image after a tedious application of the Clone Stamp Tool.

FIGURE 12.13

Use the Clone Stamp Tool to reconstruct missing areas of the image.

Creating the Final Image

If the area of the photo behind the photo subject is seriously damaged, it might be easier to reconstruct as much of the subject as possible. Move the subject to a new image window. Then create a new backdrop by adding fill layers.

The following steps show you how to move the subject in the damaged photo to a new image window:

1. Use a selection tool, such as the Magic Wand Tool, to select the subject in the damaged photo. You also can press the (**Command**) [**Ctrl**] key while clicking on the layer containing the image you want to select to highlight the image. Then, choose the **Copy** command from the **Edit** menu.

2. Choose **New** from the **File** menu and create a new document. Photoshop Elements will automatically input the width and height of the image into the New dialog box. Select a transparent background for the new window.

3. Choose **Paste** from the **Edit** menu to add the selected image into the new image window (see Figure 12.14).

FIGURE 12.14

Copy the selected image and paste it into a new image window. The gray-and-white grid indicates that the background is transparent.

4. Choose **Gradient** from the **Layer**, **New Fill Layer** menu. Type a name for the gradient layer, and then click OK. Click on the gradient in the **Gradient Fill** window. The **Gradient Editor** window opens.

5. Click in each square slider control located below the gradient bar in the **Gradient Editor** window. Click in the **Color** box to choose a new color for the gradient. Then, click **OK** in the **Gradient Editor**. You might want to adjust the angle of the gradient to match the angle of the light source in the image window. Click **OK** in the **Gradient Fill** window to add the Gradient Fill Layer to the image window.

6. Select the **Solid Color** command from the **Layer**, **New Fill Layer** menu to add a fill or adjustment layer to the image (see Figure 12.15). You can adjust the colors and opacity levels of these layers and place them in the background and foreground of the image to help blend the colors of the pasted image with the gradient and fill layers in the image window.

FIGURE 12.15

Re-create the background of the original image by adding gradient and solid color fill layers.

The final image consists of three layers. In Figure 12.16, I first copied the subject into its own layer. Then I created a fill layer to create the backdrop and used the Merge Visible command to combine the subject with the new backdrop. Next I pasted the selected subject into the image window one more time. Finally, I added a gradient layer to the foreground to blend the highlights, shadows, and colors together.

FIGURE 12.16

The final image after it has been moved to a new window.

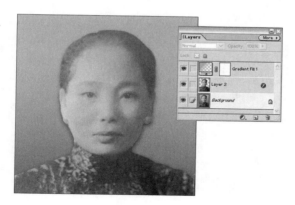

13

EXPERIMENTING WITH COMPOSITE IMAGES

A *composite image* is created when one or more images are placed overlapping and blended together in the same image window to create a unique composition. Photoshop Elements enables you to combine multiple images into a single document. Each image you paste into the image window is placed into its own new layer, above the background layer in the document. You can use Photoshop Elements to blend pixels between any two layers, or apply tools to blend the edge pixels of one image with another image to make the final picture appear realistic. This chapter introduces you to a few basic techniques you can use to create composite images.

Creating Composite Images

There are three steps involved in creating a composite: selecting an image, copying it, and then pasting it into the image window. Although the selection tools enable you to define the secondary image in a composite, the copy and paste commands enable you to duplicate and add images to an image window. A fourth step, moving and transforming the image, is optional but very likely to be part of your workflow when you're creating any realistic composite image.

Two scenarios exist for creating a composite image. The first one involves layering and possibly resizing selected images within the same image window. The second scenario involves adding one or more images to the active image window. The four-step process defines the workflow for both scenarios. The following steps walk you through this four-step process and explain some of the issues that might arise when you are creating a composite image:

1. **Selecting the image**—To define the image you want to copy, you must use a selection tool. The Magnetic Lasso Tool is probably the most helpful tool you can use to define the edges of a selection. However, you also can use the Marquee or Lasso selection tools to crop or copy a set of pixels you want to use with a composite image.

2. **Copying the image**—The **Copy** and **Paste** commands are located in the **Edit** menu. The **Copy** command enables you to duplicate pixels selected in the active image window and copy them to the Clipboard. The Clipboard is a Windows and Mac OS operating system resource designed to work hand in hand with the **Copy** and **Paste** commands. To place the contents of the Clipboard into the work area of the active image, you simply apply the Paste command.

3. **Pasting the image**—If you've already pasted an image into an image window, you've created a composite image. Each time you paste a new image into an image window, you will see a new layer appear in the **Layers** palette. The pasted image is also converted to the color mode of the new image window.

tip

If you want to experiment with an image before pasting it, you can copy and paste it into a new image window and adjust its size and color settings before combining it with other images. You also can modify each pasted image in its own layer. Select an image layer by clicking on a layer in the Layers palette. To find out more about layers, go to Chapter 10, "Working with Layers and Layer Styles."

4. **Moving, rotating, and transforming the image**—Although you can create a montage of images of any size or shape with composite images, you can also try to make the elements of the composite image blend together. The goal in this case is to make both images match the perspective of the background image, or create a logical spatial relationship resulting in a more believable picture. You may need to use the Rulers and Grid to align your images vertically or horizontally. You might also need to rotate, skew, or resize each image layer to make it fit with the rest of the picture.

If you're not sure which images you want to combine, you can save the images separately, each in its own layer. Choose the **File**, **Save As** command to open the Save As dialog box. To preserve each image in the composite in its own layer, save the image file as a Photoshop (PSD) file. Select **Photoshop** from the **Format** drop-down menu, and then click on **Save** to save the PSD file to your hard drive. When you are ready to save the final image, you can flatten all the layers into one. You also can optimize the color palette, change color modes, or apply any final adjustment layers or color corrections to the image before saving the final image to your hard drive.

Choosing Images

It's important to pick an appropriate starter image as the backdrop for the second, third, or fourth images as you define the composite image. Figure 13.1 shows a picture of daisies; it will be used as the backdrop for this first example, which will show you how to create a composite image.

Along with the content of an image, you need to consider the dimensions of the background image. Decide whether the width and height of the background image are compatible with the scale and size of the composite images you want to use. Also, check the resolution of the background image. Make sure you're working with the original, unedited source image, preferably in RGB color mode. If you plan to correct colors, apply a filter or effect, or modify the background image, you will get the best results if the image contains as many colors as possible.

One of the limitations of the **Copy** and **Paste** commands is that the Clipboard can store only one image at a time. When you choose the **Copy** command, the previous image stored in the Clipboard is deleted, and a new one is added in its place. If you want to create a composite image containing several pasted images, save each one as an original, unedited file on your hard drive.

Select an image you want to combine with the background image. You will want to choose an image that is slightly larger or one that matches the dimensions of the background image. For example, if the background image is 2000 pixels wide and 1500 pixels tall, choose a composite image that was also created at that size. Smaller images can also be added to the background image; however, if the smaller image needs to be resized into a larger, rather than smaller scale, its resolution will degrade, resulting in a pixilated image that won't match the higher-resolution background image.

FIGURE 13.1

The backdrop image has the proper dimensions and resolution for the images that will be placed here.

Before

Although each image you add to the background image defines the composition, the backdrop image can make or break a composite image. Figure 13.2 shows a pair of daffodils added to the foreground of the first image. Notice that the edges of the daffodils are soft so that they blend into the background image.

FIGURE 13.2

Adding daffodils into the backdrop photo results in a composite image.

After

Applying Selection Tools

Open an image file that contains the backdrop image you want to use to create the composite. Then, choose a selection tool from the Toolbox. Use it to highlight the image you want to paste into the background image (see Figure 13.3). You can soften the edges of the selected image with features such as the **Feather** command and the Blur Tool before moving it to another image window. You also can apply a filter or an effect to the selected image, or rotate or transform the image before copying it to the Clipboard.

FIGURE 13.3
The daffodils selected in this photo can be pasted into the image of the daisies.

The selected area in the image window behaves like a mask. The pixels located inside the marquee are editable. Pixels outside the selected area are not affected by any tools, filters, effects, or commands. After the selected area is defined, you can add adjustment or fill layers to a document. You might want to copy and paste the image into a new document window, as shown in Figure 13.4, if you want to store the selected image as a file on your hard drive.

Feathering the Selection

While the image is selected, you can apply the Feather command to soften its edges before copying it. Choose one of the selection tools to define the image you want to copy or move to another image window. Figure 13.5 shows the dashed line of the Magnetic Lasso Tool surrounding the selected image.

> **tip**
>
> You can copy an image from one layer into the selection area of a different layer to create a mask. First click on a layer in the Layers palette. Use a selection tool to outline the border of the image you want to copy. Choose the **Copy** command from the **Edit** menu, and then select the **Paste Into** command. The highlighted image in the selected layer acts as a mask to the pasted image.

FIGURE 13.4
Use a selection tool to select part of an image. Then copy and paste the selected image into a new document window.

IGURE 13.5

The Magnetic
Lasso Tool was
used to select the
daffodils.

Next, choose the Feather command from the **Select** menu or press (**Option-Command-D**) [**Alt+Ctrl+D**]. The Feather Selection dialog box will open (see Figure 13.6). Type a value between 1 and 9999 into the Feather Radius text box. If you want to create a subtle pixel feather effect, type 3 or 5 into the text box. Type a larger number, such as 12 or 15, if you want to create a more dramatic feathering effect. Click on **OK** to apply the effect to the selected area.

FIGURE 13.6

The Feather
Selection dialog
box enables you
to determine
how many pix-
els are blended
along the edges
of the area of
selected pixels.

COLOR MODES AND COMPOSITE IMAGES

Photoshop Elements supports four color modes: Bitmap, Grayscale, Indexed Color, and RGB. When you paste an image created in one color mode into another window that uses a different color mode, Photoshop Elements will convert the first image into the color mode of the target window.

RGB color mode was used to create all the images for this book. This default color mode supports the largest number of colors. If you're working with Grayscale or Indexed Color, based on a 256-color palette, you might want to convert the color mode of the composite image before pasting it into the target window. When you convert an image made up of hundreds of colors into two colors—for example, if you convert an RGB or Indexed Color image into a bitmap—you might not recognize the image as a bitmap. A bitmap consists only of black and white colors. A color image may turn into splotches of unrecognizable black and white patterns after you convert it to a bitmap.

On the other hand, when you convert a bitmap image into a higher-resolution color mode, the original image will be preserved. Because black and white are part of all the other color modes, Photoshop Elements does not need to convert them when the bitmap's color mode changes. To find out more about color modes, see Chapter 4, "Creating, Opening, and Converting Images."

Copying and Pasting the Image

Check the color mode of the image window containing the selected image before copying it. If you are planning to create composite images in Grayscale, Bitmap, or Indexed Color mode, you might want to change the color mode of an RGB image window to match the smaller-sized color palette of the target image. On the other hand, if you have converted an RGB image to Grayscale or Indexed Color mode, you might want to reopen and reselect the image in RGB mode so that you can copy as much color information as possible to the Clipboard.

When you paste an image into an image window, Photoshop Elements converts it to the color mode of the target image window. If the target window has a higher color depth than the image pasted into it, the color depth of the composite image will be preserved. However, if the target window has a lower color resolution than the pasted image, Photoshop Elements will remove color information from the composite image before adding it to the target window.

The following list describes the kinds of images and the color modes you can use with them to compose a composite image:

- **Line art**—You can work with vector graphics and Encapsulated PostScript files (EPS) in Photoshop Elements. This type of graphic image includes line art, shapes, and other black-and-white graphics, including text, with the color mode set to Bitmap. You can create composite images solely from bitmap images, or you can start from a bitmap image and then change the color mode of the document to RGB or Indexed Color if you want to add color composite images to it. For example, if the background image was created in Bitmap mode, you can change the color mode of the image window to RGB. Then you can paste Grayscale, Indexed Color, or RGB images into new layers without affecting the black-and-white background image.

- **Black-and-white photos**—You can work with black-and-white photographs in Grayscale color mode. You can combine two or more black-and-white photos, and view the composite image with a fixed palette of 256 shades of gray. This can help you pinpoint black and white levels in each image layer, and help maintain continuity across images in the final, flattened picture.

■ **Color images**—If any of the images you want to use in the composite contains color, change the color mode of the image window to RGB color mode. Choose RGB color from the Image, Mode menu. RGB color mode supports millions of colors and can help preserve the sharpness and quality of each image as you scale, rotate, or flip it in the image window.

■ **Color graphics**—*Color graphics* is a term that can refer to different kinds of graphics. The first kind of color graphic is a color image captured by a camera. The other is a color drawing or painting. In some cases, you might not be able to work with the original, full-color image that contains the RGB color information. If you plan to combine color graphics that contain 256 or fewer colors, you can work with these composite images in Indexed Color mode. However, Indexed Color mode restricts the maximum number of colors you can work with to 256. For best results, work in RGB mode until you finalize the location of each composite image and the order of each composite image layer. Then flatten the image into a single layer before converting it to Indexed Color mode.

CAN'T PASTE?

If you cannot paste an image into an image window, check your computer to see whether it is running low on memory. Click on the Applications menu if you're running Mac OS, or take a peek at the taskbar in Windows. If you have several applications open, save any files you have open, and then (**Quit**) [**Exit**] as many as you can to make more memory available for Windows or Mac OS.

The Clipboard can store a fairly large-sized image. However, the amount of memory available depends on how many other applications are running on the computer, and how much memory is available to the operating system. If Photoshop Elements cannot save an image to the Clipboard on Windows or Mac OS, you might need to (**Quit**) [**Exit**] one or more applications, or restart the computer.

You can view the contents of the Clipboard on a Mac by choosing **Show Clipboard** from the **Edit** menu in the Finder. If the copied image does not appear in the **Clipboard** window, or if no image can be pasted into the image window, the **Copy** command was not able to copy the selection into the Clipboard. You can clear the Clipboard by choosing **Purge**, **Clipboard** from the **Edit** menu.

You must use several commands to copy an image into the same window or move an image from one image window to another. Before copying or pasting an image, click on the source and target image's status bar to check the color mode of the image. The following list reviews the copy and paste commands available in Photoshop Elements:

- **Copy**—Creates a copy of the selected image and puts it in the Clipboard.

- **Cut**—Moves the selected image to the Clipboard, and deletes the original from the active image window.

- **Copy Merged**—Copies the contents of all layers of the selected area in the image window.

- **Paste**—Moves the image from the Clipboard to the active image window, creating a new layer for the image in the Layers palette.

- **Paste Into**—Enables you to paste an image from the Clipboard into the selected layer of the active image window instead of pasting it into a new layer. For example, you can use this command to paste an image into another selected image, such as a bitmap text or graphic object.

- **Duplicate Image**—Creates a new image window containing the contents of the previously active window. This command can help you view the same image at different magnification levels, or show and hide different layers in different windows.

Before you can paste an image, you must first select the image you want to copy. Then choose the **Copy** command from the **Edit** menu, or press (**Command-C**) [**Ctrl+C**] to copy the selected area to the Clipboard. Next, click on the image window where you want to add the selected image. This can be the same window you already have open, or another image window. Then choose the **Paste** command from the **Edit** menu or press (**Command-P**) [**Ctrl+P**]. The selected image will appear in the active image window. It is added to the document in a new, transparent layer. Select the **Move Tool** and click on the new layer in the **Layers** palette. Click and drag the image in the selected layer to move it to a new location in the image window.

Variations—Pasting Images

Because Photoshop Elements creates a new layer for each image you paste into the image window, anything you paste into an image window becomes a composite image. You might have noticed that there are two Paste commands in the Edit menu. The P**aste** command enables you to

note

The Composites recipe is located in the Add Elements group of recipes. Select the **Add Elements** group from the drop-down menu in the **Recipes** palette. Then, choose the **Composites** recipe to find out more about how to use selection tools, menu commands, and transform commands to work with composite images.

You can also follow recipes to find out how to remove or replace a background layer by choosing one of these topics in the **Recipes** palette.

add a new image to a new layer in the active image window. The **Paste Into** command enables you to add an image into an existing, unlocked layer. If you choose the **Paste Into** command, the selected image in the target layer becomes a mask for the pasted image. The pasted image will appear only within the boundary of the selected image, despite the fact that it might be taller or wider than the selected image.

You can apply the copy and paste commands to duplicate all or part of an image within the same image window. For example, you can enlarge or shrink a particular object in the image window, and then paste a second image behind it. The following sections show you how you can make the subject of a photo stand out from the background.

Follow the same four steps introduced in the beginning of this chapter. This time, however, you copy and paste part of the background image to place the composite image within the target image. First, use a selection tool to highlight the subject of the photo, as shown in Figure 13.7. Then, copy and paste the selected image into the same image window.

FIGURE 13.7

Place an image behind the flower by selecting, copying, and pasting the flower into its own layer.

After you paste an image into an image window, a new layer containing the selected area will appear in the Layers palette, as shown in Figure 13.8. If you're pasting the selected area into the image window from which it originated, the image window will look the same before and after the image is pasted. However, you can view the copied image in its new layer from the Layers palette.

Next, open the image you want to paste behind the duplicate composite image in the target image window. Figure 13.9 shows two yellow poppies that have been highlighted with a selection tool. Select the portion of the image you want to paste into the target image window. Then, choose the **Copy** command from the **Edit** menu, or press (**Command-C**) [**Ctrl+C**] to copy the selected image to the Clipboard.

FIGURE 13.8

The image remains the same. However, you can see that the flower now is on its own layer in the Layers palette.

FIGURE 13.9

Select the image you want to add to the first. Then add it using the Paste command.

Click on the target image window. In this example, it's the image window that already contains the composite image of the closed poppy. Then choose the **Paste** command from the **Edit** menu. The selected image will appear in the image window (see Figure 13.9). You can use the Move Tool to change the location of the selected image in the image window. If you want the second composite image to appear behind the first one, you might have to adjust the order of the image layers in the **Layers** palette. In this example, the layer containing the two poppies is sandwiched between the composite image of the closed poppy and the background image (see Figure 13.10).

WORKING WITH THE BACKGROUND LAYER

When you open an image file, the image is created in a locked background layer. You cannot change the opacity or blending mode settings for the background layer. However, you can apply selection tools, and copy and paste all or part of the background layer image into a new layer in the same image window. Depending on the image, you might want to duplicate the background by dragging and dropping it over the New Layer icon in the **Layers** palette. You can work with the copy of the background image, while keeping the background layer locked and hidden. This is a great way to keep a backup image close by if you do not want to work with multiple image windows in the work area.

Because composite images are stored in their own layer, you might want to change the state of the background layer into a regular layer. You can convert a background layer by double-clicking on it in the **Layers** palette. The Layer Properties window will open. The name of the background layer will change to Layer 0 (see Figure 13.10). Click on the **OK** button in the **Layer Properties** window to complete the conversion. Now you can apply filters, effects, or any Toolbox tools to Layer 0.

Putting Two Subjects Together

Composing a picture with objects is a little easier than trying to place two or more people in the same picture. You don't have to worry about eye contact between people or with the camera when composing a picture of flowers or other objects. Creating composite images with people or pets involves a little more work to make the images appear as if they were truly in the same place at the same time. This section shows you how to work with the Levels Adjustment layer to help two images blend together.

The background image can consist of any particular setting or location. However, the image resolution and dimensions of each of the subjects must be similar if you want the image to appear as realistic as possible. The subjects can be rotated, flipped, or transformed to match each other's height or make eye contact. When choosing the subjects for your composite picture, try to work with images that share the same color mode, and try to choose subjects that share the same general shape and size. Figure 13.11, for example, shows a cat that will be added to the picture of a dog.

FIGURE 13.11

Apply a selection tool to highlight the cat, which will become the composite image.

The easiest way to create a composite image with two or more subjects is to select a starting photo that contains at least one subject you want to include in the final picture. Next, choose a photo of another subject you want to add to the first picture. Apply a selection tool to the image to select only the portion you want to include in the final picture. Choose the **Copy** command from the **Edit** menu to move the selected image to the Clipboard. Then, click on the first image window and use the **Paste** command to add the second subject to the first picture, as shown in Figure 13.12.

FIGURE 13.12

Use the **Paste** command to add one image to another. You can use Photoshop Elements to create portraits that are difficult or impossible to set up in the real world.

As you combine live subjects into the same picture, you might need to correct color, or make tonal corrections to the background or composite images. For example, you might need to correct or adjust the tonal range, such as the highlights and shadows, so that two images from different photos fit in with the lighting in the new picture. In almost all cases, you can work on images with color correction, as well as other image-editing tools, the same way that you work with a noncomposite image.

Before you adjust the tonal range in either image, you might want to sample the black and white points of an image to determine the best tonal range. The black and white points in an image represent the darkest and lightest pixels. You also can use the Threshold command to view the black and white points in an image. The following steps show you how to find the black and white points in an image using the Threshold command:

1. Open an image in RGB mode.

2. Select a layer in the **Layers** palette.

3. Choose **Threshold** from the **Layer**, **New Adjustment Layer** menu. Click on **OK**.

4. Click on the slider control located on the left end of the **Threshold** window (see Figure 13.13). Gradually move it to the right until you can see the first hints of black in the image window. Note the threshold value in the text box in the Threshold window. That's the black point. Remember the location of the black point in the image window. You can use this pixel location to click on with the Eyedropper Tool if you need to sample the black point of the image.

FIGURE 13.13

The black pixels in the image represent the black point of the image.

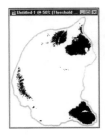

5. Next, click on the slider control on the far right in the Threshold window (see Figure 13.14). Gradually move it to the left until you can see the first hints of white in the image window. Note the threshold value in the text box in the Threshold window. This value is the white point for the image. Remember the location of the white point in the image window. You can click on this pixel location if you need to sample the white point of the image.

FIGURE 13.14

The first white pixels you can see in the image window represent the white point in the image.

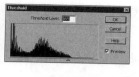

You also can use the Levels dialog box to view the black and white points of an image. The Levels command is located in the **Enhance**, **Brightness/Contrast** menu, or the **Layer**, **New Adjustment Layer** menu. The Levels dialog box (see Figure 13.15) enables you to remap the tonal distribution of pixels in an image to reduce any extreme dark or light areas of an image. Press the **(Option)** [**Alt**] key to put the **Levels** window into Auto Range mode. Then click on the black triangle control below the histogram and slide it to the right until the first black pixels appear in the image window. These pixels represent the black point in the image. If you continue to move the slider control to the right, you can see which pixels are being clipped to black. Perform these same steps with the white triangle control to identify the white points in the image, or to see which pixels are clipped to white.

Saving the Final Image

When you're ready to save the image for the Web or for printing, flatten the layers in the image. Select the **Save for Web** command from the **File** menu if you want to optimize the image for the Web. The **Save for Web** window enables you to customize color, file type, and other settings and preview the changes in a single window. Figure 13.16 shows how you can straighten the final image using the rulers and grid. You can also choose the Save or Save As command from the File menu to save the file to your hard drive.

note

When the (**Option**) [**Alt**] key is held down in the Levels window, the **Auto** button will change to **Options**. You can adjust the **Auto Range** settings for the black and white clip values in the **Levels** window. You can enter a value between 0.00% and 0.99% in each text box of the **Auto Range** window. Click on the **Reset** button (which replaces the **Cancel** button when the (**Option**) [**Alt**] key is held down) to reset the values in the Levels window to the original values when the window was first opened.

FIGURE 13.15

The Levels dialog box enables you to adjust the way pixels are distributed across the tonal range of the image. You also can use it to find the black and white points in an image.

FIGURE 13.16

Use the Grid to rotate and straighten a composite to match the alignment of the subjects in the background image layer.

Creating Special Effects with Composite Images

If you're a special-effects fan, you'll be happy to know you can create special effects with composite images. As in the other examples in this chapter, the Select and Move tools and the Copy and Paste commands play a big role in bringing two or more images together. The transform commands also help scale and size an image to fit in with the background image.

The special effects in an image can be defined purely by combining composite images that have filters or effects applied to them. You can also grow or shrink the composite image, turning a person into a giant or a midget. You can remove the color from a composite image to make that image stand out against a color background image, or add color composite images to a grayscale background image.

Choosing the First Image

One of the first things you'll need to decide is what kind of effect you want to create. This will help you pick the images you will use to create the composite image. If you're not sure where to start, pick the background image first. Figure 13.17 shows a close-up picture of a flower. Looking at this photo, you might not expect a special effect to be the first vision to pop into your head.

FIGURE 13.17

The original image, before any changes are made.

Because the flower takes up most of this photo, I added a relatively tiny person to create a giant flower effect. Take a look at the dimensions of each image you want to use before combining them. The flower is a 3-megapixel image, and the image of the person is a 640×480-pixel image. Both images are in millions of colors, and the target image window is set to RGB color mode. The dimensions and resolutions of both images enable them to come together nicely to create a composite image.

Figure 13.18 shows the completed image. The Move Tool and the transform commands are used to modify the composite image so that it fits in with the rest of the picture.

FIGURE 13.18

The same image after a composite has been added. The size of this flower makes the man at the top seem very tiny.

Transforming the Composite Image

There are many ways to transform an image in Photoshop Elements. You can resize it, rotate it, skew it, change its perspective, or flip it horizontally or vertically. To apply a transform command, you must first select the image.

Pick a selection tool from the Toolbox and use it to highlight the composite image you want to paste into the target image window. The Magnetic Lasso Tool was used to select the image shown in Figure 13.19. When the image is selected, you can choose the **Feather** command to soften the edges of the selected image, or apply a filter, an effect, or a layer style to it. You also can apply the **Rotate** or **Transform** commands (from the **Image** menu) to the selected image. However, it's easier to modify the selected image if you have the background image in the target window behind it.

> **tip**
>
> If you want a composite image to appear semi-transparent, like a ghost, you can lower the opacity value of the composite image in the Layers palette. Select the layer that contains the composite image in the Layers palette. Then type a lower value, such as 60 or 70, into the Opacity text box. The lower the value you type, the more transparent the image will appear.

FIGURE 13.19

Select the composite image and copy it to the Clipboard.

SCALING OBJECTS WITH THE TRANSFORM COMMANDS

Transform commands enable you to skew, distort, and apply perspective to an image. You can also grow or shrink the size of an image object.

You can press (**Command-T**) [**Ctrl+T**] to activate the **Free Transform** command. Most objects go into Free Transform mode when you select them with the Move Tool.

Transform commands are particularly helpful for scaling images that are pasted from one image window into another. You can shrink a large image so that it fits with the scale of the objects in the background layer of an image.

When you're ready to move the selected image to the other image window, choose the **Copy** command from the **Edit** menu or press (**Command-C**) [**Ctrl+C**]. The selected image will be copied to the Clipboard. Next, click on the target image window, which is the image window with the background image. Then choose the Paste command from the **Edit** menu, or press (**Command-P**) [**Ctrl+P**]. The selected image will appear in the active image window, as shown in Figure 13.20.

FIGURE 13.20
Paste the selected image on the left into the target image window. Use the transform commands to size the image. Then use the Move Tool to compose the new picture.

Working with Multiple Composite Images

Creating an image consisting of two or more composite images is pretty similar to putting together a single composite image. The only real difference is that there are more images to coordinate in the final composition. Figure 13.21 shows the background image that's used to create the multi-image composite image in this section.

Figure 13.22 shows the photo before any changes were made. I've added two photos of flowers and a beach sunset to it to create a new photo. Each composite image originated from a different photo, taken at different times at different locations with different cameras.

FIGURE 13.21
The golden gate bridge photo before changes. It has a lot of empty blue sky.

FIGURE 13.22

FIGURE 13.22
The same photo after it has been blended with three more photos.

Stacking Up Composite Images

If you're working with two- and three-megapixel images, you will want to preserve the dimensions of each image, in addition to all the color and image data for the selected image, by working with each image in RGB color mode. If you plan to paste several images into one file, keep an eye on the status bar. The file size of the target image will increase as you add or copy images in the Layers palette or image window.

One way to minimize the file size of a composite image is to work on some of the images prior to pasting them into the target image. Figure 13.23 shows a photo of the sun setting over the ocean. A gradient adjustment layer was added to this image to help blend it with the blue fill layer in the photo of the Golden Gate Bridge. Similarly, gradient adjustment layers were added to the photos of the sunflower and small white flowers to fade one side of each photo into the photo of the Golden Gate bridge. Saving each image in a separate image file enables you to correct colors, or customize the way it will blend with the other images in the final photo.

note

You don't have to have a background to create a composite image. You can paste images into a new document window with a white, transparent, or colored background. Then use the Move Tool to arrange the images into a photo-composition.

FIGURE 13.23

Perform any color corrections or image tweaks, such as this gradient adjustment layer, before combining with the final image.

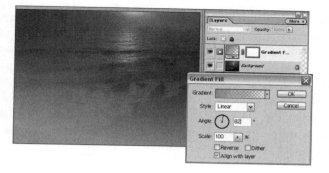

Rotating Images

When an image is pasted into an image window, it will appear in the same orientation and size as it was saved to the Clipboard. Although you can move an image using the Move Tool, you might also need to flip it horizontally or vertically, or rotate it clockwise or counter-clockwise to make the image fit in with the rest of the picture. Rotating and flipping an image are the most common corrections performed on composites. You must use several commands to rotate or flip an image. The following list briefly describes the rotate commands located in the Image, Rotate menu:

- **Free Rotate**—Rotates the selected image in any direction you choose. Click outside the border of the selected image. Then drag the mouse up or down, as desired.

- **90 Degrees Left or Right**—This moniker is somewhat of an oversimplification. But a 90-degree angle is about the same size as a quarter slice of pie. Rotate the selected image 90 degrees clockwise or counter-clockwise by choosing either of these commands.

- **180 Degrees**—Flips the selected image across the x axis. If the selected image is right side up, this command will rotate it so that it becomes upside down.

- **Flip Horizontal or Vertical**—Flips the image along an x or y axis. If you copy and paste the selected image, each of these commands can be used to create a mirror image of the original.

- **Rotate Canvas Commands**—The same commands can also be applied to the entire canvas area.

ROTATING AND RESIZING SELECTED IMAGE OBJECTS

You can freely rotate a pasted image using the Move Tool. First use a selection tool to select a portion of the background image in the window. Then copy and paste the selected area in the same image window. Select the new layer in the **Layers** palette. If you place the cursor beside the selected image, the cursor will change from an arrow to the rotate cursor (a double-headed arrow icon turned 90 degrees). Click beside the highlighted boundary (marked by a dashed line) and drag the mouse to rotate the selected image. You can grow or shrink the image by clicking and dragging any of the square handle boxes located on the boundary of the selected image.

Composing a New Photo

Each image added to a picture can either do nothing for the original or completely change the tone. Combining digital images into a composite can be extremely easy, if the source images are similar and are taken with similar cameras. Combining images that have more differences than similarities, such as combining a black-and-white image with a color one, can be a tedious task. Photoshop Elements enables you to work with any kind of image. However, the amount of time you'll spend fine-tuning the final composition will vary depending on what you're trying to accomplish, and the quality of the photo resources you have available to work with.

The composite image shown in Figure 13.24 shows how images taken with different cameras can be blended together with gradients or opacity value changes to create a complete, unique picture. When you combine images from a diverse set of source images, you likely will spend more time adjusting each image's perspective and scale using the transform commands. The Move Tool is another indispensable tool to change or tweak the location of each image. Try experimenting with the order of each of the image layers in the Layers palette. For example, you can make one image appear in front of another by dragging its layer above the other layer in the Layers palette.

FIGURE 13.24

Paste the selection into the active image window. Use the Move Tool to arrange the image and compose a new picture.

LAYERS AND BLENDING MODES

Another way you can blend composite images is by choosing a different blending mode for the image that resides in the topmost layer in the Layers palette. You can change the order of layers by clicking and dragging them in the **Layers** palette. Blending modes affect the way pixels interact with the image layer directly below it. The colors in the top layer are combined with the color in the layer directly below it to create a new, result color. To find out more about how to apply a blending mode to a layer, go to Chapter 10.

Finally, preserve the composite image and all the layer information and settings in your image file by first saving it as a native Photoshop file (*.PSD). The Photoshop, or PSD, file format preserves each layer in the image file. This enables you to continue editing each composite image at any time.

Flatten the layers to create the final image. Remember that after you flatten an image, it will be difficult to edit it as freely as you did when each composite image was in its own layer. Before you save the final image-flattened file on your hard drive, you can experiment with different optimization settings if you want to reduce the overall file size of the image. After the final file is saved, you might want to add copyright, source filenames, or photographer information into the image's **File Info** window.

PART IV

DESIGNING COMPLEX IMAGES

14

CREATING COMPLEX IMAGES

Effects, reflections, light, and shadow are some of the key elements that might not necessarily jump out at you in every photo, but definitely can make or break a picture. Some effects can improve the original composition, whereas others enable you to create entirely new ones. This chapter introduces the Liquify and Paste Into commands and teaches you how to create some cool effects. You also learn how to add a reflection or light source to an image, as well as remove shadows from an image.

Melting Images with the Liquify Filter

The Liquify filter consists of nine tools: Warp, Turbulence, Twirl Clockwise, Twirl Counterclockwise, Pucker, Bloat, Shift Pixels, Reflect, and Reconstruct. You can use these tools to perform small magical tweaks, or completely distort the pixels in a photo. The Reconstruct Tool enables you to undo any of the wacky effects created by the other tools in case you want to recall or switch back to the original image.

Open any image in RGB mode and choose the **Liquify** command from the **Filter**, **Distort** menu to access and apply the wondrous effects in the Liquify dialog box. If you are working with an image that contains more than one layer, you can apply the Liquify tools to a particular layer. If you want to apply this tool to all layers, you'll need to choose the **Flatten Image** command from the **Layer** menu to merge all layers into one first. Then, open the **Liquify filter** window and apply any of the tools to the image.

Applying Liquify Tools

To open the Liquify dialog box, choose **Liquify** from the **Filters** palette, or from the **Filter**, **Distort** menu. Click on a tool to select it. You can choose from the Twirl Counterclockwise, Twirl Clockwise, Pucker, Bloat, Turbulence, Shift, or Reflection tools located in the upper-left corner of the Liquify dialog box, as shown in Figure 14.1. In most cases, the secret to applying the Liquify tools is choosing the right brush size. Adjust the Brush Size to match 25% to 80% of the area of the image you want to change using the selected tool.

To apply any of the Liquify tools, click and hold down the mouse and/or drag the mouse on the image. Because each tool has a slightly different behavior, you'll discover that some tools work best when dragged over the image, and others create cool effects if you just click and hold down the mouse.

To apply the Warp Tool, click and drag the cursor over the image. The pixels will move in the direction of the brush. You can create high-quality image correction (for example, enlarge eyes, shrink a nose) with the Pucker or Bloat tools. Click and hold down the mouse to see the image pucker or bloat. Hold the mouse down briefly to make a subtle change to the image. Dragging the mouse around will distort the original image beyond recognition and is not what you want to do if you want the photo to look more realistic.

Press a letter on the keyboard, such as P for Pucker or B for Bloat, to quickly change between tools. Click **Revert to** remove any recent liquify effects applied to the image. The Reconstruct Tool enables you to reverse the effects created by the other Liquify tools.

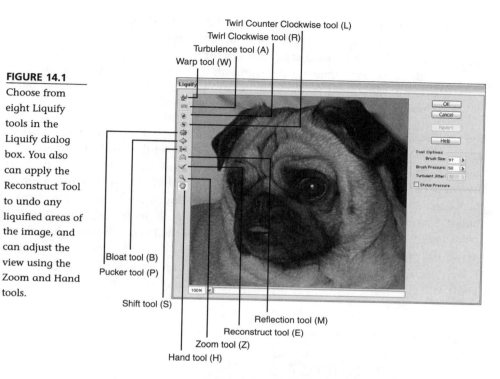

Twirl Counter Clockwise tool (L)
Twirl Clockwise tool (R)
Turbulence tool (A)
Warp tool (W)

FIGURE 14.1

Choose from eight Liquify tools in the Liquify dialog box. You also can apply the Reconstruct Tool to undo any liquified areas of the image, and can adjust the view using the Zoom and Hand tools.

Bloat tool (B)
Pucker tool (P)

Shift tool (S)

Reflection tool (M)
Reconstruct tool (E)
Zoom tool (Z)
Hand tool (H)

The following list briefly describes each tool in the Liquify dialog box:

- **Warp**—Melts pixels in the direction in which the cursor moves.
- **Turbulence**—Adds noise to the pixels directly below the cursor.
- **Twirl Counterclockwise**—Moves pixels downward and around in a counterclockwise direction.
- **Twirl Clockwise**—Pushes pixels downward and around in a clockwise direction.
- **Pucker**—Bends the pixels toward the center of the brush.
- **Bloat**—Pushes pixels from the center of the brush outward.
- **Shift**—Moves pixels perpendicular to the direction the cursor moves.
- **Reflection**—Copies pixels below the brush location in the image to the brush area. You can apply this tool by clicking and dragging the cursor on the image. The set of pixels below the brush will be reflected. If you (**Option-Drag**) [**Alt+Drag**] the pixels located above, the brush will be reflected in the opposite direction of the cursor movement. You can overlap strokes to create a reflection effect.
- **Reconstruct**—Restores pixels to the original location when the Liquify dialog box is open. You also can press the (**Option**) [**Alt**] button to change the

Cancel button into the **Reset** button. Click on the **Reset** button to remove any of the tools that have been applied to the image in the Liquify dialog box. The **Revert** button performs a similar task. If you apply one of the Liquify tools to the image, the Revert button becomes active. Click on the **Revert** button to restore the image to its original state when the Liquify dialog box opened the image for the current session.

The key to using each tool is to customize the brush size. Type a value into the Brush Size text box, or click on the arrow and use the slider to set the brush size on the Liquify Tools. The larger the number, the larger the brush. Figure 14.2 shows how the Warp Tool enables you to push pixels around with a 97 pixel-size brush. Apply short strokes to the subject's jaw line, eyes, and brow line to adjust the shape of the subject. The effect is subtle, but I moved the eye slightly to the left using the Warp Tool, stretched the edges of the right eye, and applied the Pucker Tool to reduce the overall size of the eye.

FIGURE 14.2

Reshape the pug's brow line by applying short strokes with the Warp Tool.

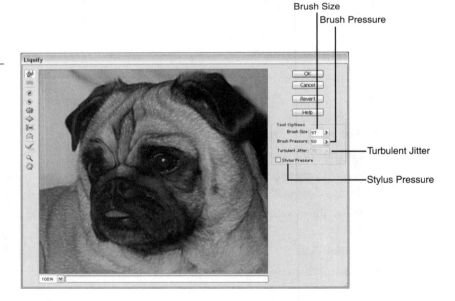

You can also adjust the brush pressure, the turbulence jitter, and, if you are using a pen tablet, the stylus pressure. The number you type in the Brush Pressure text box will determine how quickly the selected Liquify Tool applies the effect to the image. The number in the Turbulence Jitter text box enables you to add distortion as you apply the brush for each tool.

You can apply one tool to create an effect, or combine tools in any order to create elaborate effects. Figure 14.3 shows the image after the Warp, Bloat, Pucker, and

Twirl tools were applied. Each effect is subtle. You can use the Warp Tool to push up the jaw line of the subject. Bring out the subject's eye or cheek bones with the Bloat Tool, and reduce eye bulge with the Pucker Tool. You can create more dramatic effects if you apply each tool more extensively to different areas of the subject.

FIGURE 14.3

Apply the Pucker Tool to reduce the size of the subject's tongue.

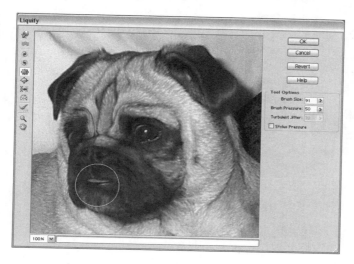

Reverse Effects with the Reconstruct Tool

The Reconstruct Tool enables you to undo any Liquify Tool applied to an image. You can also press the Revert button to return the image to its first open state. Figure 14.4 shows how the Reconstruct Tool restored the extended tongue of the subject. The Reconstruct Tool can undo any Liquify Tool applied to the image. However, when you close the Liquify dialog box, the tool changes are saved to the active image. As you work on an image in the Liquify dialog box, you can also use (**Command-Z**) [**Ctrl+Z**] with each tool to undo each step of the previous task in the image area of the Liquify dialog box.

When you click on **OK**, any changes you made to the image in the Liquify dialog box will be applied to the active image window. You can choose a previous state of the image from the History palette, or choose **Undo** from the **Edit** menu if you decide not to keep any of the Liquify filter changes.

tip

Hold down the (**Option**) [**Alt**] key, and the **Cancel** button in the Liquify dialog box will change to Reset. Click on the **Reset** button to remove any of the tools applied to the image. The **Revert** and **Reset** buttons perform the same task, restoring the image to its original state when first opened. However, the **Revert** button also returns each tool to its original settings in addition to returning the image to its original state.

FIGURE 14.4

Undo any of the
other tools by
applying the
Reconstruct Tool.

Pasting an Image into Text

The Liquify filter provides a set of tools that enable
you to create great-looking, sophisticated special
effects. Another way of creating a special effect is
to paste an image into text. You can do this by
choosing the **Paste Into** command after applying the selection tools and the **Copy** command to
an image. Unlike the Liquify filter, the **Paste
Into** command involves following a set of steps to
create the resulting special effect.

The **Paste Into** command pastes a bitmap from
the Clipboard into a selected object in the image
window. The bitmap image can be added to a
selected set of pixels in an existing layer in the
Layers palette. The following example shows you
how to fill an image into text using the **Paste
Into** command.

Creating Text to Fill with an Image

The Horizontal and Vertical Type tools enable you
to add text to a layer in the active image window.
Click on the **Horizontal** or **Vertical Type** Tool in
the **Toolbox**, and then click in the image window.

note

You might need to
increase the size of the
text object if you want to see
more of the image that is pasted
into the text. Click on the layer
containing the text object from
the **Layers** palette. Then,
select the **Move Tool** from the
Toolbox. The grow handles will
appear on the borders of the text
object. Click and drag the corner
handles away from the center of
the text object to grow the size
of the text object.

Adjust the **Horizontal** or **Vertical Type Tool** settings in the options bar. Then type some text. The text will appear in the image window (see Figure 14.5).

Text is added to an image window as a vector graphic. The Horizontal and Vertical Type tools create vector graphics stored in a special Text layer. The Horizontal Type Mask and Vertical Type Mask tools add text as a bitmap to an existing layer. If you want to apply the **Paste Into** command to text, the text object must be converted into a bitmap. You won't be able to use the Type Tool to modify the bitmap text.

FIGURE 14.5

Add text with one of the type tools. Then, scale it to a larger size with the Move Tool.

You can convert text into a bitmap by (**Command-clicking**) [**Ctrl+clicking**] the text layer, as shown in Figure 14.6. Then copy and paste the text object into the image window. Another way to convert text is to select the **Text** layer from the **Layers** palette and then choose **Simplify Layer** from the **Layer** menu. A bitmap image of the text will be created in a new layer (not a text layer).

FIGURE 14.6

Select the text object and copy and paste it to convert it to a bitmap image. Copying the image to the Clipboard converts the vector text object into a bitmap graphic.

BITMAP VERSUS VECTOR GRAPHICS

If you're not sure whether to use a bitmap or vector graphic, first decide what you want to do with the text. If you want to choose or change a font, font size, font style, or format of the text object, you'll want to preserve the original text layer created by the type tools.

You can take advantage of hiding and showing layers and convert any text into a bitmap by choosing Simplify Layer from the Layer menu. Bitmaps enable you to experiment with a filter or an effect, or apply the **Paste Into** command to a bitmap text object. To find out more about graphics, see Chapter 11.

Selecting the Image for the Text

Open another image that you want to place inside the text object. In most cases, the shape of each letter of text will prevent the image from being recognizable. Choose an image based on the way color and tonal range are distributed. Then, use a selection tool to select the area of the image you want to paste into the text, as shown in Figure 14.7. Then select the **Copy** command from the **Edit** menu or press (**Command-C**) [**Ctrl+C**].

FIGURE 14.7

Select the image to be pasted into the bitmap text object.

In the image window that contains the text object, (**Command-click**) [**Ctrl+click**] on the layer that contains the bitmap text object to select it. If you don't select the bitmapped text, Photoshop Elements won't know what to paste the second image into. Choose the **Paste Into** command from the **Edit** menu or press (**Shift-Command-V**) [**Shift+Ctrl+V**]. The image of the mushrooms will be pasted into the text object, as shown in Figure 14.8. Use the **Transform** and **Rotate** commands to customize the scale and orientation of the image as it appears in the text. Click on the check button in the options bar to save your changes.

FIGURE 14.8

Choose the Paste Into command to add the image to the text object.

You can apply filters, effects, or layer styles to the combined text and graphic. For example, in Figure 14.9, the Simple Emboss layer style was applied to the text. The Bevel and Drop Shadow layer styles give the text a three-dimensional look. You can apply more than one layer style, as well as any filter or effect. Use the **Undo History** palette to revert the image window to a previous state, or create a copy of the text layer and hide it to create a backup of your work.

Double-click on the f icon—located on the right side of a layer that has had a layer style applied to it—to open the Style Settings dialog box. You can customize any of the layer styles applied to a text or graphics layer from the Style Settings dialog box shown in Figure 14.10. Set the lighting angle, use of global light, shadow distance, outer glow size, inner glow size, or bevel size and direction, and preview any changes in the active image window.

tip

If the image with which you chose to fill your text is smaller than the text, it will not automatically resize to fill the entire block of text. You will need to use the handles on the bounding box of the pasted image to expand the pasted image so that it is larger than the text block. The pasted image then will fill the entire block of selected text wherever the text and image intersect. You can use the Move Tool to move the pasted image around until the parts of the image that you want to show appear in the text.

FIGURE 14.9

Add a layer style to the text object to enhance the effect.

Each layer style setting has a slider control combined with a text box. You can type in a value in the text box, or move the slider control to choose a new value for a style setting. If you want to save your changes, click on **OK**. Click **Cancel** if you do not want to save any changes you've made.

FIGURE 14.10

Customize the layer style settings in the Style Settings dialog box.

You also can adjust the tonal range and color settings of the bitmap text. Select the text by (**Command-clicking**) [**Ctrl+clicking**] in its layer. Then add an adjustment or fill layer specifically for the size and shape of the selected text. Experiment with different settings until you find the right combination. The final image appears in Figure 14.11.

FIGURE 14.11

The image in the text object is barely recognizable in the final picture.

Adding a Reflection to an Image

Reflections, lighting, and shadows are some of the elements that make photos seem real. For example, if you see a reflection of an image on the surface of a wall, you might think the wall is made of glass or is a mirror. You can use the Copy and Paste tools, combined with the Rotate and Transform commands, as well as the layer blending and opacity settings, to create custom reflections in an image.

For this example, a composite image is added to a background image. Then a reflection of the composite image is added to give the photo a 3-D effect. Figure 14.12 shows how the Magnetic Lasso Tool selects an Aibo dog, which is to be copied and pasted into a picture of a sunset.

FIGURE 14.12

Select the composite image for the picture you want to create.

You might need to scale the pasted image so that it matches the dimensions of the background image. The new image is pasted into its own new layer. If you see the small square handles shown in Figure 14.13, you can click on one of these handles to grow or shrink an image. Click on one of the handles on the border of the pasted image and drag it to resize the image. The border of the transform box won't always cover the borders of the composite image. Click on the **Move Tool**, and move the image to a new location in the image window.

Bitmap graphics don't retain their image quality if you try to make them larger. Photoshop Elements will interpolate the pixels to create the larger image. It does this by creating more pixels for each existing color, creating a squarish-looking, blocky image, also referred to as pixelation.

FIGURE 14.13

Scale the composite image to fit with the background image.

Although an image can be transformed when you first paste it into the image window, you can apply the Transform commands in several other ways. The following list shows you the many ways to activate the Scale, Skew, Distort, and Perspective Transform commands:

- **Move Tool**—Select the **Move Tool** from the **Toolbox**. Then, click on an image in the image window to select it and activate the Transform commands. You can click and drag the side or corner handles on the selected object to grow or shrink it.

- **Layers palette**—Click on a layer to select a text or graphic from the image window. If layers are linked, the transformations affect all linked layers.

- **Shape Selection**—Choose the **Shape Tool** from the **Toolbox**, and add a shape object to the image window. Then, choose the **Shape Selection Tool** (black arrow icon) from the **Shape** fly-out menu in the **Toolbox**. Click on the shape object with the Shape Selection Tool, and then choose the **Move Tool** to resize the shape object.

- **Transform menu**—Although some of these options are also accessible from the options bar when certain tools are active, you can skew, distort, or change the perspective of the selected object by choosing the corresponding command from the **Image**, **Transform** menu, shown in Figure 14.14.

FIGURE 14.14
Apply the Transform commands to add perspective to the composite image.

You must select an element in a text or image layer before you can apply one of the Transform commands. First, choose a selection tool and select part of an image in the image window. Then, copy and paste the image into the same window. You also can create a shape using one of the shape tools in the Toolbox, or choose **Select All** from the **Edit** menu to select the image in the active layer. Next, choose one of the Transform commands from the **Transform** menu.

When you select Free Transform, Skew, Distort, or Scale from the Image, Transform menu, several settings appear in the options bar. Choose from the buttons in the middle of the bar to rotate, scale, or skew the selected object. You can use any combination of Transform commands before saving the final transformed object.

On the far-left side of the options bar is a rectangle shape with a square on each corner and midpoint of each line, plus a square at its center. Click on one of these squares to set the center point of the selected object. Experiment with different center points combined with different Rotate commands.

Width, Height, and Rotate text boxes are also present in the options bar. You can type a new size or angle for the selected object into each text box, or click and drag the handles of the bounding box in the image window to change the size of the object. Click on the link icon if you want to preserve proportional relationships between the width and height of the object whenever a new value is typed into the width or height text box.

The following list briefly describes how each of the Transform commands works:

- **Free Transform**—Rotates the image clockwise or counterclockwise, or grows or shrinks the selected object.

- **Skew**—Extends or contracts one side or corner while preserving the proportions of the object. Creates a slanting effect.

- **Distort**—Collapses or expands a side or corner of the selected object. Stretches or squishes part of an image.

- **Perspective**—Grows or shrinks any side of an object to apply perspective to the bounding box.

After you've transformed and shaped the image, you can move it to a new location in the image window to create your composition. Identify a light source in the background image, and try to decide where the reflection of the composite image should be located. You might also want to make any tonal or color corrections to the composite or background image.

PERSERVING PROPORTIONS

When you apply a **Transform** command to an image object, you can preserve the original width and height relationship of the image by holding down the (**Option**) [**Alt**] key. Or, activate (the **Link** button will be in the down state) the Link icon in the options bar while resizing the corner handle of the object. Preserving the original proportions of the image enables you to limit the amount of distortion to the original image as you grow or shrink it.

If you do not want to preserve the object's original proportions, you can deactivate the Link button in the options bar or click and drag the corner handle to choose any combination of width or height for the object. This setting enables you to easily distort the dimensions of the selected image.

Creating the Reflected Image

The key to creating the reflection of the composite image is the Opacity setting in the **Layers** palette. Many of the skills you mastered while using the **Transform** and **Rotate** commands can also be used to create the reflected image. To create the reflection of the composite image, follow these steps:

1. (**Command-click**) [**Ctrl+click**] the composite layer, and then copy and paste the image into the image window. A new layer will be created with the copied image.

2. Use the **Move Tool** to select the copied image. Then choose **Flip Vertical** (or **Flip Horizontal**) from the **Image**, **Rotate** menu.

3. Select the layer containing the reflection, and decrease the Opacity setting from the **Layers** palette, as shown in Figure 14.15.

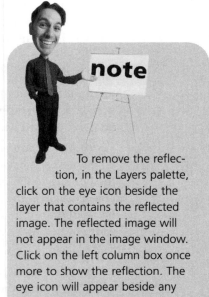

note

To remove the reflection, in the Layers palette, click on the eye icon beside the layer that contains the reflected image. The reflected image will not appear in the image window. Click on the left column box once more to show the reflection. The eye icon will appear beside any layer that appears in the image window.

Composite image

FIGURE 14.15
Create a copy of the composite image and then paste and flip it vertically. Decrease the Opacity value to create the reflected image.

Copy of composite image

Composing the Final Image

If the background image does not contain an obvious light source, move the composite image and its reflection to different locations in the image to see which positions fit best with the light and shadows in the background image (see Figure 14.16). You might also want to experiment with different opacity settings for the reflection.

FIGURE 14.16

Move the reflection around in the image to see how it matches up with the primary composite image.

After you've finalized the placement of the composite image and its reflection, as shown in Figure 14.17, you can create one more copy of the composite image for use as the composite image's shadow. As with the reflection, you can use the Transform and Rotate commands to create the shadow. With the shadow, though, you can add a Gradient Fill layer to darken the resulting image and fade it into the background image.

FIGURE 14.17

This figure shows the reflected image after the Transform commands have been applied to it.

You also can add a solid or gradient fill layer to the overall image to bring the composite and background images together. For example, if the background image contains a sunrise or sunset, you might want to consider adding an orange fill or gradient so that the composite image shares hues similar to those of the background image, as was done in Figure 14.18.

Lighten and Remove Shadows

Another conundrum of working with digital pictures is how to add more detail to dark, shadowy images. Starting with a two- or three-megapixel image can make a big difference. The more image data in the image file, the higher the likelihood you can lighten the image, although the tonal and color information won't match the rest of the lighter areas of the picture.

FIGURE 14.18

Determine the light source in the picture, and then move and rotate the reflection to match it. The background image is dimmed in this figure to emphasize the location of the drop shadow for the composite.

You can use many techniques to lighten dark areas of an image. The best approach is to work with smaller areas of the image instead of trying to fix the entire image in one fell swoop. Figure 14.19 shows an area selected with the Magic Wand Tool. You can apply the Dodge Tool to lighten the shadows in the selected area.

Lightened area

FIGURE 14.19

Select a shadow in the image with the Magic Wand Tool. Then, apply the Dodge Tool to lighten the selected area.

Dodge tool

COLOR-CORRECTION RECIPES

The **Recipes** palette contains a short list of instructions you can follow to learn how to use different tools in Photoshop Elements. For instance, you can learn how to correct colors using the **Brightness and Contrast**, **Hue and Saturation**, **Tonal Range**, and **Replace Color** commands.

Some steps have a green arrow button beside them. Click on the button to choose a menu command or Toolbox tool, or to open a tool window.

Cleaning Up Shadows with Layers

Add a new, blank layer to the image if you want to experiment with making shadows lighter. In Figure 14.20, I've created a copy of the background layer as a backup layer. Then, I clicked on the eye icon to hide the copied layer in the **Layers** palette. Next, I added a new layer that I renamed Shadow Removal. You can select dark areas of the original image and copy and paste them into this new layer to see whether the tonal range tools can lighten and blend these areas, before merging any changes with the original image.

FIGURE 14.20

Create a new layer so that you can apply any tools or effects to the image without affecting the original.

You can add a Levels adjustment layer to the image to remap the shadow, or dark pixels in the image. To select the shadowy areas of an image, do the following:

1. Open an image file. Choose the **Magic Wand Tool** from the **Toolbox**.

2. Click on the darkest areas of the shadows in the active image window with the Magic Wand Tool. Any similarly shaded pixels will be selected in the image window.

3. Choose **Levels** from the **Layer**, **New Adjustment Layer** menu. Type a name for the layer and click **OK**. The Levels dialog box will open, as shown in Figure 14.21.

4. Move the left slider to adjust the shadows level for the selected area in the image window. Then move the right slider to change the input level of the highlights. Changing the highlight setting should bring out more details in the shadowy areas.

5. Click **OK** to save your changes to the adjustment layer.

You can hide or show this layer if you want to compare the adjustment layer to the original image.

FIGURE 14.21

FIGURE 14.21

Select darker pixels with the Magic Wand Tool, and then adjust their visibility with the Levels Tool.

The lightened area of the selection might appear slightly off-color from the rest of the image. Choose **Hue/Saturation** from the **Layer**, **New Adjustment Layer** menu. The Hue/Saturation dialog box will open, as shown in Figure 14.22. Move the Hue slider control to adjust the color of the selected image area. The Saturation control will add or remove gray levels from the selected image area. Increase or decrease the amount of light in the selection by moving the Lightness slider control. If you're able to match the colors in the selected area with the rest of the image, click **OK** and save your changes to the adjustment layer. Otherwise, click **Cancel**.

FIGURE 14.22

Try to match the color of the lightened pixels with the Hue/Saturation command.

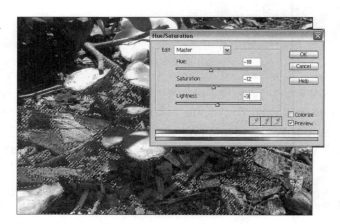

Neutralizing Pixels with the Dodge and Burn Tools

If you still have an active selection, deselect it by pressing (**Command-D**) [**Ctrl+D**]. Then take a look at the whole image. Compare the lightened areas of the image to the unchanged areas. You might find that parts of the image are a little too light compared to the rest of the picture.

You can use the Burn Tool from the Toolbox to darken pixels in the image window, as shown in Figure 14.23. The mushroom caps in this figure have been darkened to better match the overall tone of the image. When using the Burn or Dodge tools to darken or lighten pixels in an image, you'll want to use the Size, Range, and Exposure settings from the options bar. Select a brush size that generally matches the area of the image you want to correct. In Figure 14.23, I chose a soft edge brush size of 65 pixels.

FIGURE 14.23

Darken pixels that stand out by using the Burn Tool.

Darkened pixels

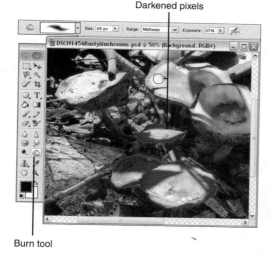

Burn tool

You can choose to darken the highlights, midtones, or shadows in the image window using the Range menu. Choose **Highlights** if you want to darken the brighter areas of the image. The Exposure slider control enables you to set a percentage (a value between 1 and 100) of how much the Burn or Dodge Tool affects the pixels in the image window. A lower value creates a more transparent effect. A higher value enables the Burn or Dodge Tool to function more like a brush with paint, having a stronger effect on any pixels touched by the tool.

The Dodge Tool lightens highlights, midtones, and shadows in an image. The Dodge Tool creates the opposite effect of the Burn Tool. You can lighten any dark areas in the image by clicking and dragging the Dodge Tool in the image window, as shown in Figure 14.24.

tip

Press the **Tab** key to hide the toolbars and palette windows from the work area. Only the image window will remain visible. Press **Tab** once more to show the toolbars and palette windows.

Press the **Shift+Tab keys** to hide only the palette windows. Press **Shift+Tab** a second time to show the palette windows.

FIGURE 14.24

Lighten pixels
by applying the
Dodge Tool to an
image layer.

Dodge tool   Lightened pixels

As you work on the image, compare the edited image to the original by opening a
backup of the original image, or by hiding the layer containing the work in
progress, and showing the original background image. Figure 14.25 shows the original photo. The edited image reveals details that were previously hidden by shadows.

FIGURE 14.25

Compare the
original on the
left with the new
image on the
right.

Adding a Light Source

A photo can have one or several light sources. Even if you can't identify a light
source in a photo, you know that photos are not possible in the absence of light.
Light plays a big role in any photo, and can also be the subject of a photo.

The Lighting Effects filter, located in the **Filter**, **Render** menu, enables you to
choose from 17 lighting effects. Figure 14.26 shows a photo taken on a cloudy day.
Although the colors are clear and the image is crisp, the lighting appears to be weak
in this photo.

FIGURE 14.26

FIGURE 14.26

Start with a photo that lacks an identifiable light source.

Choosing the Right Light

Open the Lighting Effects dialog box by choosing **Lighting Effects** from the **Filter**, **Render** menu. Several settings appear on the right side of the Lighting Effects dialog box, and a preview pane is located on the left side. Choose a light source from the **Style** drop-down menu, located at the top of the Lighting Effects dialog box.

Omni is the light type shown in Figure 14.27. Choose one of three different lights from the **Light Type** drop-down menu. Select **Directional**, **Omni**, or **Spotlight**. You can turn the light on or off by checking or unchecking the **On** check box. Click and drag the slider controls to adjust the Intensity and Focus of the type of light.

Customize the properties of the light by adjusting the settings for the Gloss, Material, Exposure, and Ambience slider controls.

Choose a light style from the **Style** drop-down menu to customize the light type for your photo.

Figure 14.28 shows some of the lighting styles available. I've selected the Parallel Directional light as a secondary light type for this photo.

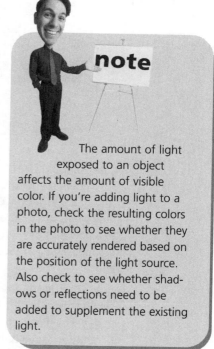

note

The amount of light exposed to an object affects the amount of visible color. If you're adding light to a photo, check the resulting colors in the photo to see whether they are accurately rendered based on the position of the light source. Also check to see whether shadows or reflections need to be added to supplement the existing light.

FIGURE 14.27
Preview the rendered light effect in the preview window.

FIGURE 14.28
Pick a lighting effect from the Style drop-down menu.

DUPLICATE A LIGHT

Hold down the (**Option**) [**Alt**] key in the preview area of the **Lighting Effects** window. Then click on the center, white circle in the light source and drag it to a new location in the preview window. Release the mouse to add the new light source to the image.

A white circle will appear in the preview pane, indicating where the first light source is positioned. Add as many light sources as you like to the image.

Click on the **Save** button if you want to save the customized settings for the light. Type a name for the light settings, and then click on **OK**. The new light should appear in the Styles list in the **Lighting Effects** window.

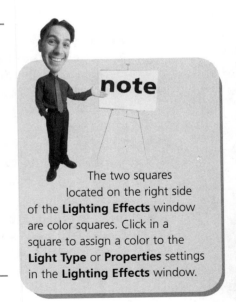

The two squares located on the right side of the **Lighting Effects** window are color squares. Click in a square to assign a color to the **Light Type** or **Properties** settings in the **Lighting Effects** window.

Applying Another Light Source

In our image, the parallel directional light brightens up the large portion of the photo dedicated to the gray, cloudy sky. The parallel directional light breaks up the upper-right half of the image by adding a gradient light pattern. However, the bridge and the flag are the subjects of the photo. Add another light source to the photo to highlight these subjects. I've chosen the Crossing light, shown in Figure 14.29, to point toward the subjects in the photo.

FIGURE 14.29

Adjust the properties of the light in the **Lighting Effects** window.

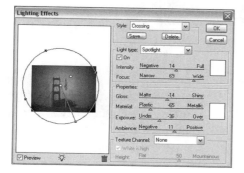

Viewing the Final Image

As you add each light source to the image, view the full image and decide whether the light source is worth keeping, or whether you should undo it and try adjusting some of the settings to create a more realistic lighting effect. Figure 14.30 shows the photo after the Parallel Directional and Crossing lights have been added to it. Although the image in the photo is essentially identical to the original, the additional light sources make it more colorful and visually interesting.

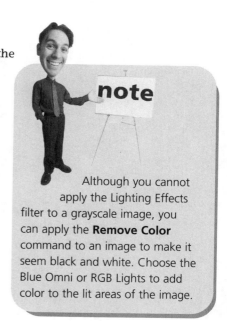

note

Although you cannot apply the Lighting Effects filter to a grayscale image, you can apply the **Remove Color** command to an image to make it seem black and white. Choose the Blue Omni or RGB Lights to add color to the lit areas of the image.

Applying Texture Channels

The Lighting Effects filter and its dialog box enable you to add texture to an image
(see Figure 14.31). First, select the image layer you want to modify with the Lighting
Effects filter. Then, choose **Lighting Effects** from the **Filter**, **Render** menu. The
Texture channel settings are located at the bottom of the **Lighting Effects** window.

Select a channel

FIGURE 14.31
Adjust texture
channel settings
in the Lighting
Effects dialog
box.

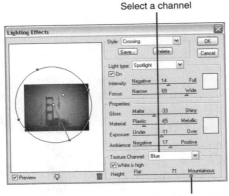

Adjust texure height

You can create a texture based on a red, green, or blue channel in the image by
choosing one of the options in the **Texture Channel** drop-down menu. Adjust the
height of the texture by moving the Height slider control to a value between 0 and
100. Check the **White Is High** check box if you want the lighter colors to rise from
the surface to create the texture.

Click and drag a slider control to adjust any of the lighting effects settings before
applying the texture channel settings to the image. Check the **Preview** check box,
located in the lower-left corner of the Lighting Effects dialog box, if you want to view
your changes in the active image window. Click **OK** to apply your changes (see
Figure 14.32), or click **Cancel** to return to the active image window.

FIGURE 14.32

The final image after the texture channel has been modified. As you increase the Height value, you will see more texture bumps appear in the preview and image windows.

15

ANIMATING IMAGES

The human eye interprets a series of changing images as motion. Animation can consist of two or more images that are played one after the other, or repeated over and over again. Full-motion animation can range from 12 to 30 frames per second. Cartoon characters, such as Bugs Bunny and Mickey Mouse, are likely to be the first cartoon characters you think of when you see the word "animation." However, over the years, digital imaging (also known as CGI, computer-generated images) and digital special effects have put animation center stage in live-action television and film, as well as for computer-generated and hand-drawn cartoons. The animation examples in this chapter show you how to create animation with photographed or scanned images.

Creating the First Frame

The first frame will contain a subject and a background. The background image can also be animated, and could be a separate photo. You will want to identify something that can be the subject of your animation for the first frame. You can then create additional key frames of animation from the first one.

Some images naturally hint at motion by the way the characters are positioned. Try to find a photo containing several discrete objects. It's easier to animate a small, recognizable object, rather than to try to animate something abstract, such as colors or shadows.

Next, decide how many frames of animation you want to create. If you want to create real-time motion, the frame rate can range from 18 to 32 frames per second (fps), although you really need 24 or more frames per second if you want to create quality animation. Depending on the size of each frame of animation, this can create a gigantic animation file.

For example, if one frame of animation contains a 1-megapixel image (approximately 500×700 pixels in a 1MB file), three frames will grow to be approximately 2MB to 3MB. You can reduce the overall size of the animation by reducing a 2000×1500 pixel image to a 640×480 pixel image. The best way to keep the file size small is to design an efficient animation. Keep an eye on the file size as you work on your animation.

Composing with Composite Images

If you're creating an animation that will share the same background image across frames, you'll probably be copying and pasting other images into each frame to create the animation. When you paste one or more images into the image window, each is added to the document as a new layer. Because the pasted image is placed on a layer above the background image, the resulting image is referred to as a composite. You can paste as many images as you like into the image window. Figure 15.1 shows two Aibo dogs copied from separate image windows into the background photo for the animation.

FIGURE 15.1

Combine a photo with composite images to create an interesting animation.

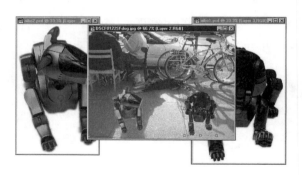

Use the Move Tool to place each image in the image window and compose the first frame of animation. As you put together the animation, try to decide how you want to light and frame the subjects in the animation. Try to think of a message, or give the animation some sort of theme. The following list describes important elements for you to consider when putting together an animation:

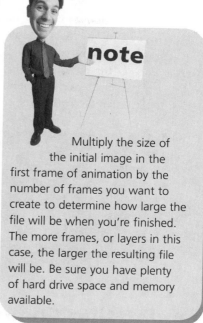

- **Lighting**—The central subject of a photo should be well-lit, crisp, and free of shadows.

- **Scale**—Larger images usually are perceived as closer to the viewer. Images that are smaller give the illusion of being farther away.

- **Perspective**—Exaggerating the background image or any props in a photo can distract the person from viewing the actual subject of a photo. Keeping the subject somewhere in the foreground of the photo in perspective with the background images can make animation easier to follow.

- **Shadows**—First, it's easiest to animate frames of animation if most of each frame is completely black or white. Regardless, keep an eye on how the shadows fall in each frame. Shadows and light give animation a three-dimensional look but are harder to animate.

- **Number of frames**—Adding more frames to an animation enables you to create smoother, more believable motion. Another way to simulate smoother motion is to add blur to one or more frames of the animation.

> **note**
>
> Multiply the size of the initial image in the first frame of animation by the number of frames you want to create to determine how large the file will be when you're finished. The more frames, or layers in this case, the larger the resulting file will be. Be sure you have plenty of hard drive space and memory available.

Finalizing the First Frame

Copy and paste as many images as you need in order to create the first frame of animation. In the Layers palette hide any layers of images you

> **note**
>
> Save your finished animation, or one in progress, as a PSD file to preserve the layer information. Each layer represents a frame of animation in a Photoshop (PSD) file. Saving in other file formats will flatten the image into a single layer.

might not want in the first frame. You can also apply filters, effects, and layer styles to add any final touches to one or all the images in the animation.

After you've decided which layers you want to use in the first frame of the animation, create a copy of the background layer so that you can create any additional frames using the same background image, as shown in Figure 15.2. Hide the copy of the background layer in the **Layers** palette. Then use the **Merge Visible** command in the **Layer** menu to merge all visible layers in the image window. Voila! You've created your first frame of animation!

FIGURE 15.2

Merge visible layers to create the first frame, or layer, of animation.

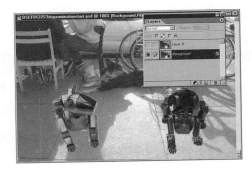

Animating Composite Images

An animation is broken down into two groups of images. The first group, *key frames*, includes the first and last frames of an animated sequence. For example, if you want to animate a stick figure walking from the left of the screen to the right, the first key frame would show the stick figure on the left side of the screen, and the last key frame would show the stick figure on the right side of the screen.

The second group of animated images is called *in-betweens* (or you might be familiar with the term *tweening*, which is the creation of these in-between frames). In-between images contain the frames of animation between the first and last key frames.

Add or select the second layer in the **Layers** palette to create the next frame of animation. You can approach putting together an animation in several ways. The traditional way is to create the first and last frames of animation. Then, create key frames of motion between the first and last frames, adding in-between frames to smooth out any motion between any of the key frames. However, you can also create each frame of animation sequentially.

It's All in the Layers

The trick to creating live motion in photos is to capture sequential images with a digital camera or video camera. If you want to experiment with motion, you can use a poseable figure and shoot it in different positions to create key frames of animation. Figure 15.3 shows two Aibo dogs placed in slightly different positions in the first and second layers of the animation.

These images were copied and pasted into the second layer of the document. Then the **Merge Visible** command was applied to the images needed for the second frame of animation. You can hide and show the first and second layers to play back the animation.

Copy and paste another set of composite images to create any additional frames of animation. In this example, two frames, or layers, are used to create a simple animation. Hide and show layers to make sure each object lines up with the previous object in the first and second layers of the animation. Then make each layer of the third frame visible. Choose **Merge Visible** to create the third layer in the **Layers** palette. Now you're ready to turn the animation into a full-fledged animated GIF file.

> **tip**
>
> You can decrease the opacity setting on a visible layer if you want to see how one layer of images overlaps with the previous layer, as shown later in Figure 15.8. This is similar to a technique used in animation called *onion skinning*, in which transparent sheets of paper hold each frame of the animation. These sheets enable the artist to see through each "frame" and make the slight adjustments from one page to the next that result in the animation you see when the frames are played in succession.

FIGURE 15.3
Hide and Show previous layers to place the composite images into the next frames of animation.

Creating an Animated GIF

An animated GIF is the file format used to store several frames of animation. It's popular because Internet Explorer and Netscape Navigator support this file format by default. You don't need to install a plug-in file to play an animated GIF in a browser window.

Photoshop Elements enables you to save layers as frames of animation. Choose **Save for Web** from the **File** menu to open the **Save for Web** window. Then choose **GIF** from the **Settings** drop-down menu. The GIF setting, located in the top-left drop-down menu, activates the **Animate** and **Transparency** check boxes shown in Figure 15.4. Check the **Animate** check box if you want Photoshop Elements to treat each layer as a frame of animation. You also can choose a palette, dither options, and the number of colors in the color palette from the drop-down menus located in the Settings area of the Save for Web dialog box.

Click on the arrow buttons in the **Save for Web** window to view each frame in the animation. Adjust the view of the image in the preview windows. The image on the left side of the **Save for Web** window is the current image in the active image window. The image on the right side of the window is the image as it would appear if the settings located on the right side of the **Save for Web** window are applied to the original image. I refer to the image on the right as the optimized image.

> **note**
>
> For Windows only (sorry, Macintosh folks), hold down the **Ctrl+Alt** keys when opening the **Save for Web** dialog box to delete any prior preference settings for the Save for Web dialog box.

FIGURE 15.4

Check the **Animate** check box to turn the image file into an animated GIF.

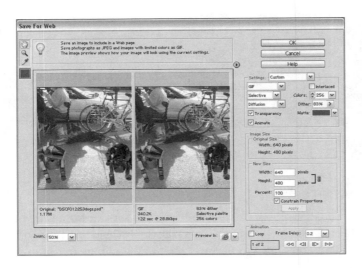

The Hand, Zoom, Eyedropper, and Color Picker tools are located in the upper-left corner of the **Save for Web** window. You can use the Hand Tool to position the preview images in their respective windows. The Zoom Tool enables you to adjust the view of the original and optimized image in the **Save for Web** window. Select the magnifying glass icon and click in either window to zoom into the image. Hold down the (**Option**) [**Alt**] key and click to zoom away. Use the Eyedropper Tool if you want to sample a color from the image windows in the **Save for Web** window. To do so, click the Eyedropper Tool icon to select it, and then click on a color in the original or optimized image. The color square located below the Eyedropper Tool will change to the selected color.

Adjusting Playback Settings

Each of the settings in the **Animation** section of the **Save for Web** window works independently of the others. For instance, the Frame Delay setting does not affect the number of frames, and it can be changed whether the Loop box is checked or unchecked.

You can adjust the amount of time between each frame of animation by typing a value in the Frame Delay text box, shown in Figure 15.5. Click on the drop-down menu arrow to choose 0, .1, .2, .5, 1.0, 2.0, 5.0, or 10 minutes. The best way to decide whether you like the frame delay settings is to preview the animation in a browser window, as described next.

FIGURE 15.5

Customize play-back by selecting frame delay and loop settings in the **Save for Web** window.

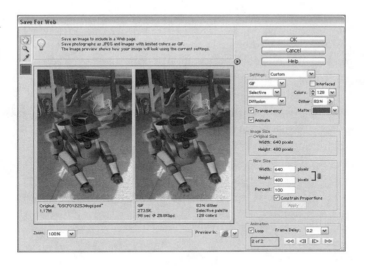

If you want the animation to play forward repeatedly, like some of the annoying Web ads found on some Web sites, check the **Loop** check box, shown in Figure 15.5. The Loop feature can help you analyze the smoothness of animation playback, as well as enable you to view frame delay timing over and over without having to keep reloading the file in the browser window.

Previewing the Animation

Choose the settings you want for your animation. Then click on the **Preview In** drop-down menu to select a browser. The icon for the browser will appear in the **Preview In** menu. Click on the browser icon to preview the animation in a browser window. Photoshop Elements will generate the animated GIF file, along with some HTML code, and open a browser window with the animation, as shown in Figure 15.6.

FIGURE 15.6

Click on the browser button in the Save for Web window to preview the animation in a browser.

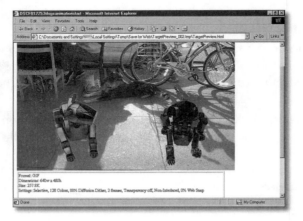

Watch each animated character in the browser window and make sure that each character appears according to the settings you made in the image window. Click on the **Back** button or **Close** box to exit the browser window and return to the Photoshop Elements work area. If you want to publish the animation as a file, click on **OK** and then type a name for the file to save it to your hard drive. Otherwise, click on **Cancel** to return to the work area. Don't forget to save the animation as a PSD file to preserve the layers of animation.

Variations—Animating People

The human body is one of the more difficult things to animate. In addition to the myriad lighting and shadow effects you must pay attention to, there are also just as many issues related to motion of the body, arms, legs, head, hair, face, and clothes. The detail needed to animate human-like subjects leads to the problem of size—image file size, animation playback speed, and memory.

note

If the browser you want to use does not appear in the **Preview In** drop-down menu in the Save for Web dialog box, choose **Other** from the menu list. Then, navigate to your hard drive and open the browser application of your choice.

Creating the First Frame

Although you can create a computer-generated background using the animated person as a composite image, this example shows you how to animate a person in an existing photo, shown in Figure 15.7. In fact, no composites are used in this example.

FIGURE 15.7

Add layers to a picture to turn a still picture into an animation.

Perform the following steps to create the first frame of the animation:

1. Open the image file. Click and drag the background layer in the **Layers** palette and drop it over the **Create a New Layer** button.

2. Rename the duplicate layer so that you can identify it as the first frame of animation. Keep a master copy of the image around so that you can use it to make additional frames of animation. Hide this master layer so that you can view your work in progress in the image window.

3. Apply the Magnetic Selection Tool and select the subject in the first frame.

4. Copy and paste the selection. The subject is now in a separate layer. Hide the copied layer.

5. Remove the subject from the first frame layer. You should see the gray-and-white checkerboard pattern where the selection was removed. The first frame of animation is divided into two layers, one with the subject, the other with the background.

Next, perform the following steps to create the second and third frames of the background photo from the first frame of animation:

1. Click and drag the layer you want to use for the first frame over the Create a New Layer button to duplicate the first layer.

2. Repeat a second time to create the third frame of animation. New layers will appear in the Layers palette.

3. Rename these layers to reflect the second and third frames of the animation, as shown in Figure 15.8.

FIGURE 15.8

Decrease the opacity settings for different frames to see how each frame overlaps with another.

You can create a copy of the layer that contains the subject (a child in this example) and create experimental frames of animation. (**Command-click**) [**Ctrl+click**] on the layer that contains the subject to select the subject. Choose the **Move Tool** and click and drag the corners of the selection to enlarge the image by about 10% to 20%. The larger animation in the second frame, compared to the smaller image in the first frame, makes the subject appear to be sliding down the beach in this example. For the final animation, the first frame shows a slightly larger subject with a slight glow and eyes closed. The second frame shows the original photo with a slight glow around the subject. The third frame shows a slightly smaller subject with the same glow as the second frame.

Select the subject, and then choose the **Feather** command from the **Select** menu. This command will blend the pixels at the edge of the selected image with the pixels surrounding it. The **Feather** command helps images blend in with the background image. Set the number of pixels in the **Feather** command to a range of 3 to 5 pixels, and then click **OK** to apply the command to the image. Fill in any transparent areas of the image by applying the Clone Stamp Tool.

Duplicate the layer that contains the subject so that you have three layers of the subject. Hide two of these layers. Select and show the layer you want to work with.

note

To find out more about the Clone Stamp Tool, go to Chapter 1, "Navigating the Work Area." To find out how to apply the Clone Stamp Tool across layers, go to Chapter 12, "Repairing Images."

To add a glow around the subject, perform the following steps:

1. (**Command-click**) [**Ctrl+click**] on the subject to select it.

2. Click on a layer that contains the background image and then choose the **Expand** command from the **Select**, **Modify** menu.

3. Type 4 in the text box, as shown in Figure 15.9, and then click **OK**. The selection area that used to represent the missing subject is now four pixels wider than it used to be.

4. Move the layer that contains the subject above the layer that contains the background in the **Layers** palette.

5. To optimize your workflow, keep layers that compose a single frame of animation organized close to each other in the Layers palette.

FIGURE 15.9
Create special effects by expanding and contracting the selection area of each frame of animation.

Creating the In-Between Frames

In-between frames transition the animation from one key frame to the next key frame. Full-motion animation can contain anywhere from 10 to 28 frames of in-betweens. In this example, only one in-between frame is needed. Follow these steps to create the in-between frame of the animation:

1. Click on the second frame of the animation. This frame will actually be a layer located in the **Layers** palette. This layer represents a layer that will be used to create a frame of animation. Use a selection tool to highlight the subject in the second layer, or (**Command-click**) [**Ctrl+click**] to select the subject.

2. Select the **Move Tool** to scale the image so that it is slightly smaller than the subject in the first frame, but larger than the one in the third frame. You can experiment with the size of the subject in the second frame by pasting it into a new layer and adjusting its size.

3. Finalize the second frame by pasting the final image of the subject into the appropriate layer. Alternatively, you can use the **Merge Down** command in the **Layer** menu to combine the subject layer with the background layer. Then delete any layers you do not want to use to create the final animation.

You've almost completed two frames of animation. Remember that comment about how difficult it is to animate the human body. Let's get your feet wet by making the subject's eye blink in the first frame of the animation as shown in Figure 15.10. Select the layer that contains the first frame of the subject. Choose **Liquify** from the **Filter**, **Distort** menu. The Liquify dialog box, shown in Figure 15.10, will open. The Liquify dialog box contains several tools that enable you to make subtle or exaggerated changes. This is a great tool for animating subjects!

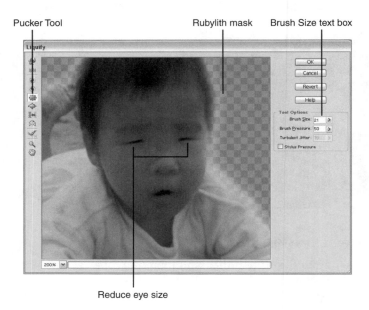

FIGURE 15.10

The Pucker Tool in the Liquify dialog box is used to reduce the size of the eyes in this frame of animation.

Perform the following steps to make the subject's eye squint, as shown in Figure 15.10:

1. Choose the **Pucker Tool**, as shown in Figure 15.10.

2. Set the brush size so that it covers the area of the photo you want to shrink. In this example, I selected a brush size of 21 pixels.

3. Place the center of the brush over the center of one of the eyes. Click to apply the Pucker Tool. Hold down the mouse if you want to continue to apply the tool to the eye. Release the mouse to stop applying the Pucker Tool. The longer you hold down the mouse button, the more intensely the tool will be applied to the image.

4. Apply the Pucker Tool to both eyes until the eyes appear closed (see Figure 15.10). Then click **OK** to save your changes.

MAKE A SLIDESHOW

If you want to be a little less ambitious, you can use the animation feature in Photoshop Elements to create a simple slideshow. Simply copy and paste each image into the image window so that each image is added into its own layer in the **Layers** palette. You can hide the layers if you want to be sure that a specific image has indeed been added to a document. To turn a set of layers into a slideshow, set a longer frame delay in the Save for Web window, which is explained in more detail at the end of this chapter.

Merging Layers

View each frame of the animation by hiding and showing each layer in the **Layers** palette. For example, if you want to view the first frame of animation, show only the beach, child (subject), and effect layer in the **Layers** palette. Move layers that will be used together to make up one frame of animation above or below each other in the **Layers** palette, as shown in Figure 15.11.

FIGURE 15.11

Organize each element of a frame of animation in the **Layers** palette. Use the **Merge Down** command to combine these elements into a single layer.

When you're ready to finalize each form of animation, merge the corresponding layers together. The eye icon should appear beside each layer in the first frame of animation. Select **Layer 2 blink**, as shown in Figure 15.12, and then choose the **Merge Down** command from the **Layers** palette drop-down menu. Layer 2 blink will merge with Layer 1. Repeat this process with the second and third frames of the animation.

FIGURE 15.12

FIGURE 15.12
The Twirl tools
can be applied
to animate the
arms as shown
here.

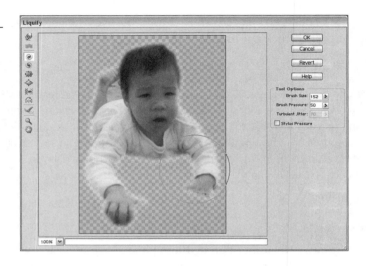

Finalizing Tweaks and Previewing the Animation

Open the Save for Web dialog box to make any final optimizations or changes to
the animation file. Many of the settings chosen in the animation created earlier in
this chapter have also been selected in this example, as shown in Figure 15.13.
Choose **GIF** and select the **Animated** check box to access the animation settings for
the active image window.

Convert layers to animation

FIGURE 15.13
Adjust the loop
and frame delay
settings in the
Save for Web
window.

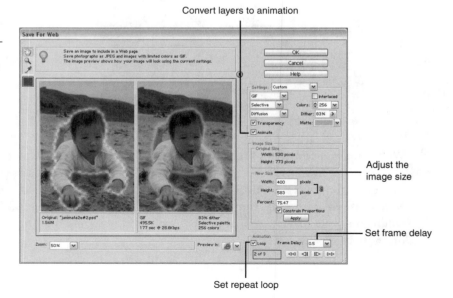

Adjust the
image size

Set frame delay

Set repeat loop

There are several default settings for the animated GIF image file. Photoshop Elements will select the optimal color palette and dither settings for the animation. If there are any transparent areas of the image, check the **Transparency** check box if you want them to remain transparent in the final image. The animation will loop indefinitely, and each frame has a delay of 20 seconds.

Before saving the file to your hard drive, preview it in a browser window. The animation should play back the same way in Internet Explorer 5 and Netscape Navigator 4.7. Click on the browser icon in the **Preview In** menu to preview the animation in a browser window, as shown in Figure 15.14.

FIGURE 15.14

Preview the final animation in a browser window before saving the final animated GIF file.

If you like the animation as it appears in the browser window, close the browser window and then click **OK** in the **Save for Web** window. Otherwise, go back to the file and change the **Frame Delay** setting, or experiment with a different GIF palette setting before saving the final file. After the file has been saved, you can upload it to a Web server and share the URL for the animated GIF file with your friends and family.

16

STITCHING TOGETHER A PANORAMA

Ever want to capture all the colors of a beautiful sunset along with the color reflecting across the local hillsides and plains? This can be an expensive task to perform with even a traditional 35mm camera. First you would have to shoot each picture of the panorama, and then you'd have to print the pictures and lay them out to identify the overlapping areas.

This more expensive process can involve splicing together the negatives, or exposing separate negatives to a large-sized sheet of photography paper. The inexpensive way to create a panorama is to mount the images to a piece of cardboard, or align them in a picture frame.

Photoshop Elements enables you to create multi-picture panoramas by laying out each picture and then merging them into a new document window, as shown in Figure 16.1.

FIGURE 16.1

Combine similar photos with the **Photomerge** command.

Shooting and Choosing Images

The first step to creating a panorama is to take several pictures of a skyline or a horizontal or vertical view of some sort of scenery. Try to apply many of the basic photography practices to take an appealing, well-composed picture. Each picture can overlap 30% to 50% with other pictures in the panorama. Also, you might want to set up a tripod to take pictures. Try not to change any of the camera settings as you take each picture.

Photo Composition for Panoramas

A panorama is composed of several photos that move along a horizontal or vertical axis. It can be difficult to decide where your panorama should start and end. Depending on how much of the view you want to include, it can be difficult to decide how much sky, or other objects, you should include in the panorama composition.

As you look through the viewfinder of the camera, try to frame the view into thirds: one-third sky, one-third hills or water, and one-third foreground or flat ground area. Composing a panorama is much easier when you are taking pictures in daylight. Digital cameras can capture darker photos under low light, resulting in unsightly tints, shadows, or hues—consider taking your first panorama photos in daylight. Figure 16.2 shows the first picture in a multi-photo panorama.

FIGURE 16.2

Include the skyline or other common elements in each picture you want to use in the panorama.

A tripod can help you maintain consistency in each picture you take for the panorama, although all the panoramas created in this chapter were shot by hand, without the aid of a tripod. However, you'll notice that the overall horizontal area of the panorama is slightly smaller because of fluctuation in overlapping areas across pictures. When I took the picture shown in Figure 16.3, I tried my best not to change the position of my arms and of the camera, overlapping part of the picture in Figure 16.2 so that I could match similar elements in both pictures.

Each photo you add to the panorama will increase the file size of the final image. However, be sure to capture each photo at the highest possible resolution so that you have as much image information to work with as possible. Adobe recommends using image files that are two megapixels in size. The images used to create the examples in this chapter were all three-megapixel images. If you want to reduce the size of the images for the panorama, you can choose 12.5%, 25%, 50%, or 75% from the Image Size Reduction drop-down menu located in the Photomerge dialog box.

note

The number of files, combined with the width and height of each image file, can help you estimate the final dimensions of the panorama. If you want to reduce the resulting image, you can do so by choosing a menu item from the **Image Size Reduction** drop-down menu. Don't forget that the pictures will overlap about 30% to 50%, too.

FIGURE 16.3

Include some overlapping areas across photos.

Clouds

Sign

For example, Figure 16.4 contains a person moving along the horizon. Because each photo is a high-resolution three-megapixel image, I can use the Clone Stamp Tool to remove whatever I don't want to appear in the final panorama. If I make the image smaller, thus removing image data, the edits to the image might not be as easy to make.

FIGURE 16.4

Don't worry if movement is absent from neighboring shots. You can edit them out if you don't want to include them in the panorama.

Boat

Figure

Before taking any of the photos, determine where the light source is. Try to stand in front of the light source. If the light source is in front of you, the foreground objects in the picture will be underexposed, or too dark compared to the light source. If at all possible, try not to include the light source in the panorama. The brightness of the sun, or other light source, can overexpose the immediate area surrounding the light.

For best results, do not add any lenses that distort the digital photos. If you attach a wide angle or fish-eye lens to your digital camera, the resulting images will be difficult to use to create a panorama.

As you take each photo, try to look for any landmarks, such as a tree or sign (see Figure 16.5) in both vertical and horizontal overlapping areas of the panorama. Distinct objects that appear in two or more images can help you reassemble each picture of the panorama in Photoshop Elements. In this example, the figures standing along the shoreline, plus the tree, and props along the right side of the photo in Figure 16.5 helped me match the overlapping areas of the images in the Photomerge dialog box.

FIGURE 16.5

Look for a landmark or other object to match the middle photos with the end photos in the panorama.

Tree

Boats

After you've taken the first set of panorama pictures, you might want to change the zoom settings or, if your camera has manual options, adjust the shutter speed or aperture settings. You might want to wait for the lighting to change. Then take another set of panorama pictures. You can use a second or third set of pictures to create and choose the best-looking panorama. Copy the pictures you want to use from your digital camera to your computer's hard drive.

Before creating the panorama, you can use Photoshop Elements to correct any color differences between the pictures, or to clean up any objects you don't want to appear in the final image. However, you can also edit the image after the panorama has been created.

tip

The optimal number of photos in a panorama depends on how much of the view you want to show, and how many pictures you've taken. If you're trying to determine how many photos to take, experiment with creating panoramas using anywhere from two to eight photos.

Introducing Photomerge

The wonderful panorama-making feature in Photoshop Elements is called Photomerge. The **Photomerge** command is tucked away in the File menu. Photomerge enables you to arrange two or more photos horizontally or vertically to create a single image file panorama.

Choose the **Photomerge** command from the **File** menu to open the Photomerge dialog box. There are two main Photomerge dialog boxes. The first one, shown in Figure 16.6, enables you to select files and allow Photoshop Elements to take a first crack at automatically arranging your photos into a panorama. The second dialog box, shown later in Figure 16.8, enables you to compose and generate the panorama.

FIGURE 16.6

Select the image files you want to use for the panorama from the Photomerge dialog box.

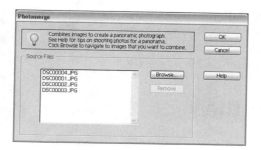

By default, any image files that are already open in the work area will appear in the Photomerge dialog box. If you don't want to include these photos in the panorama, select each one and click **Remove**. If the photos you want to include in the panorama are not already open, press the Browse button in the Photomerge dialog box. The Open dialog box will appear.

To easily locate each image you want to include in the panorama, store all the files in the same folder on your hard drive. You can hold down the **Shift** or (**Command**) [**Ctrl**] key and click on more than one file in the Open window to add multiple files to the Photomerge dialog box list, as shown in Figure 16.7. If you're not sure which photos you want to use, choose more, rather than fewer, files. You can always remove a photo from the final panorama in the second Photomerge dialog box.

FIGURE 16.7

Select multiple images in the **Open** window.

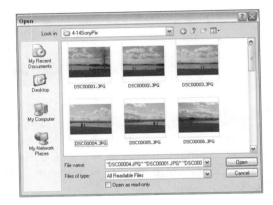

There are five buttons in the Photomerge dialog box: **Browse**, **Remove**, **OK**, **Cancel**, and **Help**. The Browse button enables you to choose each photo you want to include in your panorama. Conversely, the **Remove** button enables you to delete any file you don't want to include in the panorama. Click the **Help** button to view the panorama help information. You can click **Cancel** at any time to exit the Photomerge dialog box. After you've selected all the source files, click **OK**.

Arranging Images in the Panorama

After you've added the files you want to use to the Photomerge dialog, click **OK** and wait for Photoshop Elements to arrange the photos into a

note

Photoshop Elements will not resize any of the photos in the panorama. For best results, select photos taken at the same resolution to create the panorama. Save the original panorama and then reduce its size, or apply filters, effects, and so on.

panorama. You can watch Photoshop Elements open, resize, and then close each image in the work area. When the batch script has completed all its tasks, a new, larger Photomerge dialog box will open in the work area, as shown in Figure 16.8. Photoshop Elements will present what it thinks the panorama should look like in the larger window area of the Photomerge dialog box.

FIGURE 16.8

View the panorama in the Photomerge dialog box.

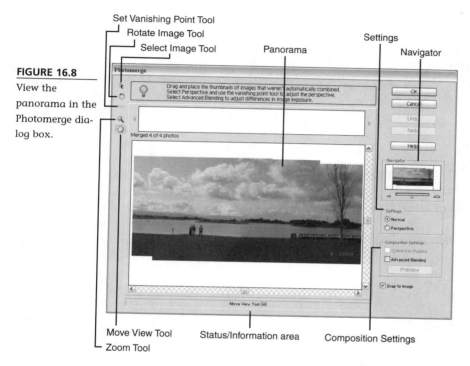

The Photomerge dialog box is divided into three general sections. There are two windows located at the center of the Photomerge dialog box. The top window stores any images selected in the first Photomerge dialog box that do not appear in the second, larger window. To the left of the windows are five tools. To the right are several buttons, such as **OK**, **Cancel**, **Undo**, and **Redo**. A mini-Navigator window is located below the buttons. It works almost exactly like the **Navigator** palette. View and Composition Settings are located in the bottom-right side of the Photomerge dialog box.

Selecting Panorama Images

Use the Select Image Tool (arrow icon) to manually arrange images in the large lower window. Click and drag any image to change its location. You can even drop it in the top window if you want to exclude it from the panorama. Any selected image will become semitransparent as you move it around, returning to its normal transparency after you release the mouse.

Click and drag the slider control in the Navigator palette to reduce the size of the photos if you want to see all or only part of the panorama. Select the **Move View Tool** (hand icon) to move the entire panorama in the Photomerge dialog box.

The following list details the tools and settings located in the Photomerge dialog box:

note

The Photomerge dialog box enables you to choose any combinations of photos you want to use to create a panorama. If Photoshop Elements fails to combine any two photos to make a panorama, the following message will appear: "Photomerge could not automatically arrange any of the images. You can manually drag the images into the work area to create a panorama." Click OK, and manually place each image in the Photomerge dialog box to create the panorama.

- **Select Image Tool** (A)—Select a photo and arrange it in the large, lower window, or place it in the unmerged area of the Photomerge dialog box. Click outside of a photo to deselect all images.

- **Rotate Image Tool**(R)—Freely rotate any photo selected in the panorama area of the dialog box. Use the **Select Image Tool** to select a photo, and then pick the Rotate Image Tool.

- **Set Vanishing Point Tool**(V)— Choose the **Perspective** radio button, and adjust the center photo of the panorama using this tool. Photoshop Elements will redraw the perspective depending on which photo you select.

- **Zoom Tool**(Z)—Click to magnify or demagnify any part of the panorama.

- **Move View Tool**(H)—Use this tool to move all images in the panorama around.

- **Navigator**—Move the slider control to the left to zoom out, or to the right to zoom into the panorama.

- **Settings**—Create a normal, flat panorama, or flare the end photos to create a Perspective. You can use the **Set Vanishing Point Tool** to select the image you want to place at the center of the perspective.

- **Composition Settings**—Apply advanced blending and cylindrical mapping to the panorama. Check the **Advanced Blending** check box and click **Preview** to see whether the Advanced Blending Tool is able to smoothly blend the panorama photos together. If the **Perspective** radio button is selected, you can check the **Cylindrical Mapping** check box. You must exit preview mode to apply any other tools to the panorama.

Any photos that could not be automatically arranged will appear in the smaller window at the top of the Photomerge dialog box. Click on the arrow icon to activate the **Select Image Tool** to select and move images into the Photomerge dialog box. Figure 16.9 shows all four images in the top window section. Use the **Select Image Tool** to move an image from the top portion of the window and place it in the larger window to compose the panorama. You can move an image within the larger window, or drag and drop it into the top window area to exclude it from the final panorama.

Identify the image you want to start building the panorama with. Choose the **Select Image Tool**, and then click and drag each surrounding image and see how close a match the two images are, as shown in Figure 16.10. The two images might not line up exactly with each other. This results in a panorama that is not completely horizontal. The corner areas of two or more pictures might not line up with each other, creating a staggered, slightly vertical panoramic image. Focus on the central content of the images to piece together the panorama.

note

Check the **Snap to Image** check box if you want the **Photomerge** command to help you align the photos in the panorama. Choose either **Ghost** or **Blend Dragging** to define how the selected image should be drawn when it is being dragged in the Photomerge dialog box. Choose **Ghost Dragging** if you want to view a partially transparent image as you drag it around in the Photomerge dialog box to help you find appropriate placement. Select **Blend Dragging** if you do not want the image to appear as you drag it around.

After you select an image in the lower, larger area of the window, click on the **Rotate Image Tool** (second from the top) if you want to rotate the image. When you place the cursor over the larger window, it will change from an arrow icon to the rotate icon. When this happens, click beside the image and drag the mouse. The selected image should rotate along its x axis as you move the mouse up or down in the window.

FIGURE 16.9

Use the Select Image Tool to move any photos from the top window to the bottom window as you put the panorama together from scratch.

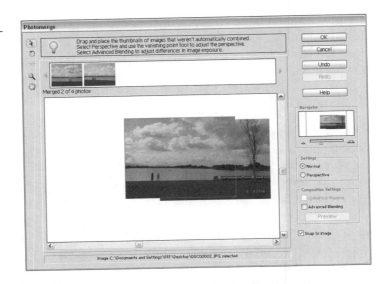

FIGURE 16.10

Select and place each photo in the panorama in the Photomerge dialog box. Scale the panorama by moving the Navigator slider control located on the right side of the window so you can view the entire panorama.

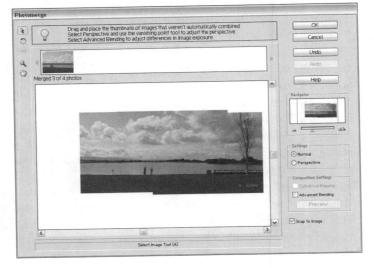

Adding Perspective

The **Perspective** radio button can work independently or in conjunction with the Set Vanishing Point Tool. Select the **Perspective** radio button if you want the panorama to be drawn so that the outer images gradually grow larger as they get farther away from the vanishing point. If you want Photoshop Elements to pick the vanishing point, choose the **Select Image Tool** (arrow icon) and click in the white space beside one of the panorama photos. Click on the **Perspective** radio button. To set the vanishing point, click on the **Set Vanishing Point Tool**, and then click on one of the center photos in the panorama. The panorama will be redrawn, as shown in Figure 16.11.

FIGURE 16.11

The **Perspective** radio button enables you to flare each end of the panorama. You can use the Set **Vanishing Point Tool** to choose a different center-photo in the perspective.

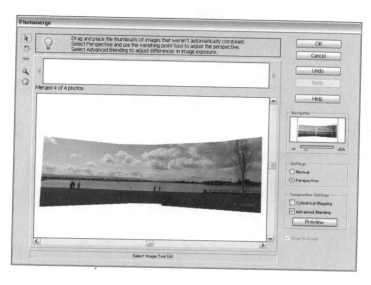

REVERSING THE PERSPECTIVE

Check the **Advanced Blending** check box before choosing the vanishing point in the panorama. Wait for the perspective to be applied to the panorama. Check the **Cylindrical Mapping** check box. Then press the **Preview** button to view the panorama. Cylindrical mapping makes the vanishing-point photo larger than the left or right photos, whose ends taper off into slightly smaller images. You must click the **Exit Preview** button to select or apply any tools in the Photomerge dialog box.

Publishing the Panorama

When you're ready to turn the panorama in the Photomerge dialog box into a new image window, click **OK**. Photoshop Elements will resize each image, create a new document window, and arrange the images to mimic the panorama defined in the Photomerge dialog box. The final panorama will appear in the work area, as shown in Figure 16.12.

After you create the final panorama image, you cannot return to the Photomerge dialog box. Review each radio button and check before you

note

Select the **Advanced Blending** check box if you want Photoshop Elements to blend the colors and tonal range across the images in the panorama.

click on the **OK** button. Figure 16.13 shows the same panorama used in Figure 16.12, but without the perspective settings.

FIGURE 16.12

A perspective panorama with the center image used as the vanishing point.

FIGURE 16.13

The same panorama minus any composition or perspective settings.

Cleaning Up the Final Image

Take a close look at Figure 16.13. Notice that most of the image is surrounded by white space, and some of the images have dates or timestamps. If you like the way the images fit together in the image window, the first thing you should do is save the file to your hard drive. Because all the images used to create this panorama were originally JPEG files, I chose to save the panorama as a JPEG file, too.

You can choose from several options to perform the final cleanup of the panorama. You can apply the Clone Stamp Tool to fill in the white areas in the image window, and apply the Crop Tool to trim away the incongruous edges of the panorama, as shown in Figure 16.14. Use the **Dodge Tool** to lighten merged photo areas, or the **Burn Tool** to darken blended areas.

> **note**
>
> You can click on the **Tutorial** button if you want to navigate Adobe's built-in tutorial. It shows you how to compose and stitch together a panorama.

FIGURE 16.14

Apply the Crop Tool to trim the edges of the incongruous areas of the panorama.

Cleaning up the image also involves removing any visual glitches or unwanted graphics. For example, the digital timestamp from the camera was removed with a 21-pixel, soft edge Clone Stamp Tool. You can also remove any people, or other small objects, from the image depending on what you want the panorama to focus on. Sometimes having a person in an image reveals the true scale of the panorama.

Variations—Working with Different Photo Elements

You can create a wide range of landscapes—from scenic hillsides or lakes, to urban cityscapes or skylines. Panoramas can contain vertically overlapping images, too. Figure 16.15 shows a pastoral hillside near Page Mill Road in Palo Alto, California. I tried to capture the dramatic cloud cover in addition to the green hillsides when I took these photos.

FIGURE 16.15

Although a group of images might be a great fit logistically, tonal range differences can be difficult to correct after the panorama has been created.

Color and tonal corrections are particularly difficult to perform on panorama images because it is difficult to know which areas of an image will overlap. For example, the top-middle portion of the panorama in Figure 16.15 is the result of two slightly lighter and darker images overlapping, resulting in a visual glitch in the image. Try correcting this tonal difference with the Dodge or Burn tools to lighten or darken areas as needed. You might also want to see whether you can correct the tonal differences by applying the Magic Wand Tool combined with a Levels adjustment layer. You can also apply the Blur Tool, located in the Toolbox, to blur the edges of the overlapping areas to help bring them together.

Experiment with foreground and background composition in panoramas. Figure 16.16 contains a bench in the left foreground with the panorama of the East Bay skyline in the background. Because the skyline is a fairly small area of the panorama, it can be difficult to line up each of the images. Try to use the clouds in each of the pictures to determine whether you've overlapped two images correctly.

tip

Select an image with the **Select Image Tool** in the Photomerge dialog box. Then, choose the **Rotate Image Tool** to freely rotate any image. After the image is rotated, it will remain in that orientation. A subtle rotation might enable you to exaggerate part of an image, such as the slope of a hill or skyline.

FIGURE 16.16

If you're not sure how many photos to use, choose more than you need and piece together a panorama with the images of your choice.

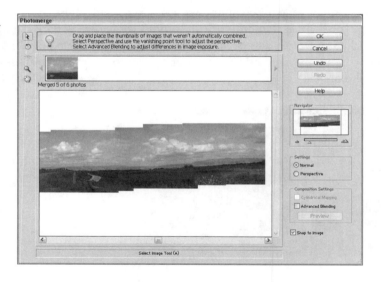

Although you can place each image in the Photomerge dialog box, you cannot modify individual images in the panorama after the new document window has been created in the work area. Look closely at the left-middle skyline area of the panorama in Figure 16.17. Even though the pictures appear to be a match in the Photomerge dialog box, the final image is slightly off-kilter. You can apply the Clone Stamp Tool to correct this visual glitch. You might also have noticed that the overlapping corners of the middle images are slightly darker than the rest of the blue sky in each photo. You can apply the Blur or Clone Stamp tools to lighten the border resulting from the overlapping images.

FIGURE 16.17

You will want to fill in the rest of the panorama with other images, or crop the continuous area of the image.

17

CREATING A SLIDESHOW AND WEB PHOTO GALLERY

Photo albums and slideshows contain a treasure chest of photographed memories. You can create traditional photo albums by printing photos to glossy paper using a color printer, a computer, and Photoshop Elements. To share photo albums with friends and family, more and more people are creating photo albums on the Web. Digital slideshows are another way you can share photos online. Photoshop Elements enables you to create both customizable slideshows and Web photo galleries.

Creating a Slideshow

Photoshop Elements enables you to take a folder of photos and turn them into a slideshow. All the photos that compose the slideshow are stored in a single PDF file. A PDF file can store text and image information. Users of Macintosh and Windows computers can view any PDF file using Acrobat reader, a free PDF viewer from Adobe. You can also install an Acrobat plug-in with Internet Explorer or Netscape Navigator and share your slideshow online.

Perform the following steps to create a PDF slideshow:

1. Choose the **PDF Slideshow** command from the **File**, **Automation Tools** menu. The PDF Slideshow dialog box will open (see Figure 17.1).

FIGURE 17.1

Create a slideshow with the PDF Slideshow command.

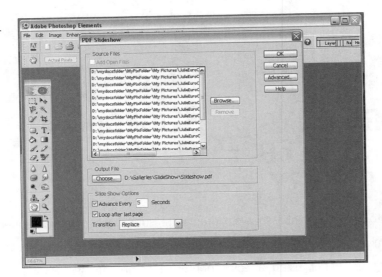

2. Click the **Browse** button and choose the files you want to add to your slideshow.

3. Click on the **Choose** button if you want to save the PDF slideshow to a particular folder on your hard drive.

4. Check the **Loop After Last Page** check box if you want the slideshow to repeat.

5. Type a number into the **Advance Every** text box to set the delay time between each slide. The default value is set to 5 seconds.

6. Click on the **Transition** drop-down menu to select a transition effect to be used as the slideshow progresses to the next photo.

7. Click the **Advanced** button to choose **PDF** options for ZIP or JPEG encoding of the slideshow images. You can choose to apply (or not apply) save transparency settings and apply image interpolation to each image.

8. Click **OK** to create the slideshow file.

To view the slideshow, drag and drop it into a browser window or open the file with Adobe Acrobat Reader (see Figure 17.2). Wait and let the slideshow progress to the next photo after the pre-set time delay elapses. The slideshow will remain onscreen when it arrives at the last slide. Press the Escape key to exit the slideshow.

note

If a non-image file, such as a text file, is located in the folder you select for the Web photo gallery or PDF slideshow, Photoshop Elements will display an error message after the automated script completes its run. Don't fret; the slideshow or photo gallery will complete successfully despite the error.

FIGURE 17.2

You can view the slideshow with a browser that has the Acrobat 5 plug-in installed, or use Acrobat Reader (version 5 or newer).

Creating a Photo Gallery

Adobe has several gallery styles you can choose from for your Web Photo gallery (see Figure 17.3). You can choose from two categories of styles: frame- and non-frame-based galleries. A frame is a part of the Hypertext Markup Language (HTML) that enables a single Web page to be divided into two or more parts. A frame-based gallery enables Photoshop Elements to place thumbnail images of your photos on one frame, while showing the full-size image in the other frame. You can choose from **Vertical**, **Horizontal Frame**, or a slew of other gallery layouts for your Web photo gallery.

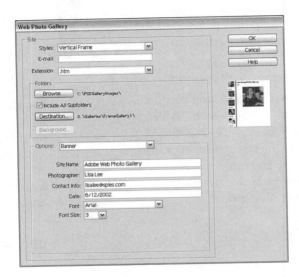

FIGURE 17.3

Photoshop Elements can create a fully functional Web photo album from a folder of image files.

The other categories of gallery styles are Simple and Tables. The Simple gallery uses HTML tags to format the thumbnail images on a Web page. Click on a thumbnail to view the full-size photo on a different Web page. Tables are another construct of HTML. Tables enable a Web page to group text or images into columns or rows, similar to the way a spreadsheet groups its data. The Tables gallery places each thumbnail image in a cell of the table in a Web page. Click on a thumbnail image to open a new Web page containing the full-size image.

Creating a Frame-Based Gallery

Choose the Web Photo Gallery command from the **File**, **Automate** menu. Photoshop Elements uses a set of scripts to automate resizing each image file, and then generates the HTML and JavaScript code to create the Web photo gallery. The Web Photo Gallery dialog box, shown in Figure 17.3, will open. The Web Photo Gallery dialog box is divided into three sections: Styles, Options, and Files. The Banner setting will appear as the default item in the Options text box. You can type the site name, photographer, and date of the photo gallery into each text field (see Figure 17.3).

The **Styles** drop-down menu contains all 15 gallery styles available for the Web Photo Gallery. The selected style determines how the final gallery is formatted. Preview the layout in the right column of the Web Photo Gallery dialog box. The following list describes each gallery style you can create with the Web Photo Gallery command:

- **Horizontal Dark or Horizontal Frame**—Places the full-size image at the top of the Web page, and a thumbnail along the bottom of the page.

- **Vertical Frame**—Splits the Web page vertically. The thumbnail images are located on the left side of the page, and the full-size image is on the right.

- **Custom Galleries**—Choose from Antique Paper, Bears, Lace, Museum, Office, Space, Spotlight, Theater, Vacation, and Wet themes for your photo gallery. Preview each one in the right side of the Web Photo Gallery dialog box.

- **Simple**—Creates a Web page consisting of a specified number of columns and rows of thumbnail images. Click on a thumbnail image to go to another Web page to view the full-size image.

- **Table**—Each thumbnail image is placed in a table, which can be customized with an HTML editor program. Click on a thumbnail image to go to another Web page to view the full-size image.

Many Web sites, including www.yahoo.com and www.msn.com (http://photos.msn.com), enable you to create and upload digital photos if you create an account on the Web site. Other Web sites, such as www.kodak.com and www.shutterfly.com, also provide Web photo-album services, plus additional services, such as converting printed photos into digital files, or printing your digital pictures onto glossy photo paper.

Click the (**Choose**) [**Browse**] and **Destination** buttons located in the middle of the Web Photo Gallery dialog box to choose the source and destination folders for your gallery. The source directory contains the files you want to include in the photo gallery. The destination directory contains the Web photo gallery files created by Photoshop Elements. If you have several directories of files—for example, folders containing other folders of image files—check the **Include All Subfolders** check box if you want Photoshop Elements to add all folders in the selected folder to the Web gallery.

IMAGE SIZES AND DOWNLOAD TIMES

You can customize the size of each full-size photo and thumbnail for each Web photo gallery you create. If you're not worried about the amount of time it will take for your Web site visitors to download images from your Web site, feel free to select the full width of the image in the Web Gallery dialog box (see Figure 17.3). If you are concerned about the amount of time it might take for your Web site visitors to download the images in your Web photo gallery, choose a smaller image size, such as 300 pixels wide for the full-size image and 100 pixels wide for the thumbnail images.

Setting Gallery Options

The **Options** drop-down menu enables you to customize each photo gallery. You can review each set of options by choosing each menu item from the **Options** drop-down menu. Customize settings for the banner, gallery images, gallery thumbnails, custom colors, and security. Simply select each menu option, and configure each drop-down menu or text box.

If you're not sure whether you should customize the numbers of rows or columns in a gallery, leave the default settings untouched and create a photo gallery. The Vertical Frame gallery is shown in Figure 17.3, as are the settings for the **Banner** option. Type the name of the photo gallery, photographer, contact info, and date, and set the font family and font size.

Notice that the thumbnail images are not exactly the same size. Photos taken in portrait mode are not turned on their side. Similarly, vertical photos that remain in landscape mode are not automatically turned right side up.

The following list summarizes each of the menu settings available in the **Options** menu:

- **Banner**—Type in the site name, photographer, date, and font settings for the gallery. This information is added to every page of the gallery.

- **Gallery Images**—Choose the border size, image size, and JPEG image quality for the full-size image that will appear in the photo gallery.

- **Gallery Thumbnails**—Select a caption, font, font size, image size, and number of rows and columns for the thumbnail images (if you're creating a Simple or Table gallery). You can also change the border size of each thumbnail.

note

If the photos were scanned in at 300 ppi, or a different resolution, the batch script will convert the resolution of each image to 72 ppi.

■ **Custom Colors**—Modify the HTML color settings of the background, banners, text, links, active links, and visited links for each Web page in the gallery.

■ **Security**—Customize a copyright notice, or add the filename, a caption, a title, or credits to each photo in the gallery.

You can navigate the Web gallery in two ways: view and click thumbnails, or select a thumbnail to view a larger photo. Some Web galleries include navigational arrow buttons that enable you to move from one page of thumbnails to another. Frame-based galleries, like the Horizontal Frame gallery shown in Figure 17.4, enable you to click on a thumbnail to change the full-size image in the larger frame in the browser window. The Simple gallery, shown in Figure 17.4, enables you to click on a thumbnail to view the larger photo. Click an arrow button to navigate through each page of thumbnails.

FIGURE 17.4

Click on a thumbnail image at the bottom of the browser window to make a larger-size image appear in the top frame.

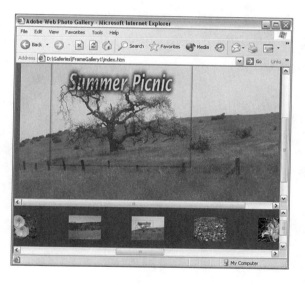

Creating a Simple Gallery

The Simple gallery style enables you to navigate pages of thumbnail images by clicking on arrow buttons. Click on a thumbnail image to view the full-size image. The Simple gallery Web page layout, shown on the right side of Figure 17.5, does not use any fancy HTML elements such as frames or tables to create the gallery layout, just straight, simple-as-can-be HTML tags. This gallery format works with any browser program.

If you want to see how each gallery layout looks and feels with your photos, choose a different Destination folder, and select a different style each time you open the Web Photo Gallery window. You can view each gallery from your hard drive by opening the `index.html` file with a browser application. Open the folder containing the Web gallery images. Then drag and drop the `index.html` file into a browser window. Figure 17.6 shows the images previously shown in the Horizontal Frame gallery laid out as a Simple gallery.

FIGURE 17.5

The **Preview** window on the right side of the Web Photo Gallery dialog box enables you to preview a gallery layout—in this case, the Simple photo gallery.

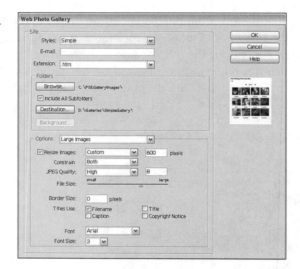

FIGURE 17.6

Compare different gallery styles and decide whether you want to use custom settings for thumbnails or gallery images.

Making a Table Gallery

The best feature in the Table gallery is the Background button. You can customize the background of the Table gallery with any photo. Choose **Table** in the **Styles** drop-down menu, and then click on the **Background** button, shown in Figure 17.7, to select the photo from the Table gallery.

You can customize your gallery's colors to create a unique color scheme. Click on the **Options** drop-down menu and choose **Custom Colors** to view the custom color settings. Choose a custom color for the background or banner areas. Or select a custom color for static or link text.

The **Security** options, shown in Figure 17.7, enable you to customize the content of each photo. You can add custom text, a filename, a title, credits, a caption, or a copyright notice to each photo in your gallery. Set the font family, font size, color, opacity, position, and rotation of the security content, too.

Customizing Thumbnail Settings

Gallery thumbnail images exist in each gallery style. Unlike the frame-based galleries, which show a gallery photo beside the thumbnails, the Simple and Table gallery styles use only thumbnails in the Web photo gallery index pages. You must click on a thumbnail to view the larger, full-size photo.

You can choose **Gallery Thumbnails** from the **Options** drop-down menu to view the page layout settings of the thumbnail images in the gallery. Check the **Use Filename** check box if you want the name of each file to appear below each thumbnail image, as shown in Figure 17.8. The filename will appear below the thumbnail if you choose any gallery style except for the Horizontal Frame gallery, in which the name appears in the upper-left corner of the browser window. You also can determine the size of each thumbnail image, as well as how many rows and columns of thumbnail images you want to appear on each Web page.

FIGURE 17.7

Customize the security options for your photos.

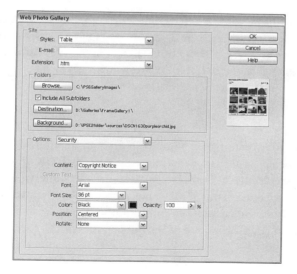

FIGURE 17.8

Customize the
size of the
thumbnails and
set the number
of rows and
columns for a
Table gallery.

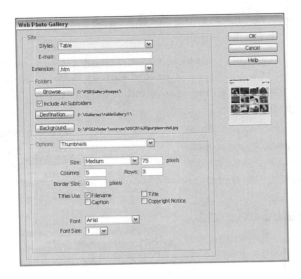

Try to keep the thumbnail images in smaller columns and rows. More images will mean that each page takes more time to download. And more than likely, your Web visitors will need to scroll through three or more rows of images if they don't have the luxury of a huge desktop.

CREATING CUSTOM WEB GALLERIES

The gallery template files are stored in the Preset folder, located in the Photoshop Elements folder on your hard drive. Open the WebContactSheet folder to access the template files for the Horizontal Frame, Simple, Table, and Vertical Frame HTML files that Photoshop Elements uses to lay out the Web galleries.

Make a copy of any template you want to modify. Then customize the HTML files using a text editor program, or an HTML editor application such as BBEdit, Adobe GoLive, or Macromedia Dreamweaver. Choose **Web Photo Gallery** in the **File**, **Automate** menu to view your new gallery template, or select it to make a new gallery.

Navigating the Gallery

After you've added your custom information to the banner, gallery thumbnail, gallery image, and color settings for the photo gallery, click **OK**. Photoshop Elements will generate the resulting HTML and image files for your gallery, as shown in Figure 17.9. The Table gallery creates an HTML table, similar to a spreadsheet. Photoshop Elements will add either the custom background photo you chose or a texturized background image to each Web page of the Table gallery.

Navigate a Table gallery by using the arrow buttons located at the top of each page. Customize the background of a Table gallery with one of your own photos.

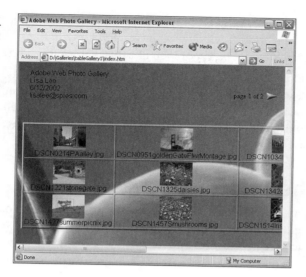

As part of your gallery options, you can customize the size of each thumbnail image. Figure 17.10 shows what the gallery looks like in its final form with larger thumbnail images previewed in a browser window. The person viewing the images will have to use the horizontal and vertical scrollbars in the browser window to gain access to all the thumbnails.

FIGURE 17.10

Customize the size of the thumbnail images to fill the layout with larger-size photos.

Relative and Absolute Paths

Each Web page is a text file that can be stored in any directory on your hard drive, or on a Web server. Photoshop Elements uses relative paths to locate the image and Web files created for each gallery. This means you can move the gallery folder to a

Web server or any directory on your hard drive, and each link will work. Each picture will appear in the browser window when you load any of the HTML files in a browser window. A relative path might look like this: `\images\GreatWall.jpg`.

One thing to avoid using is an absolute path. An absolute path includes an exact directory path to each Web page, link, or image. An absolute path might look like this: `C:\ProgramFiles\MyWebGallery\Images\GreatWall.jpg`. If you move the gallery out of the `ProgramFiles` folder, this link no longer will be able to locate `GreatWall.jpg`. The lesson here is to use relative paths whenever possible.

Working with the Photo Gallery HTML Files

Photoshop Elements creates each Web gallery by processing each image in the source directory and creating full-size and thumbnail images. Then, it generates HTML code for each Web page in the photo gallery. As mentioned earlier in this chapter, HTML is an acronym for Hypertext Markup Language, the language that enables a browser to view a Web page. When you create a Web photo gallery, Photoshop Elements creates several folders on your hard drive. The `images` folder contains the full-size images for the gallery. The `thumbnails` folder stores all the thumbnail images, and all the HTML files for the gallery are located in the `pages` folder.

You can view the HTML code for one of the Web pages in the gallery in one of two ways. One way is to drag and drop the HTML file into a browser window to view an HTML file as it will appear in a browser window of any Windows or Mac desktop. This enables you to view the file located on your hard drive. The other method is to post the file on a Web server and visit the Web site. In both cases, you can choose the **Source** command from the **View** menu to take a closer look at each Web page in your photo gallery. Although you don't need to have an understanding of HTML to create a Web photo gallery, the following sections provide a brief overview of the HTML code that is used to create the Web photo galleries in Photoshop Elements.

Viewing the Photo Gallery's HTML Source Code

While viewing the Web photo gallery in the browser, you can take a look at the HTML source code for the Web page. The HTML source code enables you to view the tags and URLs for each image and file in the gallery, which can be helpful if you want to troubleshoot any problems navigating the gallery images. If you're using Internet Explorer, choose the **Source** command from the **View** menu, or press (**Command-E**) [**Ctrl+E**]. If you're using Netscape Navigator, choose **Source** from the **View** menu. A window will open containing the HTML code, as shown in Figure 17.11.

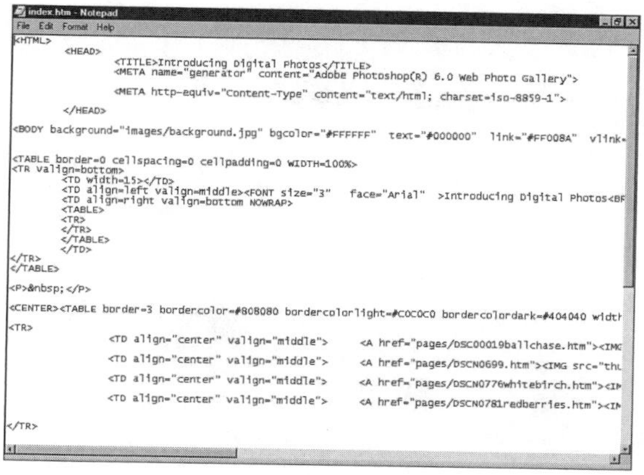

FIGURE 17.11

Choose the View Source command in Internet Explorer to view the HTML code.

This code is interpreted by the browser program, which enables you to view a Web page in a browser window. If you look closely, you'll notice that some of the text matches what you see in the initial browser window. Viewing the source code can be helpful if you notice a typo or misspelled word in your photo gallery and want to find out where that word appears in the HTML code for that Web page. You also can use a text editor program to view and modify the HTML code for the Web photo gallery pages.

Modifying the Gallery with a Web Editor

You can customize any of the HTML code in any pages of the Web photo galleries using an HTML editor application, such as Notepad in Windows, or SimpleText on a Mac. Several commercial HTML editor applications are also available, enabling you to view the HTML source code, find errors in your HTML code, and perform other helpful functions. Some of the more popular HTML editor applications are Microsoft FrontPage, Macromedia Dreamweaver, Adobe GoLive, and, for Mac users, BBEdit.

The home page of the Web gallery will have the filename of either FrameSet.htm or index.htm. In addition to having a separate thumbnail image, each image in the photo gallery will have its own HTML page. Each Web page is named with the filename of each image file in the photo gallery. If you want to customize text on each Web page, you must open each one and modify the text in the gallery.

The first index.htm file contains the main layout of the gallery. The following examples use Microsoft FrontPage to open the gallery HTML files. Choose **Open** from the **File** menu. The **Open File** window, shown in Figure 17.12, will open in the work area. Double-click on the index.htm file.

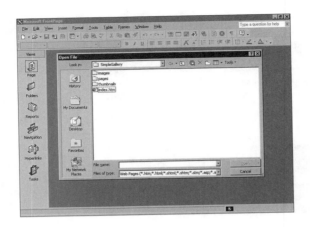

Although you can customize some of the text that appears in each page from the
Banner Options settings in the Web Photo Gallery dialog box, you can add other
kinds of information using a text editor. The following list outlines some of the elements you might want to add to each gallery Web page:

- **Titles**—The site name of the Banner Options page appears as the title on
  each Web page of the photo gallery.

- **Copyright**—You can type copyright information into the Photographer or
  Date fields in the Banner Options settings in the Web Photo Gallery dialog
  box. You also can customize each image with the Horizontal or Vertical Type
  Tool, and add copyright information to each image before you create the
  photo gallery.

- **Captions**—Photoshop Elements can add the filename for each thumbnail
  image as the caption. Check the Use Filename check box in the Gallery
  Thumbnails Options page in the Web Photo Gallery dialog box if you want
  to add this information to each file in the photo gallery. You can modify the
  name of an image by changing its name in index.htm and changing the filename for the HTML file for that image in the Pages folder of the photo gallery.

- **Links**—Photoshop Elements creates a link for each image in the photo
  gallery and places it in the index.htm or FrameSet.htm file. If you change the
  name of an HTML file in the photo gallery, be sure to change the filename in
  the link in the index HTML page, too.

HTML Tags

The index.htm file opens in the FrontPage work area. HTML uses language elements
referred to as *tags* to define how the text appears in the browser. Each tag, such as
<HTML>, begins and ends with a bracket (see Figure 17.13). The text following this tag

follows the language syntax associated with the `<HTML>` tag. Each tag also has a closing tag, noted by the forward slash (/). If you scroll to the bottom of the `index.htm` file, you'll find a `</HTML>` end tag.

FIGURE 17.13

The `index.htm` page open in FrontPage.

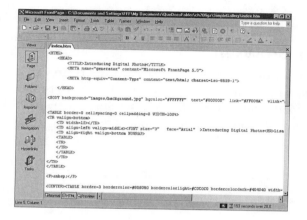

The HTML language has changed over the years. The World Wide Web Consortium (W3C) was created in 1994 and is responsible for defining new additions to HTML, such as XML. It currently has more than 500 member organizations, 50 team members, and an advisory board. However, each browser can implement HTML, as well as any other Web language, such as JavaScript, as they like. Keep this in mind if you notice that your Web photo gallery appears with a slightly different layout in one browser program, but not another.

There are many tags you can use to put together an HTML Web page. Photoshop Elements uses only a subset of HTML tags to create the Web photo galleries. The following list reviews some of the HTML tags used to create the Web photo galleries:

note

To find out more about HTML and Web-related languages, visit www.w3.org, www.htmlcompendium.org, www.webmonkey.com, or www.webreview.com.

- **Page-related tags**—Such as `<HEAD>`, `<BODY>`, `<TITLE>`
- **Formatting tags**—Such as `<CENTER>`, `<P>`, `<bgcolor="#FFFFFF">`
- **Table-related tags**—Such as `<TABLE border=0 cellspacing=0 cellpadding=0 WIDTH=100%>`, `<TR>`, `<TD>`

- **Frame-related tags**—Such as `<FRAMESET frameborder=1 rows="80%,20%">`
- **Link-related tags**—Such as `<A href="index_2.htm">`
- **Tags for images**—Such as `<IMG src="images/next.gif" height="30" width="30" border="0" alt=Next>`

HTML for Nonframes Browsers

Photoshop Elements shows an error message when you try to view a gallery made with frames using an older version of Internet Explorer or Netscape Navigator (which do not support frames). Open the `FrameSet.htm` file to view the frame-related code. The following code appears at the bottom of the page:

```
<NOFRAMES>
<BODY>
Viewing this page requires a browser capable of displaying frames.
</BODY>
</NOFRAMES>
```

If someone visits your Web site using a browser that cannot display frames, the message located between the `<BODY>` tags tells the viewer that this page requires a browser that can display frames.

Glossary

A

adjustment layer   A special kind of layer you can add to an image that enables you to adjust the levels, brightness/contrast, hue/saturation, gradient, invert, threshold, or posterize commands without altering the image layers located below the adjustment layer in the Layers palette.

alpha channel   An alpha channel represents the fourth channel that composes a 32-bit graphic image. It contains 256 shades of pixel data reserved for storing transparency data, but it is also responsible for defining how the pixels in each eight-bit red, green, and blue channel are overlapped with each other to create the resulting full-color image.

analog-to-digital converter (ADC)   A device containing one or more chips that converts analog data into digital data. For example, a Charge Coupled Device (CCD) converts light information into digital image information. CCDs are used in scanners and digital cameras.

animation   Two or more images that play back and forth to create the illusion of motion. Photoshop Elements enables you to use layers to create an animated GIF, a commonly used file format for animation files viewable on Web pages.

anti-alias   A software option that enables the program to smooth out the edge pixels in an image, blending them with the background color.

aperture   In a digital camera, the aperture setting determines the amount of light exposed to the CCD. Increasing the aperture can affect the depth of focus on the camera.

Automation Tools   Two automated commands are stored in the File, Automation Tools menu. These commands use scripts to automatically create a PDF slideshow or convert a multi-page PDF to a Photoshop (PSD) file.

B

background color   The color of the background of the image window in the Photoshop Elements workspace. It also can be the background color of a Web page.

background layer   The bottom layer of an image file, or the bottom layer in the Layers palette. See also *layer*.

bitmap graphics   A matrix of pixels that form an image. Digital pictures are created as bitmap graphics. Most of the tools in Photoshop Elements enable you to work with bitmap graphics. See also *vector graphics*.

BMP A standard bitmap file format supported by Photoshop Elements, and more commonly created and used with PC computers.

brightness The luminance of a color across pixels in an image.

browser An application that can read Hypertext Markup Language (HTML) documents.

Brush Tool A drawing tool selectable from the Toolbox. Can be used to define the masked or unmasked areas of a channel, layer, or quick mask.

Burn Tool A tool that resides with the Dodge Tool in the Toolbox. It can darken pixels in the image window.

button A graphic element used in applications to enable users to perform specific actions, such as to accept changes or to bring up a new dialog box. If clicked, a button indicates a transition to a unique set of information in the same or different window, toolbar, or dialog box.

C

calibration The process of configuring one device, such as a monitor, to match certain settings. These can be color settings, a predefined set of values, or the values of a second device, such as a printer or scanner. You can use the Adobe Gamma control panel to calibrate your computer monitor.

canvas Actual work area of an image file. Non-canvas areas of an image window are marked with a gray color.

cast A light shade of a color, usually created by a reflection of a brighter color in an image.

CCD An acronym for Charge Coupled Device. CCDs are used with most popular digital cameras and scanners. A CCD is a device the size of a microchip. It contains a group of light-sensitive components that translate light into digital data, which is in turn processed and stored as a file on a camera's storage card or sent from a scanner to a computer.

channel In an RGB image, a channel consists of eight bits of red, green, or blue image information. Each channel contains a set of pixels that can range in value from 0 to 256. You can view the pixel distribution for each channel from the Histogram or Levels window.

check box A graphic element used in an application which, when checked, indicates that a particular feature is active. If it is unchecked, the feature is not active.

chroma Synonymous with saturation color levels.

CIS An acronym for Contact Image Sensor. A low-cost image sensor used in some scanners.

Clipboard An area of memory managed by the operating system that stores cut or copied data from an application. Images stored in the Clipboard can be pasted into an image window.

Clone Stamp Tool A tool located in the Toolbox that enables you to copy part of a bitmap image and apply it elsewhere in the image window.

CMOS An acronym for Complementary Metal Oxide Semiconductor: a method for building low-power chips. CMOS chips are used by some digital cameras and scanners to capture light information. Palm handhelds and cell phones are a couple of examples of handheld devices that use CMOS-driven digital cameras.

CMYK An acronym used to express Cyan, Magenta, Yellow, and Black color values. Each color component has a value between 0 and 255. Some applications and printers do not use the black channel of a CMYK image file. Photoshop Elements does not support opening or converting images to CMYK. It supports RGB, Grayscale, Indexed Color, and Bitmap image modes.

Color Management The color model that Photoshop Elements uses that enables you to view, modify, and save photos. You can assign a specific color profile to define the color model, or color management system used by Photoshop Elements or for Windows or Mac OS color management.

Color Picker A window containing a palette of colors. Select a color to work with from the Color Picker window. Click on a foreground or background color in the Toolbox to open the Color Picker window. You also can choose to use the Adobe or Windows or Mac OS Color Picker window, from the General Preferences window.

color space A general term used to define a particular method for determining color on a computer. For example, RGB is the name for the red, green, and blue color space. Hue, Saturation, and Brightness (HSB) is another color space supported by Photoshop Elements.

ColorSync Apple's name for its color management software installed with Mac OS 9 and Mac OS X. Choose ColorSync from the Apple, Control Panels menu to assign a color profile for your computer monitor.

composite An image created by combining multiple images. For example, if you paste one photo into an image window, the pasted image is placed in a new layer located above the image in the existing layer below it. The resulting single image is called a *composite*.

contrast The difference between light and dark pixel values in an image or object.

convert Usually refers to changing the file format of an image from one format to another.

crop A tool that enables you to retain the subject of a photo, but remove unselected image areas.

D

digital camera A consumer electronic device, similar to a traditional analog camera, that can capture digital images and store them on a removable card.

Dodge Tool A tool that resides with the Burn Tool in the Toolbox. It can lighten pixels in the image window.

download To copy a file from another computer on a network or from the Internet to your computer's hard drive. For example, if you want to edit your Web pages, you can log in to your Web site and download a file to your computer using a network connection.

dpi An acronym for dots per inch, a measurement used to define screen and printer resolution.

E

edit To change, adjust, or reorganize text or image objects.

editor   An application or feature in an application that edits text or graphics.

effect   One or more ways to enhance the way an image appears in the image window. Most effects consist of a combination of filters that are applied to all or part of the active image window. Some effects can be added as a separate layer, while others are applied directly to the selected image layer.

eraser   This tool erases pixels from an image. Photoshop Elements has three kinds of erasers: Eraser, Background Eraser, and the Magic Eraser Tools.

export   A command used to convert the active image window into a special file format. Export file formats are defined by a plug-in file. Photoshop Elements plug-in files are installed in the Import/Export folder located in the Plug-ins folder in the Photoshop Elements application folder.

Eyedropper   A tool that can capture a color from an image and be used as the foreground or background color in the Toolbox.

F

f-stop   Also referred to as shutter speed. A setting on a digital camera that can affect the simulated shutter speed. This impacts how long the CCD will be exposed to light.

file format   A generic term for describing the way a file is saved. GIF, PSD, JPEG, and PNG are examples of graphic file formats.

filter   Photoshop Elements includes image-editing filters that adjust contrast, brightness, and other types of filters to improve your images. You can view filters in the Filters palette or the Filter menu.

font   A character set of a specific typeface, type style, and type size. Some fonts are installed with the operating system on your computer.

foreground color   The upper-left color in the color well in the Toolbox. If the Pen, Pencil, Paintbrush, or other drawing tool is selected, the foreground color is used with the selected tool.

frames   A feature of HTML that can be used to divide a Web page, enabling you to view and navigate more than one page in a browser window. Photoshop Elements enables you to create a Web photo album containing frames.

FTP   File Transfer Protocol. You can use a browser application to download files from an FTP site. An FTP application enables you to upload or download files to the Web or network server that has an FTP server.

G

gamma   Also known as the gamma correction setting. Not synonymous with Grandma. You can adjust the gamma setting for your monitor from the Adobe Gamma control panel. In the Levels window, gamma is synonymous with midtones.

GIF   Pronounced "gif," (with a hard "g") the Graphics Interchange Format is one of the two most common graphic file formats used on the Web. The GIF format is most effective at compressing solid-color images and images with areas of repetitive color. In addition to supporting background transparency (which is great for animation), up to 256 colors can represent a GIF image. Best used with illustrations, text, and line art.

gradient A progression of colors that gradually blend or fade into each other. Create a gradient within an object or across frames and layers.

grayscale Represents a percentage of black where 0 is white and 100 is black and intermediate colors are shades of gray.

H

halo An off-colored ring of pixels that appears around borders of a graphic. Most noticeable around the edges of a mask.

hard disk A hardware component commonly used in computers to store files and folders of data.

hexadecimal A term to express red, green, and blue color values. Each component value is represented by a hexadecimal value, such as FF-FF-FF for white.

highlight color The color used as a visual interface to identify selected text or graphics.

hints Similar to tool tips. Hints are located in the Hints palette. Click on a tool in the Toolbox to view its tool information in the Hints palette. The text in the Hints palette is more informative than the word or words that appear in the tool tips.

How To palette A window containing a group of instructions for a single task or group of tasks that can be applied to an image, a selection object, or a layer.

HTML An acronym for Hypertext Markup Language, which is the language used to create Web pages. Photoshop Elements generates HTML code to create Web photo gallery files.

hue/saturation Hue is an adjustable range of colors from 0 to 360, or plus or minus 180. Saturation values encapsulate color intensity within a range of 0 to plus or minus 100.

I

ICC Profile The color profile you can save along with a color photo in the Save or Save As dialog box in Photoshop Elements.

image A bitmapped matrix of pixels that represent a picture.

Image Mode Located in the Image, Mode menu, enables you to set the number of colors you can work with in the image document to RGB (full color), Indexed Color (a fixed set of colors), Grayscale (256 shades of gray), or Bitmap (two colors.

Import The command used to acquire an image from a scanner or digital camera. It can also be used to convert a nonsupported document into Photoshop Elements.

Impressionist Brush Tool One of the drawing tools in Photoshop Elements. Combines pixel colors with the Brush Preset and size settings. As it is applied to an image, it creates and smoothens and blends the colors in an impressionist-like painting style.

Indexed Color One of the color modes supported by Photoshop Elements. This color mode uses an indexing algorithm to reduce the number of colors in the image and also reduce its file size. Indexed Color mode enables you to work with up to 256 colors in an image.

Info palette Displays the location, size, and colors of a particular object in the image window.

interpolation The process for calculating color when pixels are added to or removed from an image during transformations. Bicubic interpolation creates the best results but is usually the slowest method of interpolation. Photoshop Elements also enables you to apply nearest neighbor and bilinear interpolation processes. Choose the Image Size command from the Image, Resize menu to select an interpolation method for an image.

J

JavaScript A scripting language created by Netscape. The Web photo gallery in Photoshop Elements uses JavaScript to move from photo to photo as you click on each image, or view a slideshow.

JPEG Created by the Joint Photographic Experts Group, JPEG is a popular graphic file format used on the Web. The JPEG file format preserves broad color ranges and subtleties in brightness and image tones and supports up to millions (24 bits) of colors. JPEG uses a lossy compression format that can remove some of the image data when a file is compressed. Best used with images and photographs. See also *PNG* and *GIF*.

JPEG 2000 A new file format supported by Photoshop Elements 2. The JPEG 2000 format enables you to adjust the compression level and image quality of the JPEG image, sort of a customized JPEG file format.

L

Lasso A selection tool that enables you to select a freeform set of pixels. Photoshop Elements has three kinds of Lasso tools: Lasso, Polygonal Lasso, and Magnetic Lasso.

layer A particular plane in a document window that enables you to store simple or complex graphics. You can rearrange, add, remove, show, hide, and lock a layer in Photoshop Elements. You can work with only one layer at a time in Photoshop Elements.

layer styles A collection of effects that can be applied to a selected object in the image window. Layer styles are located in the Layer Styles palette.

lossy compression An image file compression format used to compress a JPEG image. Lossless JPEG compression preserves the original image, without losing any image data. Lossy compression can lose image data when compressing a file. Photoshop Elements lets you choose between 12 levels of JPEG compression. The lower the level you choose to save the JPEG image, the more image data is lost due to compression. The image will not lose any additional data each successive time you save a JPEG image at the same compression level.

M

marquee Rectangular or elliptical tool that enables you to select an area of pixels in an image.

mask A selected area of pixels that can be modified with a tool or menu command. The pixels outside the selected area cannot be modified with tools or commands.

megabyte Abbreviated MB. Equivalent to a million bytes, or more exactly, 1,048,576 bytes.

megapixel A million pixels. A measurement used by digital camera manufacturers to measure the total number of pixels captured by a camera. Most of today's cameras can capture 2- or 3-megapixel images.

memory   Also known as RAM. Refers to the amount of physical memory (in chips) installed on your computer. Virtual memory is the amount of memory or hard disk space allocated for use by the operating system and applications on a computer. As you use the software on your computer, data is swapped from the hard drive into memory, and data stored in the physical memory chips is swapped to the hard drive.

Photoshop Elements creates a scratch disk with its own form of virtual memory to store image information on the hard drive as you modify an image in the work area. Memory, in regard to an application such as Photoshop Elements, represents the amount of space required for an application to run its routines and functions.

menu   A user-interface element originating from the operating system and containing commands for an application.

O

opacity   The degree of transparency applied by a blending mode onto an object.

optimize   To reduce the size or image quality of a document in order to decrease the loading time of a Web page.

options bar   Contains additional settings and tools in the Toolbox. It is located at the top of the Photoshop Elements work area.

P

Paint Bucket Tool   A fill tool selectable from the Toolbox. Works with the foreground color in the color well to fill a selected object with a particular color.

palette   Similar to the term *floating palette*; synonymous with *panel*. A window containing a set of tools and icons. Some palettes also contain a custom menu.

palette well   Located in the toolbar, this is the storage place for all palette windows.

PDF   An acronym for Portable Document Format. A file format capable of preserving text and image information that can be viewed with a PDF viewer application such as Adobe Acrobat.

Pencil Tool   A drawing tool located in the Toolbox. Used to draw with a single pixel of color in the image window.

Photomerge   A menu command located in the File menu that enables you to create horizontal or vertical panoramas.

pica   A format of measurement of approximately 1/6 of an inch. Originated with the typewriter, where 10 characters were roughly equivalent to a horizontal inch, or six lines of type for a vertical inch. You can create a new document with the width and height in picas.

pixel   An atomic element of color; pixels can be grouped together to form a picture or image.

pixels per inch (ppi)   A measurement of a monitor's screen resolution. This is usually set to 72 ppi. For this reason, images created for the Web use the resolution of 72 ppi.

plug-in   A special type of file that can be placed in a folder on your hard drive. Each plug-in file extends the features available in Photoshop Elements. If the plug-in preferences are configured correctly, all plug-ins will appear in the Filter menu.

PNG   The Portable Network Graphic is a newer graphic file format growing in popularity on the Web. Effectively compresses solid-color images and preserves details. The PNG format might require a plug-in to be added to a browser, but it can support up to 32 bits of color, in addition to transparency and alpha channels. It uses a lossless form of compression. It is best used for creating high-color graphics with complex live transparency, and general low-color graphics. See also *PSD*, *GIF*, *JPEG*, and *lossy compression*.

preferences   Application and document-specific settings you can customize to increase your productivity within Photoshop Elements.

process   A set of steps that, when followed, complete a task.

processor   The central processing unit of a computer. A faster processor will display graphics more quickly than a slower processor.

PSD   The native file format of Photoshop Elements. Preserve layers, layer sets, channels, and masks by saving them in a Photoshop Elements file. The Windows version of Photoshop Elements shows this file format in the Save As window as Photoshop (*.PSD or *.PDD). The Macintosh version shows this file format as Photoshop.

Q

QuickTime   Apple's technology for storing and playing back still frame, audio, and video on Macintosh and Windows computers. Photoshop Elements 2 enables you to import one frame of video into a new image window.

R

radio button   A user-interface element found in applications and Web pages that has an on or off state.

RAM   See *memory*.

rasterize   The process of converting a vector graphic, such as text, into a bitmap so that it can be displayed onscreen or printed.

Recipe   See *How To palette*.

Red Eye Brush Tool   An exclusive Photoshop Elements tool. You can use it to replace colors in the active image window. The letter Y on the keyboard is the shortcut key you can press to quickly access this tool.

resolution   The number of horizontal and vertical pixels that make up a screen of information.

RGB   Red, green, and blue values used to express a color. Each value is within a range of 0 to 255.

S

samples per inch (spi)   A measurement used by scanner devices to measure the resolution of captured images. Samples per inch combines the number of sensors (600 to 1200) on the scan bar located below the glass surface with the amount of vertical distance the bar moves for each scanned line.

Save   A command used to convert an image stored in memory into a file on the hard drive.

scale   A term used to indicate the size—larger or smaller—of an original object or image.

scanner   A computer peripheral that usually connects to the USB port. A scanner can be powered by the USB port, or powered by an external power source. Images are captured line by line and converted into digital data, viewable on your computer screen. Today's scanners can capture 24- or 36-bit images ranging from 600 dpi to 2400 dpi, or higher resolutions.

Selection Brush   A new selection tool in Photoshop Elements 2. This tool enables you to select pixels using a custom brush style and size. You can view the selected area using the traditional marching ants graphic, or using the red hue to mark uneditable areas of the image window.

Send Via Email   A button located on the shortcuts bar or File menu that enables you to resize a photo and send it to a friend using an email program installed on your computer.

shortcuts bar   The toolbar located below the menu bar. Click on a shortcut icon to quickly access a command, such as the Save, Copy, Paste, or Print commands.

shutter speed   A setting on a digital camera that can affect the simulated shutter speed. This impacts how long the CCD is exposed to light. Synonymous with f-stop.

swatch   Not a watch by any means. A swatch is a single square of color stored in the Swatches palette. The Swatches palette enables you to select, add, or remove a single color, or change to a particular group of colors for the active image.

T

text   Also referred to as type. Alphabetic, non-alphabetic, and numeric characters that make up a font. Use the Horizontal or Vertical Type Tool to add text to an image window.

Create a mask in the shape of text with the Horizontal and Vertical Type Mask tools.

tonal range—A term used to describe a range of shadows, midtones, and highlights that define the pixel distribution of an image. You can adjust the tonal range of an image from the Levels dialog box. You can use tonal range settings to correct contrast, change brightness levels, identify and change the black and white points of a photo, and so on.

Transform   A set of commands that enable you to scale, rotate, flip, distort, or skew all or part of an image in the image window.

TWAIN   A special kind of plug-in file that enables Photoshop Elements to communicate with a scanner or digital camera. Each device can have its own specific TWAIN plug-in file installed onto a computer. Any installed TWAIN plug-ins are accessible from the File, Import menu or from the Connect to Camera or Scanner button in the Welcome Window. The Select Import Source dialog box opens and displays a list of TWAIN plug-ins if you click the Connect to Camera or Scanner button.

U

Undo   A menu command that enables you to reverse a previous command in the image window. Set the number of undo levels in the General Preferences window.

Undo History palette   Stores a list of states as you work on image files in Photoshop Elements. Each state is a command that has been performed or a tool that has been applied to a Photoshop Elements document. The Undo History palette does not store zoom or view changes, or the scroll location of the image window.

upload   The process of copying a local file or folder to another computer.

URL   An acronym for Uniform Resource Locator. Type a URL (such as http://www.adobe.com) into a browser window to go to a Web site or Web page on the Internet.

V

vector graphics   A type of graphic composed of paths and points. Vector graphics use an algorithm to retain crisp, high-resolution versions of an image if scaled larger or smaller than the original size. You can use the Shape and Type tools to create vector graphics. Use the Simplify Layer command to convert vector graphics into a bitmap.

W

Web   Also referred to as the World Wide Web. A group of computers running Web server software connected to an extended network around the world.

Welcome window   The menu window that opens when you first start Photoshop Elements. Open a file, acquire or paste an image, or access the help or tutorial files by clicking on an image in the Quick Start window.

Windows Media Player   Microsoft's technology for viewing still-frame photography, or playing back audio or video on a Windows computer. Photoshop Elements 2 enables you to import one frame of a Windows Media Player video file into a new image window in the work area.

Z

Zoom Tool   A tool that enables you to magnify the contents of the image window. Use with the Hand Tool (H) to move the page while it is magnified. Press the Z key as a shortcut to select the Zoom Tool from the Toolbox. Press the (Command) [Ctrl] plus or minus key combos to zoom into and out of an image in the image window.

Index

How can we make this index more useful? Email us at indexes@quepublishing.com

How can we make this index more useful? Email us at indexes@quepublishing.com

How can we make this index more useful? Email us at indexes@quepublishing.com

How can we make this index more useful? Email us at indexes@quepublishing.com

How can we make this index more useful? Email us at indexes@quepublishing.com

W

Y-X-Z